WHO'S WHOSE?
A No-Nonsense Guide to
Easily Confused Words

PHILIP GOODEN

BLOOMSBURY

A BLOOMSBURY REFERENCE BOOK
www.bloomsbury.com/reference

First published in 2004 by
Bloomsbury Publishing Plc
38 Soho Square
London W1D 3HB

A catalogue record for this book is available from
the British Library

ISBN 0 7475 7231 3

3 5 7 9 10 8 6 4

All papers used by Bloomsbury Publishing are natural,
recyclable products made from wood grown in
well-managed forests. The manufacturing processes
conform to the environmental regulations of the
country of origin.

Typeset by Refinecatch Limited, Bungay, Suffolk
Printed and bound in Great Britain by
Clays Ltd, St Ives plc

INTRODUCTION

Who's or *whose*? *Disinterested* or *uninterested*? *Ameliorate* or *alleviate*? Is there anybody who hasn't at some point had to consider, when faced with a choice between these or other similar-sounding words, which one will better convey the required shade of meaning? Or, more simply, hasn't stopped to wonder which word is the right one?

All of us, in practice, choose the language which we use. And we choose all the time, whether consciously or not. The expressions in an e-mail will be different from those used in a formal letter; the words said in the pub aren't necessarily the same as the words heard in the workplace. Almost everybody adjusts the register of his or her language, according to circumstances and company. A lot of this may be instinctive, but it is an instinct which is constantly being modified and refined. We learn about the words we use as we go along.

English is a wealthy language. The number of words available to any speaker or writer of it comfortably exceeds half a million, at least in theory. Anybody who has a working knowledge of just 5% of that total can claim to have an extensive vocabulary, much more than is needed for everyday purposes. Buried in this great heap of words are many duplicates or near-duplicates, terms that mean the same or almost the same as other terms. And, more deceptively, there are words that *look* or *sound* as though they mean the same as others. This book is a guide to some of the most frequent and interesting confusables in English – or confusibles (there's a choice here too).

Anybody who writes about English usage needs to face the question: Does it matter? Is the misuse – or abuse – of language truly important? We generally manage to make our meaning clear, even if our vocabulary is pretty basic, perhaps especially if it is pretty basic. Are slips of the tongue where one says *less* instead of *fewer*, or uncertainties about whether to write *phase* or *faze* really significant? Sometimes, the answer must be no. Your listener or reader may not care about any mistake, may not even notice any mistake. But, of course, the reverse is also true. That listener or reader may notice, may care.

I wouldn't, however, want to base a defence of correct usage solely on what others might think – that makes the whole business too nervy and defensive. Speaking and writing English is about communicating with others, naturally, but much of the benefit of using language well is for the sake of the user. There is a great increase in confidence and, yes, an increase in pleasure in saying what one wants to say, in having a firm grasp of the intricacies of vocabulary – or some of the intricacies, since there will always be that other half a million words or so to get familiar with. And English does not become much more intricate or tangled than in the area of confusables.

There are several reasons why all of us confuse words, whether often or occasionally. It may be no more than a matter of spelling (*advice/advise*) or uncertainty about which way round a term applies (*reliable/reliant*). At other times the distinction between expressions may be subtle (*defective/deficient*) or hard to pin down (*recourse/resource*). And there is yet another category where people assume a difference but where, in practice, none exists (*stanch* and *staunch*; *inoculate* and *vaccinate*). Confusables have always existed, of course, but reliance on the spellchecker, and the general speeding-up of the publishing process, mean that we see more and more confused spellings and usages in print.

Of course, the words in *Who's Whose?* are just the tip of the iceberg. Or – thinking of those half million or more still to go – the tip of the tip. But this is the part which is the most visible.

The entries in this book are organised alphabetically, sometimes with the more familiar form/spelling coming first (e.g. *bizarre/bazaar*). An opening sentence or two helps to outline the reason(s) why the two or more terms are mixed up. The main part of each entry defines the terms, with examples generally drawn from the newspapers, although with a few from other sources such as fiction. (Where I have not found particular usages I have made up examples.) At the end of each entry is an **Embarrassment rating** which rates – on a scale from nil (represented by ○○○) through moderate (represented by ●○○) to high (represented by ●●●) – the 'seriousness' of confusing the words under discussion. And finally, under the heading of **How to avoid**, there is some guidance on telling the confusables apart, how to avoid writing one for the other, etc. In some cases the guidance may perhaps be trickier to recall than the original words, and I would always suggest that, in cases of doubt, the user should consult a dictionary or a reference book like this one rather than struggle with memory aids. Sometimes, the best advice that can be given over English usage is simply: be careful. And the next best is: use a dictionary. It helps, too, to be aware of words which are likely to cause you, or others, problems.

The newspapers which I have gone to for examples – mostly of correct use but sometimes of misuse – are *The Times*, the *Guardian*, the *Daily Telegraph*, the *Independent*, and occasionally the *Daily Mirror* and the *Sun*.

In looking for right and wrong usage, I haven't deliberately picked on the broadsheet papers (incidentally, at least two of these are now in the process of rebranding themselves as *compacts*, an interesting choice of word since it distinguishes them in style if not in size from the *tabloids*). It is rather that this end of the press is more accessible, not least through the excellent websites of the *Guardian* and the *Telegraph*. It is also that, in the nature of things, the style and range of prose used in the broadsheets tend to be more ambitious than that found in the tabloid press. They are therefore handier as a source of illustrations.

In some examples, an ☒ has been used to indicate a usage which is better avoided, i.e. a slight mistake; a double ☒ ☒ to show a usage which should be avoided, i.e. a serious mistake. The correct version appears [in squared brackets] alongside.

Philip Gooden

AAAA**A**AAA

ABUSE *or* MISUSE

Two words which have a considerable overlap of meaning. Different contexts require the use of one rather than the other.

Of the two, *abuse* is the more serious term, constantly appearing in phrases like child *abuse* or *abuse* of power. To *abuse* means to 'make bad use of'. As noun or verb it can describe the physical (usually sexual), verbal or psychological mistreatment of others. When applied to drink and drugs, the word suggests an excessive, uncontrolled intake of the substance in question (arguably, people should really refer to alcohol *misuse*, but *abuse* is more attention-grabbing):

> . . . new 'drinking warehouses' and superpubs are fuelling a culture of alcohol abuse. (Daily Telegraph)

To *misuse* is to 'use for the wrong purpose'. The two words are often used interchangeably but there can be a useful distinction. To use a book as a doorstop is a *misuse* of it as an object, but to take the contents of that book and deliberately misrepresent what the author is saying would be an *abuse* of it. Another distinction is that an *abuse* is generally a conscious action while a *misuse* may be committed unawares. It's more forgivable, as in this example:

> . . . it is not uncommon for any of us to misuse language when hoping to convey a truth. (Daily Telegraph)

Embarrassment rating: ●●○ To accuse someone of *misusing* something is a lot less offensive than accusing them of *abuse*, especially now that the word is so frequently linked to children.

How to avoid: Most people are very sensitive to the overtones of *abuse*, and will instinctively shy away from the word unless they feel it is really justified. This is particularly so in professional (i.e. social work) circles where, for example, substance *abuse* has now become *misuse*.

ACCEPT *or* EXCEPT

Probably because of the tendency in spoken English to pronounce the opening vowels similarly, these two words are occasionally confused despite having almost opposed meanings.

To *accept* is to 'receive':

I accepted her kind offer of help.

The less common verb to *except* means to 'take out', to 'exclude':

He was excepted from the criticism which the rest of the committee earned.

(*Except* is also a preposition meaning 'not including'.)

Embarrassment rating: ●●◐ This is a fairly elementary mistake because *accept* and *except* (as a preposition) are so much part of everyday use.

How to avoid: Go back to the related noun forms, *acceptance* and *exception*. These should guide you to the appropriate verb.

ACETIC *or* ASCETIC

Two words quite easily confused in their spelling. And, perhaps at some subconscious level, the vinegary sense of one suggests the self-punishing sense of the other!

Acetic defines a 'type of acid' which, in a diluted form, is vinegar:

You can sweeten onions even more by rinsing them in vinegar: the acetic acid in it will mask the remaining sulphur compounds. (Guardian)

The adjective *ascetic* means 'denying oneself bodily pleasure for moral or religious reasons'. Somebody who lives like this full-time is an *ascetic*.

So you cut out coffee, cigarettes, carbohydrates, dairy products, red meat – anything to keep up the ascetic high. (Guardian)

Embarrassment rating: ●◐○ Even if the words are misspelled, the context will generally make the meaning clear.

How to avoid: The chemical term, *acetic*, has the same first two letters as 'acid'. *Ascetic* is connected to *a* self-denying outlook.

ACQUIESCE, ASSENT *or* AGREE

These three words occupy the same sort of area but have different shades of meaning.

To *acquiesce* is to 'consent without showing opposition':

He acquiesced in the plans although he had no part in making them.

To *assent* has a slightly formal tone to it and means to 'comply', to 'agree to' (usually without much eagerness). *Agree* covers these two senses but also extends to more positive meanings: to 'be of one mind with', 'be compatible with'.

Embarrassment rating: ●○○ But a careful writer/speaker can convey enthusiasm – or the lack of it – by the right choice among these words.

How to avoid: There is perhaps not much to avoid here. It's more a matter of degrees of enthusiasm. *Acquiesce* and *assent* are terms more likely to occur in writing than speech (where they could sound pompous), and anyone using them on paper is likely to be aware of their shades of meaning. *Agree* can be conveniently neutral when put in writing, whereas we all know that, when spoken, it can convey anything between eagerness and a grudging acceptance.

ACTIVE *or* PROACTIVE

The choice between this pair of closely connected words has more to do with fashion than meaning.

There's something about *proactive* which sets my teeth on edge. A few years ago *proactive* was a buzzword, an unwelcome newcomer on the fringes, but it has made the transition into ordinary English, or at least as ordinary as the English you find in officialese. I can't believe that many people use it in everyday conversation – and am not sure they'd be worth listening to if they did – but reluctantly I have to admit that *proactive* has its place. Not as a synonym for 'very active', which is sometimes how it's used (with the underlying thought of 'You may be active but I'm proactive'), but in the sense of 'instigating change' or 'acting without being prompted'. The word is really the counterpart of 'reactive', as it is used here:

Online recruitment may be a growth area, but few people believe it will replace traditional methods of finding a job through word of mouth,

recommendation or even contacting a company direct. It's likely these kinds
of proactive job-seeking will always have the edge because the internet
remains a reactive way of finding work. (Guardian)

Embarrassment rating: ○○○ Nil, unfortunately. If you move in the
kind of circles where *proactivity* is desirable, then you'll win brownie
points by employing it wherever you can.

How to avoid: Don't use *proactive* unless you have to.

ACTOR *or* ACTRESS

**One of a group of word-pairs describing professions (see below for
other examples) where the neutral form has traditionally been
reserved for the male sex. The problem comes with the 'feminine'
form of each pair, use of which is frequently seen now as not PC.**

The tendency is to avoid words that designate the sex of the person
carrying out a particular job, thus 'firefighter' is preferred to 'fireman'.
An *actor* describes a person who acts on stage, film or TV, irrespective
of sex:

First, there is the fact that she is generally considered an extremely bad
actor indeed – chronic, even. (The Times)

(The difference between 'actor' and 'star' would make for an
interesting little excursion – not all actors have star quality, but most
stars refer to themselves as actors when they want to be taken
seriously.)

Other art forms are also home to unisex terms like 'author',
'poet', 'sculptor'. There are feminine forms of some of these terms
('authoress', 'poetess') but they not only sound out of date but have
a slightly patronising air, as if the women were merely dabbling in
the activity. Even in ballet, the feminine 'ballerina' has generally
been replaced by 'dancer'. In those few areas where men and women
have long been on a more equal footing, the feminine form may
sometimes be retained – waiter/waitress; steward/stewardess;
headmaster/headmistress – although, as far as the last two are
concerned, there is a preference now for the sexually unrevealing
'flight attendant', and 'principal' for the head of a school. Job
advertisements, wary of accusations of discrimination, may also
announce that they are looking for strange, hybrid beings called
'waitpersons' or 'postpersons'. One of the fields where the sex
difference still holds is the host/hostess distinction. 'Hostess' leads a

kind of double life: ultra-respectable at a dinner party but slightly sleazy in a clip-joint or nightclub. 'Host' can be used for either sex, however.

Embarrassment rating: ●◐○○ When it comes to actors, it depends if you're talking to a luvvie or a serious actor. The latter might just be offended, I suppose.

How to avoid: Play safe and refer to all artistic practitioners by the neutral form: actor, sculptor, etc. But it's difficult to believe that many people would naturally say 'waitperson' rather than 'waitress'.

AD HOC *or* AD LIB

Both of these Latin expressions are concerned with things done at short notice, and are sometimes treated as though they are interchangeable. They're not.

Ad hoc means '(organised) for a particular purpose' rather than being permanent. *Ad hoc* arrangements tend to be makeshift:

> *No longer would massed-start races, on open roads from town to village and back again, be organised in that ad hoc way, without permanent facilities or even the vaguest notion of safety precautions.* (Daily Telegraph)

Ad lib (from *ad libitum* – 'at will') means 'spontaneous', 'unrehearsed'. It generally applies to off-the-cuff speakers, who will get a reputation for *ad-libbing* if they make a habit of it:

> *On stage, he was a seasoned raconteur and ad lib humorist.* (Daily Telegraph)

Embarrassment rating: ●●○ Anyone who knows enough to use these two phrases should be able to distinguish between them.

How to avoid: *Ad-libbing* is generally connected with speech/performance so some association between 'lib' and 'lip' might be helpful. *Ad hoc* is almost always tied to structures, arrangements, committees, etc.

ADOPTED *or* ADOPTIVE

A pair of words that describe different sides of the same process, the second being less familiar than the first.

Adopted applies to the person who is being adopted (or to the plan, suggestion, etc.):

The adopted children were likely to go through great . . . turmoil. (Guardian)

Adoptive describes those who are doing the adopting – this word can only be applied to those adopting children, not to the children themselves:

They faced the prospect of being caught between adoptive parents worried that the adoption may be overturned and birth parents . . . (Guardian)

Embarrassment rating: ●○○ But confusion may result if you get them the wrong way round: to characterise a couple as *adopted* would mean that they themselves have been adopted, and the term would tell you nothing about the status of their children.

How to avoid: Think which side of the coin you're looking at and choose accordingly. The '-ive' suffix tends to imply active (thus, those who do the adopting).

ADVERSE *or* AVERSE

Two adjectives with a one-letter difference, both carrying a general sense of 'against'.

The adjective *adverse* means 'opposing' or 'unfavourable':

Adverse weather conditions delayed the ferry crossing.

Averse means 'reluctant', 'unwilling', and generally describes people's responses:

Averse for years to anything so sweaty as 'live' performance, the Pet Shop Boys compensated in the late 1980s with the Discovery tour. (Guardian)

Averse is very often coupled with 'not' – as in 'I'm not averse to your suggestion'. Although this phrase is sometimes objected to as a faintly pedantic understatement, it suggests a willingness to be persuaded rather than enthusiasm about something, and so carries a valuable shade of meaning.

Embarrassment rating: ●●● High if you make a reference like 'averse weather' since the word makes little sense in this context. You might describe a person as being *adverse* (to some idea, suggestion, etc.) but it would be preferable to use a more familiar term like 'against'.

How to avoid: *Adverse* generally goes in front of a noun such as 'conditions' or 'report'; *averse* usually relates to people and is likely to be preceded by a noun or pronoun and 'not' and followed by 'to' ('They were not averse to . . . ').

ADVICE *or* ADVISE

This is one of a group of words where the spelling differs by one letter between the noun and verb forms. Noun and verb? The decline in knowledge about parts of speech makes mistakes over spelling more likely since many are no longer certain of even the basic elements of language – and telling a noun from a verb is pretty basic. All I can say is that not knowing whether you're using a noun or a verb is rather like putting up a shelf and not knowing the difference between a nail and a screw. Such information should not be confined to dedicated DIY-ers. So ends a fogeyish lament about falling standards.

When it comes to *advice/advise*, mistakes like the following are quite usual:

☒☒ . . . *you will be introduced to your personal shopper who will give you all the advise* [should be *advice*] *you need* . . . (Metro)

Advice is the noun form and the one which should have been used in the example above, while *advise* is the verb:

We received some good advice [noun]/*He advised us well* [verb]

(But the person giving the *advice* is an *adviser*.)

Embarrassment rating: ●◐○ Low to moderate, because the mistake is quite frequent and often goes unremarked. Nevertheless, the wrong spelling will irritate those who notice such things because only a little care is required to put it right.

How to avoid: The pronunciation differs according to whether you are using the noun or the verb. If in doubt, say the word aloud. The change from the 'c' sound in the noun (*advice*) to the 's' in the verb (*advise*) is a guide to the changes in a number of other words (e.g. *device/devise*) which switch between 'c' and 's' spellings. In all cases they conform to the *advice/advise* pattern. *Device/devise* have the same pronunciation change as *advice/advise*, so use this pair for reference if in doubt.

AFFECT *or* EFFECT

Two words that sound very similar and which are frequently mixed up. To add to the confusion, the noun which relates to the main meaning of *affect* is *effect*.

As a verb *affect* means to 'have an impact on', 'make a difference to':

> *Peter's drinking affected his health more than his personality.*
> (Independent)

Also, as a verb *affect* has the less usual meaning of to 'put on', to 'pretend':

> *Donovan wasn't ready to affect his Yorkshire accent at a press conference yesterday.* (The Times)

To *effect* is to 'bring about', to 'carry through':

> *They effected the most dramatic transformation almost overnight.*

In the next sentence *effect* has been used wrongly instead of *affect*:

> ☒☒ *Concern about job security now effects [should be **affects**] everyone from mandarin to road sweeper.* (The Times)

The noun which relates to the verb *affect* and has the same general sense of 'impact' is not, as one might expect, *affect* but *effect*:

> *The harmful effects of cigarette smoking are now well established.*

So the following are wrong:

> ☒☒ *And he had the same affect [should be **effect**] on his players.*
> (Sun)

> ☒☒ *. . . the crash of 1929 had profound affects [should be **effects**] on law and order.* (Independent on Sunday)

Embarrassment rating: ●○○ Almost everybody mixes up their *affects* and *effects* from time to time. The general sense of what you are writing is unlikely to be *affected*, but it's still a mistake.

How to avoid: *Affect* is the more common of the two verbs, so the chances are that it will be the right word if you are looking for a verb. However, if your sentence contains a word like 'change', 'transformation', 'improvement' then it is likely to be preceded by *effect*, i.e. 'bring about'. When it's the noun you want, *effect* will almost certainly be right (since the rarely found *affect* has the specialist, psychological sense of 'emotion' or 'desire'). But knowing whether you are looking for noun or verb depends on knowing parts of speech . . . There's no shortcut here. Just consult this book.

AFFLICT *or* INFLICT

Two similar-sounding words, both suggesting suffering and punishment.

If a condition *afflicts* a person or animal it causes them 'trouble' or 'distress':

> *Travellers' diarrhoea is a more widespread problem, afflicting at least two-fifths of all international travellers.* (Daily Telegraph)

To *inflict* is to 'impose something unpleasant on someone'. This word focuses more on the punishment, condition, etc. than the victim of it:

> *In my book, it is perfectly fine to inflict the emotional torture of letting your mother watch as you throw yourself out of a plane from 3,000ft.*
> (Daily Telegraph)

Embarrassment rating: ●●◐ Moderate to high if you get them the wrong way round, for example by referring to being 'inflicted with diarrhoea' or 'afflicting torture'.

How to avoid: Getting these two straight is quite tricky and it may be helpful to think of the noun forms where the difference is plainer to see – *affliction* meaning a 'state of distress or what causes it', and *infliction* meaning the 'imposition of some penalty' – and work backwards from there.

AGGRAVATE *or* ANNOY

These two words were separate once. But popular use has transferred the meaning of *annoy* to *aggravate*, so that it has become *annoy* with knobs on. Maybe it is the similarity of the word to 'aggression' that causes the error.

The primary meaning of *aggravate* is to 'make worse' – as in the following example, where it is balanced against the idea of making better or easing a situation:

> *It stands to reason that the Iraq venture was always going to aggravate not relieve the so-called War on Terror.* (The Times)

By contrast, *annoy* often means no more than 'irritate':

> *She was annoyed by the frequent interruptions to her work.*

Embarrassment rating: ○○○ Nil in speech but low to moderate in formal writing, since the principal sense of *aggravate* is still alive and well, although I suspect it will sooner or later be pushed to one side by the informal sense of 'deeply irritate'.

How to avoid: In formally correct English, you can *aggravate* a condition or a situation but not a person – therefore if an individual is the object of your *aggravation* the chances are that you are misusing the word.

ALIBI *or* EXCUSE

Two words connected with establishing innocence – or at least with avoiding trouble. The impressive, legalistic overtones of *alibi* perhaps account for its use in contexts where *excuse* would be more appropriate.

An *alibi*, more precise and forceful than an *excuse*, is a defence (often produced in court) that a person could not have committed some offence because he/she was 'elsewhere at the time' (this is its literal meaning from Latin). Some proof of the *alibi* is usually required, in the form of witnesses, photos, etc., and, if shown to be true, it must be accepted. There are, of course, false *alibis*:

> Aimed primarily at cheating spouses who need an excuse to get away from home for a day or two, or explain away a lost night after an unplanned indiscretion, Dmitry Petrov sells copper-bottomed alibis for as little as £120. (Daily Telegraph)

An *excuse* is sometimes just an 'explanation', as in the first line of the *Telegraph* sentence above, but more often it means a 'plea offered for some failure or shortcoming'. Unlike an *alibi*, an *excuse* may not be accepted and, even if it is, it's likely to leave the person offering it on the back foot.

> Her excuse for being late was that her alarm clock hadn't gone off.

Embarrassment rating: ●○○ But if you talk of having an *alibi* when you really mean an *excuse*, people will prick up their ears because the first word hints at something more serious, if not criminal.

How to avoid: *Alibi* should be restricted to formal, official contexts such as those involving the law. It's not really a word for everyday cock-ups, failures to make appointments, and so on.

ALLEVIATE *or* AMELIORATE

There's no particular trap here since these two are close in meaning; they are not absolutely identical, however.

To *alleviate* is to 'make lighter'. It's generally applied to moods, emotional burdens, pain, or states of mind:

. . . the various friends whose inconsolable grief at my departure is to be somewhat alleviated by the legacy of some trinket or other. (The Times)

To *ameliorate* is to 'bring about an improvement'. The tendency is to use the word about physical conditions (illness, poverty, etc.):

. . . if they linked those machines up to a generator, it might produce enough juice . . . to sell back to the grid, which along with wind farms would certainly help ameliorate the looming energy crisis.
(Observer)

That said, you could exchange the two words in the examples above without producing a significant change in meaning!

Embarrassment rating: ○○○

How to avoid: There are some situations where one word may simply 'feel' more appropriate than the other.

ALLOT, A LOT *or* ALOT

One of these words does not exist. Guess which.

Allot means to 'parcel out' (the noun is *allotment*). It has nothing to do with *a lot* (i.e. a 'large quantity'). But the real error comes when these last two words are written as one – 'alot'. People do this either because pronunciation runs them together, or perhaps influenced by such spellings as 'aloud' and 'alone'. Whatever the excuse, *alot* is always wrong:

☒☒ *. . . you will have alot* [should be *a lot*] *of client contact.*
(recruitment ad)

Embarrassment rating: ●●● I'm afraid that this is an error on the borders of illiteracy.

How to avoid: Nobody writes 'abit' as one word. So why *alot*?

ALL RIGHT *or* ALRIGHT

Probably under the influence of words such as 'already' and 'altogether', there is a growing tendency to run together the two parts of *all right*.

Alright is especially common in informal contexts – 'It'll be alright on the night' – but is regarded by what is probably a diminishing number as less correct than *all right*. Even so it is better avoided in formal writing.

Some would claim that there's a possible distinction in meaning between the two spellings, as here:

He got those answers all right. (i.e. all correct)

He got those answers alright! (where the word works as a part of an emphatic exclamation)

Embarrassment rating: ●○○

How to avoid: As suggested above, in formal usage *all right* is the preferable form.

ALLUSION, ILLUSION *or* DELUSION

Three nouns which differ only in their first two letters. The second two are quite close in meaning.

Of these three nouns *allusion* has a meaning distinct from that of the other two. An *allusion* is an 'indirect reference' and it's often found in discussion of music, films, and so on (where it indicates references to other bits of music, verse, etc.):

. . . they have succeeded in creating an album with more allusions than Ezra Pound's Cantos. (Observer)

Illusion and *delusion* are both to do with a 'mistaken idea' or a 'false belief'. Of the two *illusion* is the milder word. Having *illusions* suggests ignorance but the experience may be a pleasant one – before they are, in any case, destroyed by harsh reality:

For a time the negotiators had the illusion that they would quickly achieve peace.

A *delusion*, however, is not something that is easily driven away by argument or brutal fact, as it may be a sign of madness:

He began to suffer from the delusion that he was Napoleon.

Embarrassment rating: ●●○ if you use one of the other two for *allusion*. But potentially high if you suggest someone is suffering from *delusions* rather than *illusions*. Curiously, to say that someone is *deluded* doesn't carry quite the same charge.

How to avoid: Remembering the adjectives which derive from these words may help to keep clear the difference. *Illusive* and *illusory* describe nothing worse than false appearances but to describe a person as *delusional* (rather than *deluded*) suggests that they are in the grip of illness.

ALTAR *or* ALTER

Identical pronunciation sometimes causes confusion over spelling.

The *altar* (noun only) is the 'communion table' in church or a 'place for making sacrifices'. *Alter* (verb only) means to 'change' (noun: *alteration*).

Embarrassment rating: ●●◐, since this is a fairly elementary spelling error.

How to avoid: Cut the noun spelling *alteration* in half to get *alter*. Alternatively, *alter* comes from a Latin word of the same spelling meaning 'other', as in *alter ego*.

ALTERNATE *or* ALTERNATIVE

There's a clear distinction between these two, but they both contain the ideas of 'otherness' and 'change' and are frequently confused.

Alternative can be used as a noun or adjective, and indicates that a 'choice' is being offered. Originally the word was restricted to contexts where no more than two options were available, but it's often used now to indicate a wider range of choices:

> *Prime ministers are often unpopular; yet they can still win large general election victories if voters nevertheless believe the government is doing a better job than the alternatives.* (Guardian)

Alternate is both adjective and verb. As an adjective, it means 'occurring by turns', 'every other':

> *We make deliveries in your area on alternate Thursdays.*

As a verb, *alternate* means to 'shift from one thing to another, and then back again':

> *Her moods alternated between euphoria and gloom.*

The adjectival form of *alternate* shouldn't be used as a substitute for *alternative*:

> ☒ *The city was an alternate* [should be ***alternative***] *target and was bombed two days earlier than planned.* (Guardian)

(This suggests that the city was bombed by turns with another target.)

Alternative also describes technology, medicine, comedy, etc. which is not mainstream.

Embarrassment rating: ●◑○, since the writer's or speaker's meaning may be obscured. This may not happen often, but there is a real difference between the sentence 'The boy spent alternate holidays with his father', meaning that he holidayed with his mother or someone else the rest of the time, and 'The boy spent alternative holidays with his father', meaning that they dropped in on a commune.

How to avoid: If in doubt which to use, try rephrasing the sentence. If a choice between two or more items is involved then *alternative* is the right word, but if time/frequency are in question then *alternate* is probably right.

ALTERNATIVE *or* DILEMMA

By a kind of linguistic drift, the harsher associations of *dilemma* have become muted so that it is frequently used where *alternative* would be more correct.

Alternative suggests a 'choice between two possibilities' (see previous entry). *Dilemma* has the same meaning but in its original definition both the choices were unpleasant ones – so a *dilemma* presents a genuine problem:

> But once there, Langsdorff [the German captain of the Graf Spee] faced a dilemma – either blow up the ship or have her interned and risk sensitive information falling into the hands of the British. (Daily Mirror)

Embarrassment rating: ◑○○, since people happily use *dilemma* to indicate a difficulty in choosing between attractive *alternatives* (what to wear, what to eat). It would be a pity if the proper application of *dilemma* – as shown in the example above – disappeared altogether.

How to avoid: The phrase 'on the horns of a dilemma' tends to suggest that it is not a comfortable position to occupy.

ALTOGETHER *or* ALL TOGETHER

Like a number of words and phrases involving the prefix 'al-' and the complete word 'all' – 'already/all ready', 'alright/all right' – these are sometimes confused, particularly because the two words run into one when spoken aloud.

Altogether (an adverb) means 'entirely', 'with everything included':

The newly married couple were altogether delighted with their presents.

He made seven trips during the year altogether.

All together means occurring 'simultaneously' or 'in the same place':

At the end of a traditional whodunnit the suspects are summoned all together for the unmasking of the murderer.

Embarrassment rating: ●◑○ But there is room for ambiguity if the right form is not chosen. 'They left the house altogether' suggests they left the house, not intending to return. But 'They left the house all together' means that they left the house at the same time, and does not imply that they won't be returning.

How to avoid: If you are referring to time or place then *all together* will probably be correct. If 'entirely' or 'in total' can be substituted without changing the meaning of the sentence, then *altogether* is right.

AMBIGUOUS *or* AMBIVALENT

These two are used pretty casually to describe situations or attitudes that are hazy or in conflict so there is an ironic aptness in their confusion.

Ambiguous is an adjective meaning 'unclear', 'of doubtful meaning', and people may be *ambiguous* either through failure to make their meaning clear or, alternatively, because they don't want to make it clear:

Astrologers usually couch their predictions in ambiguous terms.

Being *ambivalent*, however, involves a more thought-out position since it means 'being in two minds' or 'experiencing conflicting emotions about something' (approval/disapproval; attraction/revulsion):

Segal is ambivalent about the benefits of the female pill – applauding women's freedom to make sexual choices, but decrying the health risks that were glossed over in the way it was sold to us. (Guardian)

(The nouns forms are *ambiguity* and *ambivalence*.)

Embarrassment rating: ●○○ There may even be some overlap between the two states of mind since being *ambivalent* about something may cause you to be *ambiguous* in your comments on it.

How to avoid: Try substituting 'in two minds' for either word. If this still conveys your meaning, then *ambivalent* is the right choice (on the other hand, you could simply stick to 'in two minds'). If the sentence doesn't sound right, then you probably mean *ambiguous*.

AMEND *or* EMEND

Both verbs have very similar pronunciation and the same general sense but the second is used only in a very particular context.

To *amend* is to 'improve by changing or correcting':

President Bush has signalled that he will support amending the federal Constitution to prevent same-sex couples from getting married. (The Times)

To *emend* has the more restricted sense of 'make alterations in a written text':

She emended the proof copy before returning it to the printers.

(The nouns from each verb are *amendment* and *emendation*.)

Embarrassment rating: ●◐○ There is a difference between *amending* a rule and *emending* it, since the second implies no more than making physical changes to the wording.

How to avoid: *Amend* has a much more general application and is likely to be the correct form/spelling. Only use *emend* and *emendation* where texts, drafts, etc. are concerned.

AMIABLE *or* AMICABLE

Both adjectives are to do with friendliness but have different applications.

Amiable means 'friendly', 'likeable':

He was popular for his easy-going and amiable manner.

Amicable means 'in a friendly spirit', and tends to be found in situations where differences of opinion have been resolved without a quarrel, or where bad relations might be expected:

They divorced 12 months later and all seemed amicable. (Daily Mirror)

Embarrassment rating: ●◐○ But *amicable* is a more formal term than *amiable* and the context where one is used is not necessarily appropriate for the other.

How to avoid: *Amiable* is used of people and their manner, smiles, facial expressions and so on. *Amicable* applies rather to situations, understandings, agreements, etc.

AMNESTY *or* MORATORIUM

These two words are sometimes confused, probably because both refer to a specified period in which some normal process is suspended.

An *amnesty* is a 'general pardon' or describes a 'period in which crimes can be admitted to without penalty':

> . . . *the government renewed the amnesty offered to paramilitary organisations which decommission weapons.* (Guardian)

A *moratorium* describes a 'stretch of time when an activity is halted'. It is often applied to the suspension of debt payment but has wider uses:

> *There has been little support from the conservation community for the Botswana government's four-year moratorium on lion hunting.*
> (Guardian)

Embarrassment rating: ●●○ If you know enough to employ these slightly specialist terms, you should know the difference between them. It would be incorrect to change them round in the examples above.

How to avoid: The organisation that campaigns for the rights of political prisoners and against state torture is called Amnesty. Less helpfully, *moratorium* derives from a Latin word meaning 'delay'. A clue, however, is that *moratorium* is generally followed by 'on'.

AMONG, AMONGST *or* BETWEEN

There are some word distinctions where people choose correctly without having to think about it. If they do stop, however, they may wonder whether there are any fine shades of meaning. This is one such distinction.

There's no difference between *among* and *amongst*, although the first version of the word is more widely used. There's no great difference between *among* and *between*, either, although *between* rather than *among* is used where there is a connection involving only two items (as at the beginning of this sentence and the previous one). It's sometimes claimed that *among* should be used with larger numbers, as in 'We shared the costs among the six of us' but *between* would do just as well here. If the larger number is seen as a unit rather than individuals, however, then *among* ought to be used:

They distributed the leaflets among the crowd.

Embarrassment rating: ○○○, if only because this is not an error likely to be made by a native English speaker (e.g. by mistakenly referring to *among* the two of us).

How to avoid: Your ear tells you which to use.

AMORAL *or* IMMORAL

These two look alike and may even describe the same sort of outlook or behaviour, so what's the distinction between them?

Amoral means 'outside accepted systems of morality'. The word implies lack of the conception of right and wrong. Animals are *amoral*, for example. The term is often used of large groups which supposedly operate without regard to standards, or even without knowledge of them:

. . . her [Princess Diana's] campaign against landmines threatened the profits of an amoral and sometimes ruthless international industry.
(The Times)

By contrast, *immoral* means 'contrary to accepted standards of morality'. The word frequently has a sexual application. Terming someone *immoral* implies that they know what ought to be done but choose to flout the 'rules':

. . . critics of the system say it is immoral for [Members of the European Parliament] to claim the money when they have no intention of working in the parliament that day. (Daily Telegraph)

Embarrassment rating: ●●○ Both *amoral* and *immoral* are pejorative terms. I think that the first is 'stronger' but it's arguable.

How to avoid: *Amoral* seems more appropriate for groups, where individual responsibility may be hard to pin down, while *immoral* is more applicable to the individual. Both words should be used with care, however.

ANNEX *or* ANNEXE

There's a difference between the noun and verb forms of this word, and it is easy to confuse the two.

To *annex* (pronounced with a stress on the second syllable) is to 'attach', 'take possession of':

> *There's a lot of bitterness towards the army, who've annexed the scenic mountainside for a commando base.* (Observer)

An *annexe* (with a final 'e' and pronounced with the stress more on the first syllable) is an 'extension', a 'building attached to a larger one':

> *The buildings caught up in the development agreement are the old general market building, its annexe (once a fish market), a cold store . . .* (Guardian)

(In the US the noun tends to be spelled without the final 'e'.)

Embarrassment rating: ●○○ If you refer incorrectly in writing to an *annex*, your meaning is clear – still a mistake though.

How to avoid: There's no simple way to remember this. Like many people, I would have to check a dictionary or reference book before writing the noun.

ANOINT *or* APPOINT

Two similar-sounding words which are to do with formally establishing someone in a position.

To *anoint* was originally to 'smear with oil as an act of consecration'. Anointing still takes place during the coronation of monarchs or the consecration of archbishops. But the word is quite widely used now in the sense of to 'install in an important position' – and the context doesn't have to be serious:

> *. . . the nation's favourite gay man and the Radio Times's recently anointed most powerful person in comedy* (Guardian)

To *appoint* is simply to 'select for a position':

> *She was appointed managing director at a relatively early age.*

Embarrassment rating: ●●○ if you say something like 'she was anointed managing director . . . ' – unless you're being ironic.

How to avoid: Although *anoint* has moved away from royalty and gone downmarket, it shouldn't be used about everyday appointments.

ANTICIPATE *or* EXPECT

These two verbs are widely treated as if they were interchangeable but there is a useful difference in meaning between them.

To *anticipate* is not merely to believe that something will happen (i.e. *expect*), but to 'take some action to prevent or lessen the consequences of what will occur'. Where *expect* is largely passive:

They're expecting it to rain tomorrow.

anticipate has more active overtones:

Anticipating rain, she took her umbrella with her.

Embarrassment rating: ●○○, since so many people use *anticipate* when they really mean *expect*. It is worth trying to preserve this distinction, however, since there is no other single word in English which combines the idea of expectation and action in the way that *anticipate* does.

How to avoid: This is a question of precise use. Before using *anticipate* you should ask yourself whether the subject of the sentence has actually done anything to deal with whatever is expected. If they haven't, then the simple *expect* would be more correct.

ANXIETY *or* ANGST

This is what one might call a lifestyle difference – or confusion. People who wouldn't like to admit to suffering *anxiety* might be quite happy to confess to *angst*.

Although *anxiety* has a specialist medical application (describing an aspect of depression) the general sense of the word is 'worry', a 'nagging concern':

When a disaster like a flood or stock market crash happens, do you, like most of us, purge your anxiety with an indignant search for explanations? (Daily Telegraph)

Angst (from the German) also means 'anxiety', but it has philosophical overtones suggesting troubled soul-searching. *Angst* is anxiety with attitude. Most uses of the word, however, have an ironic tinge to them. In this example the writer seems to be distancing himself slightly from the London middle classes and their concerns:

And it is a relief not to be overwhelmed by the angst about secondary education that grips the London middle classes. (Independent)

Embarrassment rating: Probably ○○○, since people who use the word *angst* do not get embarrassed.

How to avoid: The British only use *angst* ironically. If you are suffering from *anxiety*, you are not being ironic.

APOLOGIA *or* APOLOGY

Despite the look of the first word, it has almost nothing to do with saying sorry or expressing regret.

An *apologia* (pronounced with the stress on the long second 'o') is a 'formal statement in defence or justification of a particular position', while the person who makes such a statement is an *apologist* (pronounced with a stressed first 'o', as in *apology*). There's no suggestion of regret in an *apologia* – rather the reverse:

> In his passionate foreign policy apologia in Sedgefield last week, [Tony Blair] declared Britain to be 'in mortal danger'. (Spectator)

An *apology* is an 'expression of sorrow or regret', sometimes on others' behalf but usually for oneself. How heartfelt the *apology* is depends entirely on the context and the speaker's sincerity: the 'apologies for absence' which precede a meeting, for example, are about as meaningful as the Dear X which begins a letter.

Embarrassment rating: ●◐○ Any error here is likely to be on the side of the listener/reader who may assume that a person making an *apologia* is expressing remorse.

How to avoid: *Apologia* is a bit of posh vocabulary. 'Justification' will often do the same job and be more readily understood. But the word has its place when describing a systematic, formal defence of someone's position.

APPRAISE *or* APPRISE

These bureaucratic-sounding words are quite easy to mix up, not only because of their similar sound and spelling but because they can occur in the same sort of context.

The verb *appraise* means to 'sum up', to 'estimate the value or quality of' something or somebody (not usually in a monetary sense):

> . . . his intense skull and cold blazing eyes appraise you with a look of narcissistic derision. (Spectator)

(The noun is *appraisal* – a pseudo-technical-sounding word now most often applied to the way in which employees are assessed by their bosses.)

To *apprise* (slightly formal rather than in everyday use) is to 'give notice to', 'tell':

> *[Sylvia] Plath, who has already apprised her husband of two earlier suicide attempts, resents his way with the ladies, and begins to suspect that he is having an affair.* (Guardian)

Embarrassment rating: ●●○ The two words have nothing to do with each other, as is shown by comparing the sentences 'She was apprised of the situation' and 'She appraised the situation'. To confuse them is to show ignorance.

How to avoid: As a rule of thumb *appraise* cannot be followed by 'of', whereas *apprise* has to be. There are simpler and perhaps preferable expressions for these two – 'judge' or 'assess' for *appraise* and 'tell' or 'inform' for *apprise*. Use these if in doubt.

ARBITER, ARBITRATOR *or* MEDIATOR

These three terms, all describing people who assess situations and sort out problems, are sometimes used interchangeably but they have distinct shades of meaning.

An *arbiter* is an 'umpire', one who lays down the law or sets a standard of taste. The word is often found in connection with fashion or public opinion:

> *Her treatment also raises the danger that populist newspapers like the Sun . . . will become the arbiters of public confidence.* (Guardian)

An *arbitrator* is 'someone brought in to settle a dispute'. This word, rather than *arbiter*, tends to be used in trade disputes and the law:

> *Mr Justice Popplewell . . . once sued a paper for libel for saying he was asleep when he wasn't. The arbitrator, the late Lord (Gareth) Williams QC, awarded him £7,500.* (Guardian)

A *mediator* is an 'individual who acts as a go-between', sometimes when two or more parties are in disagreement but often simply to keep things running smoothly:

> *Mikhail Fradkov, the new prime minister, is the former Russian envoy to the EU and will act as a mediator to improve relations.* (Guardian)

Embarrassment rating: ●◐○ There is a blurring of meaning between the first two, but even so one should not refer to, say, an *arbitrator* of fashion.

How to avoid: *Arbiter* can be used generally, although it contains the notion of judgement which may not always be appropriate for the *mediator's* role.

ARCHETYPE *or* STEREOTYPE

A pair of words which are to do with pattern-makers and models. The difference between them is that between an antique and a reproduction.

An *archetype* is the 'original model from which copies are produced':

> *Hollywood . . . also captured the world's imagination with a whole series of American archetypes: the cowboy, the gangster, the little tramp.* (Telegraph)

Almost by definition there can only be one *archetype* for each pattern but the adjectival form of the word – *archetypal* – is very often used to mean one of many rather than the 'first' of many. In this sense, 'typical' or 'standard' or even 'stereotypical' is more accurate:

> ☒ *Even the hardiest club cricketer is likely to enter the archetypal [**stereotypical** would be better] ramshackle village pavilion with a wrinkled nose.* (Daily Telegraph)

A *stereotype* is a 'clichéd image', 'something which conforms completely to a standard pattern', and there is usually a negative shading to the word (as there is to the verb *stereotype* and the adjective *stereotypical*):

> *Terence Stamp leaves no stone unturned as he delivers every American's idea of the classic English servant stereotype.* (Daily Mirror)

Embarrassment rating: ●○○ But it is preferable to be clear as to whether you're talking about an original, an *archetype*, or the copy, a *stereotype*.

How to avoid: The 'arch-' part of *archetype* may suggest something high and so outstanding, original. If you want to sound critical rather than neutral, use *stereotype*.

ARDENT or ARDUOUS

Two adjectives with deceptively similar beginnings but no connection of meaning.

Ardent means 'burning with enthusiasm':

In the eyes of the more ardent cricket nationalists, the inescapable vagaries of luck and form are always suspect. (Guardian)

Arduous means 'difficult to achieve' or 'tough' (when applied to working conditions):

. . . most of us knew nothing about Britain's cockle industry – a bleak and arduous trade worth over £20 million a year. (Observer)

(The respective nouns are *ardour* [US *ardor*] and *arduousness*.)

Embarrassment rating: ●●○, since substituting one word for the other will obscure meaning.

How to avoid: *Ardent* can only be applied to individuals and their attitude/spirit; *arduous* can never be applied to people but only to tasks, duties, journeys, etc.

AROMA or ODOUR

Two nouns meaning 'smell'. But is one more positive than the other?

If there's a difference it is that *aroma* tends to be applied to pleasant scents, particularly from food or drink:

I can still recall the delicious aroma of teas from around the world. (Guardian)

while *odour* is more neutral and wide-ranging. In fact, my unscientific survey suggests it's generally associated with the less attractive smells such as body odour. To take a random example:

A thick ashen odour still hung in the air. (Guardian)

Embarrassment rating: ●○○ But one could imagine the embarrassment level shooting up as the result of a careless reference to the *odour* of someone's cooking, rather than the *aroma*.

How to avoid: Any advice here is more to do with etiquette than correct usage. Remembering 'body odour' and 'deodorant' may help.

AROUSE *or* ROUSE

Two very similar words connected with coming to life from a sleepy or passive state. They are not quite interchangeable.

To *arouse* is to 'excite', to 'provoke', and is usually applied to reactions (interest, concern) or feelings (suspicion, anger):

The proposal to build a by-pass through the unspoiled countryside aroused controversy.

Arouse is also used of sexual responses, as is the associated noun, *arousal.*

To *rouse* is to 'awaken', to 'stir up' and generally takes a person or animal as its object:

The church bells roused him from his sleep.

(A speech, song, etc. should be described as *rousing*, not *arousing*.)

Embarrassment rating: ◑○○ But if you refer to someone being *aroused*, it will almost certainly be taken in a sexual sense whether you mean this or not.

How to avoid: Sex aside, *arouse* usually takes an abstract noun as its object (see above) – think *a*rouse and *a*bstract – while *rouse* applies to people and animals.

AS IF *or* LIKE

This isn't a confusion so much as a whinge about the colloquial use of *like* when *as if* would be better English.

The use of *like* as a link-word (conjunction) instead of *as if* or *as though* is very frequent:

She looked like she had some good news to tell. (rather than the more correct . . . *as if she had* . . .).

In recent years the habit has spread from spoken English to written English:

☒ *Timberlake wore something that looked like* [should be *as if*] *it had come from the Young Casuals department at M&S.* (Daily Telegraph)

☒ *Twain's whole wardrobe looked like* [should be *as if*] *it cost less than the £50 she charged for a ticket.* (The Times)

Embarrassment rating: ○○○ Non-existent most of the time, regrettably. I'd like to say that the use of *like* instead of *as if* is still an informal usage, not acceptable in more formal prose, blah, blah. But I'm afraid the truth is that it *is* acceptable, as the examples above show. You wouldn't get it in the most formal writing and to me it still sounds self-consciously hip and laid-back. But this is a usage which is really well dug in. In fact, in some contexts, it would be embarrassing to use the rather formal *as if* construction.

How to avoid: If this sense of *like* jars on your ears or eyes, then you will avoid using it. If it doesn't, you won't.

ASSUMPTION *or* PRESUMPTION

There is no real difference between the verbs *assume* and *presume* in the sense of to 'take for granted' but there is a distinction between their noun forms, *assumption* and *presumption*.

An *assumption* can be a 'supposition which isn't supported by evidence'; 'false' is the adjective often partnered with it and, even if it turns out to be correct, it has more the sense of a 'guess':

   . . . the assumption was that, following his messy public divorce in a Cape Town court, she picked him up and dusted him down. (Daily Telegraph)

A *presumption* has more the sense of a 'probability', i.e. it is more than guesswork:

   Every village these days is set within a so-called developmental envelope, which governs planning decisions. Within the village envelope, there is a presumption that some degree of development will be allowed.
   (Daily Telegraph)

Under English law, courts work on the *presumption* of innocence rather than the *assumption* of it.

   (*Presume* can also carry the sense of 'be bold enough to', as in 'I wouldn't presume to tell you how to do your job'. Another related sense attached to *presumption* is 'arrogance', 'insolence'.)

Embarrassment rating: ◑○○ But the careful user will observe the shade of difference between a belief which isn't much more than a guess (*assumption*) and one which has, say, past experience to back it up (*presumption*).

How to avoid: See above. A *presumption* is a *rea*sonable belief; an *assumption* could be *su*spect.

ASSURE, ENSURE *or* INSURE

These three verbs, all containing some idea of 'guarantee', are related but have different applications.

To *assure* is to 'guarantee', to 'give certainty to someone':

They did their best to assure him that he was welcome.

To *ensure* is to 'make something safe or certain':

Careful preparation helped to ensure the success of the expedition.

To *insure* is to 'protect oneself (financially) against loss or damage':

We've insured for the trip after last year's disaster.

(The noun *assurance* can describe 'anything which is intended to inspire confidence or belief' such as an encouraging remark. When used in the context of the insurance market, *assurance* relates to those policies which cover an individual's life and pay the beneficiaries on his or her death. *Insurance* can also be used to describe [life] *assurance* policies, and is applied to everything else against which one can insure: accident, fire, theft, etc.)

Embarrassment rating: ●◑○ If there's any confusion, it's likely to occur with the first two. The difference is shown by 'The general assured his men that their superior skills would ensure victory'.

How to avoid: *Insure* and *insurance* are always connected to financial payments or some other security against disaster. *Assure* and *assurance* and *reassurance* are usually related to words or symbolic gestures. To *ensure* (there is no noun equivalent) suggests the taking of physical measures to achieve something.

AUGER *or* AUGUR

The obscure sources of these words and their identical pronunciation sometimes cause mistakes in spelling.

Both of these words are to do with somewhat remote worlds, unless you're an advanced DIY-er or a Roman fortune-teller. An *auger* (noun only) is an 'instrument for boring holes', usually in wood. An *augur* is a 'fortune-teller', the word deriving from the ancient Roman practice of telling the future through bird flights (which were seen as auguries). Despite this exotic source, *augur* is quite often found, more often as a verb than a noun – things are said to *augur* well or badly for the time to come:

[In Bolivia] a dried frog augurs wealth and is apparently doubly effective if it has a cigarette in its mouth. (Daily Telegraph)

Embarrassment rating: ●○○, although the popularity of *augur* in talking about sporting chances or financial prospects should encourage the regular user to get the right spelling.

How to avoid: *Augury* is to do with the future, and like that word contains two 'u's. An *auger* is a bor*er*.

AURAL *or* ORAL

Both words are adjectives with a near-identical pronunciation and both are often connected with types of exam. Any problems over use are likely to be connected with the less familiar *aural* and to occur in speech rather than writing.

Aural means 'of the ear':

In the secular songs of England's supreme composer, Henry Purcell, romance is given its consummate aural shape. (The Times)

Oral means 'relating to the mouth':

Video on-demand technology installed in dentists' chairs is the latest attempt to make oral surgery appear less of an ordeal. (The Times)

As a noun, *oral* describes an examination where the candidate gives spoken answers. Confusion sometimes arises when the words are used in this context. An *aural* examination in French would test the candidate's ability to hear and understand that language when spoken. But a French *oral* tests the candidate's capacity to speak the language.

Embarrassment rating: ●○○ Confusion over which is meant in speech is easily resolved. To take one example: no one is likely to think that *oral* sex refers to the ear – if *aural* sex existed it would presumably be the same as phone sex.

How to avoid: Some speakers distinguish between the two words by pronouncing the first syllable of *aural* to rhyme with 'ow'. Try remembering that an *or*ator speaks, or *or*ates, whereas an *au*dience listens.

AUTHORISED, AUTHORITARIAN *or* AUTHORITATIVE

These adjectives are connected to the noun *authority*. All appear in different contexts, two conveying a kind of approval and the other being critical. The first and third are particularly likely to be confused.

Authorised means 'proper', 'permitted by recognised authority':

The inspectors made an authorised visit to the nuclear plant.

Authorised is frequently tagged to biographical revelations, where it suggests that the author has been given access to the subject's life and secrets, warts and all. (Paradoxically, the opposite term *unauthorised* is often used as a selling point since the word hints that you will discover things which the subject would prefer to have kept hidden. In this sense *unauthorised* is a euphemism for 'scandalous', 'dirt-digging'.)

Authoritarian is often applied to governments rather than individuals, but more generally it defines an attitude or style 'rating obedience to authority more highly than individual freedom':

Could the tide now turn, and by liberating parents to be more authoritarian, bring about a swing back to a more orderly society?
(The Times)

Authoritative means 'possessing authority', and is applied to people and sources which can be relied on to produce the right answer:

You can almost believe a timetable when it is printed in authoritative type.
(Independent)

Embarrassment rating: ●●○, because the meaning is mangled if the wrong word is used. For example, a person who is *authorised* (to do something) will not necessarily be an *authoritative* person. Conversely, an *authorised* biography may not be an *authoritative* one. And an *authoritarian* individual may be neither *authorised* nor truly *authoritative* – merely someone who likes laying down the law.

How to avoid: There is no really simple way to remember the distinction between these three. *Authoritarian* has echoes of 'disciplinarian', and *authorise* can be paired with 'legitimise'. With *authoritative*, however, you are on your own.

AVENGE *or* REVENGE

These two are frequently interchanged and both carry the meaning of 'seek for vengeance'. Even so, there can be a useful distinction between them.

To *avenge* means to 'look for retribution' for a harm done not to the avenger but to somebody close to him/her:

> . . . *long-held traditions dictated that a man could fully avenge the murder of a family member only by killing the perpetrator.* (Daily Telegraph)

To *revenge* is to 'harm in exchange for a wrong done to oneself':

> *The side revenged their previous trouncing with a very convincing win against their old opponents.*

Embarrassment rating: ○○○, since the distinction between the two words is almost worn away, encouraged by the noun use of *revenge* in such phrases as 'revenge killing'. Why raise it then, if it doesn't matter? Simply because the difference is worth preserving – or resurrecting.

How to avoid: The old saying 'revenge is sweet' underlines the personal aspect of revenge: it's payback for a defeat or humiliation dished out to *you*. An avenger is a loftier, perhaps more terrifying figure, as in the Biblical avenging angel.

BBBBBBB

BAIL *or* BALE

There are so many meanings associated with this simple pair of words that uncertainty over which form to use on which occasion is almost bound to occur.

Bail is a noun and verb with several meanings. An accused person will obtain *bail*, or be *bailed*, in court, i.e. 'gain release from custody before trial by providing some security' (usually financial) which will be forfeit if the defendant disappears. To *bail* also means to 'clear water out of' something, and to 'parachute out of an aircraft'. And finally, cricket stumps are topped by *bails*.

   Bale can also be used as a verb in two of the senses above (*baling* water; *baling* out of a crashing aircraft). As a noun *bale* means a 'bundle' (a *bale* of cotton); as a verb, to 'do up in bundles' (*baling* hay).

Embarrassment rating: ●○○ As indicated, these words not only have a variety of meanings but can, in some contexts, be used interchangeably.

How to avoid: *Bale* is the more adaptable form, covering everything from bundles to aircraft escapes. The only places where the *bail* spelling must be used are in a legal setting ('Bail was set at £20,000') and on the cricket field.

BALMY *or* BARMY

The spelling of the first of these very similar words sometimes causes problems because of the unsounded 'l', and the temptation is to use the second spelling since everybody is familiar with it.

Balmy (from balm, a healing ointment) means 'gentle', 'soothing'. Its most usual application is to the weather:

   Since then we've been spoilt by winters often so balmy that the slightest flurry of snow has become national news. (The Times)

Barmy derives from barm, the froth on the head of fermenting liquor. So it means 'frothy' and therefore 'foolish', 'not right in the head' (although, to confuse things, the word with this meaning can also be spelled *balmy*):

> . . . *the show was over-ambitious, challenging, weird, and completely barmy – and that's got to be good.* (Guardian)

Embarrassment rating: ●○○, since these two words are not often committed to paper, at least in formal writing. Despite its dictionary meaning, *barmy* is not particularly insulting. In fact, there's sometimes a tinge of affection in the term (as in 'Barmy Army' to describe avid followers of English cricket). And to describe the weather as *balmy* is to resort to a rather unsatisfactory cliché, since to most people the word doesn't convey anything more exact than 'nice'.

How to avoid: The root of *balmy* in *balm* should help with the spelling. The rhyming association between *barmy* and 'army' provides help with that one, if required.

BEASTLY *or* BESTIAL

Both of these words derive from *beast* but they have ended up in rather different places. One is almost a joke while the other is deadly serious.

Although *beastly* can mean 'like an animal', it has never recovered from being part of what dictionaries once termed 'society slang' – beastly bad show, what? Even when the word is being used semi-seriously, it rarely suggests any condemnation stronger than 'not very nice':

> *Beastly gossips suggested that he had sacked 20 per cent of his staff while claiming an £800,000 pay packet.* (Daily Telegraph)

Bestial, by contrast, is the real thing since it still conveys strong disapproval, even abhorrence. Here it is synonymous with 'inhuman', 'vile':

> *Both in Europe and in America he has spoken publicly about the bestial slaughter in his country.* (Daily Telegraph)

Embarrassment rating: ●●● *Beastly* behaviour may not be very attractive but it's far removed from *bestial* behaviour.

How to avoid: *Bestial* should not be used unless really justified by the context. *Beastly* is often tongue-in-cheek.

BEGIN *or* COMMENCE

A pair of synonyms. All words may be equal but some are more equal than others.

Plenty of people think that the bunged-up, bureaucratic word *commence* sounds better than its synonyms 'begin' or 'start'. Some language guides will tell you that *commence* is for formal use – so that a ceremony or a meeting *commences* rather than starts – but it still sounds constipated to me.

Embarrassment rating: ●○○ This isn't a confusable in the ordinary sense, but its appearance in an everyday context – 'They commenced their journey at Heathrow' – sounds pompous, and the user should feel highly embarrassed.

How to avoid: Keep off *commence*.

BENEFICENT, BENEFICIAL, BENEVOLENT *or* BENIGN

All of these words have positive overtones connected with the doing of good but they crop up in different surroundings, and the wrong choice can sound odd.

Beneficent is a fairly high-flown word meaning 'kind or charitable' and tends to describe people and their actions or outlook:

It set the seal on an event of joyous anarchy, as if the composer's beneficent shade were with us . . . (Daily Telegraph)

Beneficial can mean simply 'useful', as in 'a beneficial exchange of views', but its most usual context is probably to do with 'promoting health or well-being':

The doctor suggested that a change of scene would be beneficial.

Benevolent falls somewhere between *beneficent* and *benign*, in that it can describe somebody who's merely 'well disposed' towards others as well as suggesting actions that are more positively 'charitable' – it's in this second sense that societies once incorporated *benevolent* into their titles, although any charity setting up now would avoid the word since it has overtones of patronage.

Benign, with the sense of 'kindly', is more to do with attitude than action (a *benign* smile, a *benign* presence) and has a specialist sense in describing a 'non-cancerous' growth – the opposite of 'malign/malignant'.

Embarrassment rating: ●○○, since this is a question of shades of meaning. However, to describe a medicine as 'benevolent' instead of 'beneficial' or to refer to a charity donor as 'benign' rather than 'benevolent' would suggest an uncertain grasp of language.

How to avoid: *Benevolent* (showing goodwill) is the opposite of 'malevolent' (showing ill-will). *Beneficial* is linked with effects, therapies, diets, and is often followed by 'to', with the sense 'of *benefit* to'. *Beneficent* is extremely rare so unlikely to trouble you. But generally only the context of the word, and some sensitivity to its overtones, will tell you which to use.

BEREAVED *or* BEREFT

Two words connected with death and loss that are often used inappropriately.

Bereaved means 'deprived of by death', and should be used only about those who were genuinely close to the dead person. *Bereft* (originally having the same meaning as *bereaved*) generally means 'deprived of something or somebody significant', without having a necessary reference to death. The death of Princess Diana in 1997 may have left many people *bereft* but it didn't, strictly speaking, leave them *bereaved*, whatever they may have thought. There's an overtone of hopelessness to *bereft*, properly used, and its force is weakened if it's simply used as an alternative for 'without', as it is here:

> *Bereft of anything close to evidence to support it, the report has barely been followed up by any besides the tabloid press . . .* (Independent)

Embarrassment rating: ◑○○ In new touchy-feely Britain people are quite happy to talk about being *bereaved* or *bereft* when their favourite reality TV show is off air, and hardly distinguish between these two states.

How to avoid: Restrict the use of *bereaved* and *bereft* to genuinely painful circumstances. Ber*eaved* describes the grief produced by d*eath*; ber*eft* the sadness of being *left* without something.

BESIDE *or* BESIDES

These two everyday words are often used as though they were completely interchangeable. They aren't.

Beside means 'next to' ('the table stood *beside* the window'). *Besides* means 'in addition to' (*'besides* the table, the room contained several chairs') and 'apart from' (*'besides* the table and chairs, the room was empty'). *Besides*, generally followed by a comma, also has the sense of 'moreover' (*'Besides*, there was nothing to be seen in the room!').

Embarrassment rating: ◑○○ There is a potential ambiguity in a sentence such as 'Beside the table, several chairs were found in the room', where it may not be clear whether the writer means that the chairs were near the table or that they were simply scattered about the place. Technically the first interpretation is the correct one.

How to avoid: If you mean 'by the side of' then put *beside*. Use *besides* for anything else.

BIANNUAL *or* BIENNIAL

These terms to do with time and frequency are easy to mix up but there is a significant distinction between them.

Biannual means 'occurring twice a year':

> . . . *in addition to the one-off registration fee there may be costly annual or biannual administration charges.* (Daily Telegraph)

Biannual ought not to be used to mean 'occurring every two years', as it seems to do in the following example from the same newspaper – if the 'biannual returns' really are two years overdue there should be four of them!

> ☒ *With its biannual* [should this be **biennial**?] *return more than two years overdue, Indigo Capital PLC is classified . . . as a 'company not in good standing'.* (Daily Telegraph)

Biennial means 'occurring every two years' and describes festivals or conferences which conform to this pattern or, as a noun, it applies to a 'plant which flowers or fruits only in its second year'.

Embarrassment rating: ●●◑, since the wrong word conveys the wrong meaning and will cause genuine confusion.

How to avoid: This is one of those confusions where the uncertain user needs to check the dictionary. Alternatively, pick another expression such as 'half-yearly' or 'twice-yearly' for *biannual*, and 'every two years' or 'every other year' for *biennial*.

BIAS *or* PREJUDICE

Although these two words are sometimes used as equivalent accusations, particularly in the adjectival forms of *biased* and *prejudiced*, there is a difference between them.

Bias is a milder form of *prejudice*, and the use of the word does not necessarily convey any criticism of the person or group displaying it (even if *biased* is often pejorative). *Bias* suggests an 'inclination', a tendency to be for (or against) a side in an argument, for or against a political party, a team, etc.

> *Brashness and bias are the occupational tendency, if not hazard, of a free-market press.* (The Times)

A *prejudice* is an 'already formed opinion or reaction', i.e. one which isn't reasoned but usually emotional or instinctive. The word is found most frequently in the minefields of race and religion. Although it is possible to show a *prejudice* in favour of something, the word generally appears in a negative context, as here:

> *Nor would they be surprised at the prejudice – levelled against Jews, Muslims, and Christians – that warps so much of contemporary debate.* (Observer)

Embarrassment rating: ●●○ As suggested above, *prejudice* generally reflects badly on the person showing it whereas *bias* is a less judgemental term. So care should be taken when laying either word at anybody's door.

How to avoid: *Prejudice* seems such a loaded term now, albeit one casually flung about, that a self-imposed ban on its use might be healthy for all of us.

BIZARRE *or* BAZAAR

These two words have nothing to do with each other but their similar pronunciation and quirky spelling sometimes cause. confusion, perhaps enhanced by some overlapping ideas of strangeness/foreignness (*bazaar* derives from Persian).

Bizarre means 'odd to the point of being fantastically strange':

> *Certainly it seems bizarre not to allow nail-clippers into an airline fuselage, but to legislate for the guaranteed presence of a gun.* (Independent)

A *bazaar* is a 'market-place' but it carries exotic overtones of crowded muddle:

> *I don't think I've been to Terminal 3 before. It's like a bazaar: teeming and brightly coloured and terrifically cheery . . .* (Daily Telegraph)

Embarrassment rating: ●●○ This is really a matter of spelling rather than a confusion of meaning.

How to avoid: The association of a *bazaar* with a market-place may be reinforced by the frequency of the 'a's in both words.

BLOND *or* BLONDE

The second word is so frequently applied to women that people don't know or have forgotten that there is a masculine form.

Blond, meaning 'fair', 'light-coloured', applies almost exclusively to hair colour. Both noun and adjective take the final 'e' if the subject is female:

> *Still, Page is more than a woman trading on being yesterday's blonde bombshell.* (Guardian)

but when the word is applied to a masculine subject it should, strictly speaking, be spelled without the 'e':

> *He has never yet revealed whether his unruly, peroxide blond crop is a hairpiece or not.* (Sun)

Embarrassment rating: ●●○ A man would not like to be described as a *blonde*. But then many men wouldn't like to be called *blond*, either, accurate though the description might be, because of the inescapable Marilyn Monroe-ish associations of the word.

How to avoid: Stick to *blonde*. If using the word about men, it's probably safer to change to 'fair-haired' unless you're poking fun, as in the *Sun* quote above.

BON VIVANT *or* BON VIVEUR

Two terms, apparently from French, which have a humorously sophisticated air to them and sound almost the same. They're not. *Bon viveur* is the one more often found but *bon vivant* is the one more often intended.

To take the more usual one first: a *bon viveur* is a 'pleasure-lover', a 'man about town'. Oddly, the original expression isn't used by the

French ('nom de plume' is another example of this). Perhaps because of its fake-Frenchness, *bon viveur* has a rather dated naughtiness about it. Think of winks, nudges and twirled moustaches.

An "emotional" court hearing in London revealed the tangled love life of the screen-writer and notorious bon viveur, *who married three times and embarked on a love affair with Miss Minutolo in his 70s.* (The Times)

Just to confuse things, the term *bon vivant* is used in France with the meaning of 'jovial', although its feminine form *bonne vivante* is not found there – perhaps because joviality isn't regarded as a feminine attribute by the French? Anyway, in correct 'British' usage a *bon vivant* is a 'good companion' and 'someone who has a discriminating taste in food and drink':

. . . as any bon vivant will tell you, you rarely expect anything [in a station buffet] other than a smeared glass of gassy lager and an indigestible sausage roll when close to rolling stock. (Daily Telegraph)

Embarrassment rating: ●◐○, because if you want to impress by using these phrases you should know the difference between them.

How to avoid: Anybody wanting a word to convey a 'good-bloke-who-likes-a-drink-or-two', which is what *bon viveur* is generally taken to mean, should probably be using *bon vivant*. But then someone will say, 'Don't you mean a *bon viveur*?' or tell the speaker off for pedantry. Personally, I wouldn't use either expression.

BORN *or* BORNE

This is a tricky pair to get right, as the switch from the version without an 'e' to the one spelled with an 'e' sometimes seems almost arbitrary.

Borne is the past participle form of the verb *to bear*. It is applied to the carrier:

Used to guns, he had borne arms almost from the time he learned to walk.

or to the thing or person carried:

So we beat on, boats against the current, borne back ceaselessly into the past. (Scott Fitzgerald, *The Great Gatsby*)

When *bear* is used in the sense of to 'give birth', the form *borne* is used if the mother is the subject of the sentence:

She had borne him four children.

Otherwise the correct form is *born*:

Four children were born to her/Charles Dickens was born in Rochester.

It's quite easy to lose your bearings over *born/e*, as the following demonstrates:

☒ ☒ *This mistake is typical not of Conservatives but of the Left – borne* [should be *born*] *of the notion that a society is like a machine . . .* (The Times)

Embarrassment rating: ●●○ This seems to me a genuinely awkward distinction, and so any error is fairly forgivable. Also, the meaning of the sentence is unlikely to be impaired by any slip.

How to avoid: If the writer can substitute 'carried', then the *borne* spelling will be correct. (This test works for the *Times* quotation above, since 'carried' <u>cannot</u> be substituted and therefore *born* should have been used.) When it comes to birth or babies, remember that *borne* is only usable where the mother is the subject; otherwise it's *born*.

BRAKE *or* BREAK

These versatile words are sometimes confused, partly because of their identical pronunciation and probably also because of some association of ideas between pauses, gaps and stopping.

As a verb, *brake* has only two related meanings: to 'slow down' or to 'apply a brake'.

The noun describes the 'mechanism for slowing down/stopping', literally or figuratively:

. . . his tax credit system will put a brake on the ambitions of almost every couple with a combined income of less than £20,000. (Guardian)

Break has a variety of meanings as a verb from 'interrupt' to 'damage', and as a noun from 'crack' to 'pause for rest':

The cast took a well-deserved break after several hours of rehearsal.

The two are occasionally confused, as in the incorrect spelling 'tax brake' – a brake on taxes might be a good thing but the right version is 'tax break', referring to a legitimate way of avoiding tax and so gaining 'respite' from it.

(*Brake* also has the noun meaning of a 'clump of trees'.)

Embarrassment rating: ●●◑ Although the spellings are easily mixed up, the words are very much in everyday use.

How to avoid: Since the scope and applications of *break* are much wider than those for *brake*, the former is the word more frequently found. If *brake* is misused for *break*, it is probably because the context suggests that it might be the right word (as in the erroneous 'tax brake'). When the mistake occurs the other way round – as in applying the 'breaks' on a car – some notion of stopping or resting (i.e. taking a *break*) may lie behind the confusion, unless it is a simple oversight. Anyway, the only rough and ready rule is to use *break* unless the context is cars or driving, or a driving metaphor such as 'putting the *brakes* on spending'. Otherwise there is no simple memory trick to distinguish these two. Some pairs of words ought to come equipped with red flags: user beware.

BRAVADO *or* BRAVERY

These two are related but distinct, and should not be confused.

Like a cheap cracker, *bravado* goes off with a big bang to reveal nothing inside. Having the sense of a 'display of bravery', it shades into an 'aggressive showing off':

The main characteristic of teenage boys is bravado. (Daily Telegraph)

Bravery is the genuine article, 'courage':

. . . *the ingenuity and bravery of the young airmen who dug a 330-ft tunnel out of the notorious prison camp have passed into modern mythology.* (Daily Telegraph)

Embarrassment rating: ●●●, since *bravado* is generally pejorative while *bravery* is complimentary.

How to avoid: Beware *bravado* unless you wish to cast aspersions.

BREACH *or* BREECH

Two words with a one-letter difference. Vague associations between 'openings', 'guns' and 'trousers' may encourage this confusion!

A *breach* is an 'opening' – as in the famous speech which Shakespeare gave to King Henry V, 'Once more unto the breach, dear friends'. Metaphorically, it is a 'break in a contract' or a 'breakdown in relations between two groups':

. . . *[he] also had to ensure that no breach occurred between Danish amateurs and professionals in the field.* (The Times)

Breech describes the 'part of a gun behind the barrel' or the 'back or buttocks' (hence *breech* delivery, when the baby emerges buttocks- or feet-first). Apart from its connection with firearms, the word tends to appear in its plural form of *breeches*, meaning 'trousers'. The word is old-fashioned, of course, and specifically describes leggings which only reach to the knee:

> *A gloomy-looking Lord Falconer of Thoroton, the lord chancellor desperate to abandon his wig and breeches . . .* (Guardian)

This second spelling should not be used when *breach* is meant:

> ☒ ☒ *. . . into this information breech* [should be **breach**] *have leapt a whole raft of new-wave space capitalists . . .* (Guardian)

Embarrassment rating: ●●○, because *breach* is a common word – and if you put *breech* in error, then unavoidable images of climbing into a gun or a pair of trousers come to mind.

How to avoid: A *breach* is a brea*k*, and may be literal or metaphorical. If you are referring to *breech* or *breeches* you must be talking about a concrete object, e.g. part of a rifle.

BRIDAL *or* BRIDLE

Two identically pronounced words which are sometimes mixed up, particularly when it comes to a bridle path (perhaps through some association between brides-churches-aisles-paths?).

Bridal means 'relating to a bride'. A *bridle* is 'part of a horse's headgear', and therefore 'anything which restrains'. A bridle path is one on which horses can be led or ridden.

Embarrassment rating: ●●○ The joke will be on the user if he/she writes about 'bridle wear' (obviously an interesting wedding night is planned). The erroneous 'bridal path' would be ambiguous, since it ostensibly refers to the route taken by a bride.

How to avoid: *Bridle*, connected with horses, contains all the letters of 'ride'. *Bridal*, like nupti*al*, ends in '–al'.

BROACH *or* BROOCH

The second word is probably more usual than the first, yet is sometimes misspelled perhaps because the '-oa-' form looks more familiar, by analogy with 'coach' or 'poach'.

Broach, a verb, generally occurs in two contexts: to *broach* a topic, to 'introduce' it into conversation, often with the suggestion of difficulty:

> *. . . clients on her assertiveness training courses see broaching such matters with their bosses as an enormous emotional challenge.* (Guardian)

and – less often – to *broach* a bottle (i.e. 'open' it).

Brooch, a noun, is an 'ornamental clasp':

> *Across her chest she wore a diamond brooch in the shape – and almost the size – of a tree branch.* (Observer)

(Both words are pronounced in the same way, to rhyme with 'coach'.)

Embarrassment rating: ●●○ The general mistake (putting *broach* for *brooch*) is fairly easily made and will not affect the sense. It is a basic spelling error though and best avoided.

How to avoid: *Broach* is always a verb and so will be preceded by a subject, noun or pronoun, and usually followed by 'topic', 'question', etc. *Brooch* is a noun only and so will tend to have 'a/the' in front of it.

CALENDAR, CALENDER *or* COLANDER

Almost identical spelling and pronunciation often results in the first two being mixed up.

A *calendar* is a 'table for telling the date' or simply a 'list':

> *The nude calendar, with carefully placed objects à la Austin Powers, raised £578,000.* (Guardian)

It's quite common to find the wrong word used when *calendar* is meant:

> ☒ ☒ *St Patrick's Day celebrations are firmly fixed on the national party calender* [should be *calendar*]. (Observer)

But *calender* is a word not in everyday use since it's restricted to a couple of specialist applications: a 'machine for rolling cloth or paper' or (still more obscure) a 'member of a Persian religious sect'.

Neither word should be confused with *colander*, the 'kitchen container used for straining food':

> *With more holes in its plot than a colander,* Last Day in Limbo *rollicks along with a cast of 2-D characters . . .* (Observer)

Embarrassment rating: ●◑○ Even if you get the spelling wrong with the first two, your meaning will not be mistaken. As long as you don't refer to looking things up in a colander . . .

How to avoid: An almanac is a register of days, events, etc. – note the 'a's of almanac, like the end of calend*a*r. More practically, *calender* is such a specialist term that the '-er' spelling is almost always going to be the wrong one.

CALLOUS *or* CALLUS

Any problem with this pair of closely related words is likely to come with the spelling of the second one, which doesn't 'look' English.

Callous (which can be used to describe 'hardened' skin) is an adjective with the principal meaning of 'without feeling', or 'ruthless':

> *Cruelty does not simply consist of a neutral act, but of delighting in the hurt – or being callous towards the suffering – so caused.* (Daily Telegraph)

Callus, which comes direct from Latin, is the noun for a 'patch of toughened skin':

> *The presence of calluses on the forehead of a Shi'ite Muslim, by contrast, is a sign of great religiosity.* (Daily Telegraph)

Embarrassment rating: ●◑○, if you put the first spelling in place of the second ('he had callouses on his hand'). The meaning is clear but it's still a mistake.

How to avoid: The grammatical rule is that words ending in '–ous' tend to be adjectives, like *callous*, and those ending in '–us' are usually nouns. Otherwise there is no neat way to remember the difference. *Callus* is a fairly specialist term, at least when it's written down, and I suspect that most people would reach for some alternative phrase like 'rough patches' before using it.

CAN *or* MAY

Two very simple words which are used interchangeably but which can – or may – convey subtly different meanings.

Can denotes ability:

> *She can speak five languages.*

(but is often used in the sense of 'has permission':

> *She's just been told she can come on the trip*).

May indicates possibility:

> *It may rain tomorrow.*

and permission:

> *You may leave when the job's finished.*

There is a small potential ambiguity in a sentence like the one above, which could mean 'You might take it into your head to leave . . . '.

There is a stronger ambiguity in a sentence like 'He may drive across'. Context and tone of voice will tell the listener whether it's a matter of permission or possibility.

Embarrassment rating: ○○○ Long, long ago a pedantic teacher or parent might pick on a child's question 'Can I do X?' by saying 'Of course you *can* do X. What you mean is, *may* you do it?' But no one talks like this any more, do they?

How to avoid: Despite the above, it's sometimes worth considering in formal writing the distinction between *can* and *may*. Do you want to imply capability or permission?

CANNON *or* CANON

As with the example of 'calendar/calender' earlier, the identical pronunciation of *cannon/canon* sometimes causes the wrong spelling to be used.

A *cannon* is a 'large gun' or a 'type of shot in billiards'. By contrast, *canon* has a variety of different applications: a 'priest attached to a cathedral'; a 'principle or rule' (as in 'accepted *canons* of decency'); the 'body of work attributed to a particular author' (the Shakespearean *canon*, for example, covers all those works considered to have been written by him and not attributable to another author). *Canon* also has an adjectival form, 'canonical'.

The two words are sometimes mixed up, generally with *canon* being used for *cannon*. In this example, a clergyman is apparently on the rampage:

⊠ ⊠ *Stoddart, an uncomfortably outspoken loose canon* [should be ***cannon***] *in the secretive world of formula one* . . . (Guardian)

Embarrassment rating: ●●◑ Moderate to high if you put the wrong word, since there is comic potential in the idea of firing off priests or, alternatively, installing guns in cathedrals.

How to avoid: *Cannon* is frequently associated with 'loose', as in the example above. 'Loose' has a doubled letter in the middle; so does *cannon*. If you're not talking of guns or games, but of priests, rules, or art, then *canon* is likely to be the appropriate spelling.

CANVAS *or* CANVASS

Mistakes are sometimes made over the spellings of these two (see below), perhaps because of some half-conscious association between making pictures and establishing views.

Canvas is 'material used for painting on, for making ship's sails', etc.; its plural form is 'canvases'.

To *canvass* (verb) is to 'gather support in a political setting' or simply to 'ascertain other people's views':

> *The President of the United States himself was canvassed for his opinion on the matter, but it seems that he took the precaution of falling asleep in front of the telly on Sunday, before the beast could spring its attack on his tender sensibilities.* (Daily Telegraph)

Canvass also operates as a noun with the same sense of 'estimating numbers', 'gathering support for a vote'. It should not be confused with the other word and spelling, as it is here:

> ❌❌ *. . . the first full canvas* [should be ***canvass***] *of Tory MPs suggested that Mr Major would win by a comfortable margin.* (The Times)

Embarrassment rating: ●●○ The sentence quoted above is confusing because it suggests a group portrait of Tory MPs, and makes a kind of halfway sense.

How to avoid: To *canvass* is to try to *assess* the opinions of others – note the shared 'ss's. Everything else to do with boats, material, paintings, etc. is the single 's' *canvas*.

CAPITAL *or* CAPITOL

Two words with near-identical pronunciation, both suggestive of something powerful or important.

Capital has a range of meanings as a noun describing an 'important city' or 'seat of government', 'invested money', and generally 'stock'. As an adjective it means 'principal', 'connected to the head', 'involving the death penalty', etc. *Capitol*, on the other hand, has a very restricted meaning, originally describing just two imperial edifices: 'the temple to Jupiter in ancient Rome' (built on the Capitoline hill) and 'the area in Washington, D.C. where the Senate and Congress are sited', also on a hill. *Capitol* is slightly stressed on the last syllable. (In the US the word is also applied at state level to describe the place where a state legislature meets.)

Embarrassment rating: ●○○, if only because *capitol* is a relatively rare word. Slight confusion may arise over the fact that Washington is the US *capital*, while the *Capitol* is a building or area within the city.

How to avoid: Anyone writing *Capitol* is likely to be aware of the distinction but it might help to remember that the Capitol was originally built *on* a hill.

CAPTIVATE *or* CAPTURE

Two words which contain the idea of an 'involuntary taking over'. Confusion may occur because, while a *captive* is a prisoner and *captivity* is imprisonment, the verb to *captivate* has quite different and more pleasant associations.

To *captivate* is to 'fascinate', to 'enchant':

Much like the rest of the crowd, he was captivated by González's oratory . . . (Guardian)

(The distinction needs to be observed between the adjectival forms *captive* and *captivated*: a *captive* audience is one which can't get out; a *captivated* audience is one which is delighted to be there.)

To *capture* is to 'gain control of'. Although frequently used in a neutral sense ('to capture someone's attention') it also carries the meaning of to 'seize by force':

The prisoner was captured after five hours on the run.

Embarrassment rating: ●●◐, since neither of these words can be substituted for the other. A prisoner might be *captivated* by his freedom, but he wouldn't be so delighted after being *captured* and returned to *captivity*.

How to avoid: This is quite a tricky set of distinctions – particularly that between *captive* and *captivated* – since the boundaries between the words are blurred. Some rhyming association between *captivate* and 'fascin*ate*' may help.

CARAT *or* CARET

Perhaps because neither of these words is found in everyday vocabulary – unless you are a proofreader or a buyer of gold – it is easy to slip up over the different endings.

A *carat* is a 'unit of weight used for assessing precious stones and gold'. The quality of gold in an alloy is measured in carats, each carat being one twenty-fourth of the total – hence 24-carat gold is pure gold. (The US spelling is usually *karat*.)

A *caret* is a 'symbol used in writing or proofreading showing where to insert something that has been left out'. It does look something like the tip of a carrot, perhaps, but that is only to add another layer of confusion.

The original two words shouldn't be confused:

⊠ ⊠ *The canine furniture is water-gilded with 24 caret* [should be *carat*] *gold.* (Observer)

Embarrassment rating: ●●○ Moderate, if anyone spots the mistake. Meaning isn't obscured but it is pleasing to think of gold being composed of a string of typographical marks, as in the example above.

How to avoid: A *caret* (which comes from a Latin word meaning literally 'there is missing') is a symbol indicating that *care* should be taken over a missing word.

CAREFREE *or* CARELESS

This is apparently one of those 'shade-of-meaning' differences, but the distinction is wider than that. The '-free' suffix implies liberation, while the '-less' suffix indicates a lack of something. One is fairly positive, the other negative.

Carefree (often implying approval) means 'without anxiety', 'easy-going', while to be *careless* (always pejorative) is to be 'unconcerned', 'negligent'. It's quite possible that the same behaviour or personality could be characterised by either word, depending on the point of view of the speaker.

Embarrassment rating: ●○○, but since the words we pick often say as much about us as the people we're describing, the choice here shows up our own approval or disapproval.

How to avoid: It's not a question of avoiding error so much as picking the word which conveys your (positive or negative) attitude.

CATHOLIC

The meanings of *Catholic* and *catholic* differ according to whether the word begins with an uppercase letter or not.

When spelled with a capital 'C', *Catholic* as noun or adjective refers to the Catholic Church:

The writer Evelyn Waugh became a Catholic in 1930.

When spelled with a lower-case 'c', *catholic* means 'varied', 'wide-ranging', and is usually applied to a person's tastes:

Bill Clinton apparently had more catholic tastes than most of his predecessors, enjoying Baz Luhrmann's Strictly Ballroom *and Jane Campion's* The Piano. (Guardian)

Embarrassment rating: ●◑○ As with other religious denominations within Christianity – Anglican, Methodist, Baptist – it is usual practice to capitalise the word. There is a small potential for ambiguity in a spoken sentence such as 'She has a catholic outlook', although the context will generally make clear whether 'broad-minded' or 'religious' is meant.

How to avoid: Most uses of the word are likely to be the 'religious' one, *Catholic*. The lower-case *catholic* rarely stands by itself but will be linked with taste, the arts, etc.

CAVALRY *or* CALVARY

Another spelling confusion. When the 'l' in the middle of the word changes position an entirely different meaning emerges.

Cavalry is used to describe the 'troops who fought on horseback' and is now applied to the 'armoured and motorised part of an army'. *Calvary* was the 'place near Jerusalem where Christ was crucified'. Also *calvary* (occasionally spelled without the capital 'C') can be used to mean a 'period of great mental or physical anguish':

'You have no idea what the Tour de France is. It's a Calvary.' (quoted in the Guardian)

The two words – which are anagrams of each other and very close in sound – are quite often confused:

⊠ ⊠ *[Stanley Kubrick] began pre-production work and even hired Romania's 5,000-strong calvary [should be **cavalry**] division.* (Daily Telegraph)

Embarrassment rating: ●●○ Putting *calvary* where you mean *cavalry* – the usual mistake, as in the last example – makes nonsense of the sentence.

How to avoid: Some association between the horse-riding *caval*ier and *caval*ry should help with the beginning of the word.

CELIBATE *or* CHASTE

These two are sometimes treated as an interchangeable pair of heavenly twins but there are differences between them.

Celibate is an adjective or noun which describes someone 'unmarried'. Because the word was most often applied in the past to those in religious orders who were necessarily unmarried and because – a big because, this – the friars, monks and nuns were supposed to lead a sexually abstinent life, *celibacy* became equated with a sex-free existence. This may be a lifestyle choice now, especially in the US, where young people are encouraged to save themselves for marriage by remaining *celibate*. But over in unreformed old Britain there can still be something a bit high-minded and priggish about the word:

After his marriage broke up Aitken claimed to be living the life of a celibate who could not conceive of a relationship with another woman. (Guardian)

Chaste doesn't have to mean 'going without sex', although this is generally implied. It carries the sense of 'modest', 'restrained':

. . . they find themselves aimlessly passing the time in a Tokyo hotel, unable to relate to the alien Japanese culture but finding a deep, though chaste, connection with each other. (Guardian)

Embarrassment rating: ●○○ Chastity, so highly valued in Victorian novels (at least for the heroine), has become something of a liability. I suspect many people would rather be 'accused' of being *celibate* than *chaste* since, as suggested above, this can be seen as a matter of lifestyle rather than morality.

How to avoid: *Celibate* can be applied to an individual's current status – it does not imply a *chaste* past or future, and this second term should be reserved for individuals or circumstances that really deserve the accolade of modesty and purity.

CENSOR, CENSURE, CENSER *or* SENSOR

Four words of quite similar sound and spelling. The first two are connected by ideas of disapproval; the second two are physical objects.

As a verb *censor* is to 'check material so as to assess its suitability for 'publication'' (this covers letters, film, TV, etc.). Wartime provides a natural context:

> *All the officer patients in the ward were forced to censor letters written by all the enlisted-men patients . . .* (Joseph Heller, *Catch-22*)

The person who does this is the *censor* (as in the British Board of Film Censors [BBFC] though the last word usually appears now as Classification).

To *censure* is to 'judge unfavourably', to 'rebuke', while the noun carries the same meaning of 'harsh criticism':

> *I know one woman who had to put her make-up on outside, to escape the censure of her strict, puritanical eight-year-old daughter.* (Independent)

A *censer* is a 'vessel for burning incense':

> *Sordi discovered his comic vocation when, as an altar boy in Rome, he raised giggles when he waved the censer too boisterously.* (Guardian)

And a *sensor* is an 'electrical device for registering sound, movement, etc.', usually installed for security.

Embarrassment rating: ●●○ Moderate if you confuse any one of these four with the other. Despite the overtones of the word, a *censor* does not *censure* material; he/she merely assesses its suitability for publication, etc. And neither word has any link to incense-burning or to burglar alarms!

How to avoid: The spelling of *censor* can be checked against *censor*ship. The 'u' in *censure* can be linked with the 'u' in equivalent words like reb*u*ke or j*u*dge. The *censer* is for burning in*cense*. And a *sensor* *sens*es what is going on around it.

CENSORED *or* CENSORIOUS

Both these words derive from *censor*, but the meaning of the second has more in common with the meaning of *censure* (see above for both).

Censored describes a book, play, film, etc. from which material has been cut on grounds of taste, potential for causing offence and so on. The word also applies to the excluded material:

Fifteen seconds were censored from the film when it was shown on TV.

Censorious is an adjective meaning 'fault-finding', and carries with it an overtone of pettiness:

He enjoyed finding ways around the restrictions placed on smokers by an increasingly censorious society. (The Times)

Embarrassment rating: ●○○ Any error is likely to arise from the belief that a censor is necessarily *censorious*.

How to avoid: *Censored* can only be used of things; *censorious* can only be applied to people or groups or their attitude.

CENTENARY *or* CENTENNIAL

This is really a false distinction, in that US usage is affecting the British one, perhaps giving the impression of two separate meanings.

Centenary (noun and adjective) is a British English usage meaning a 'hundred-year anniversary'. *Centennial* is a rare adjective meaning 'happening once in a hundred years'. However, the US noun usage of the term to mean a hundred-year anniversary (as in '1965 was the centennial of Abraham Lincoln's assassination'), like *centenary*, is increasingly found in Britain.

Embarrassment rating: ◐○○ *Centennial* still retains its American flavour, however, and some users may prefer to stick with the British form.

How to avoid: Not applicable.

CEREAL *or* SERIAL

If the spellings of these two identically pronounced words are mixed up, the results are somewhere between embarrassing and humorous. In fact, I seem to remember a TV commercial capitalising on this with the punning claim of a child at the breakfast table to be a 'cereal killer'. If it ever existed, it must have been quickly withdrawn on grounds of taste.

Cereal is 'edible grain' (barley, wheat, etc.). As an adjective *serial* means 'occurring in a series' (*serial* number, *serial* killings); as a noun, it applies to the 'episodes in a continuing story' in a magazine, on TV, etc. This word implies a stronger degree of continuity than *series*.

Embarrassment rating: ●●● These are such familiar words, there's no excuse for confusing them.

How to avoid: *Cereal* derives from *Ceres*, the Roman goddess of crops. A *serial* applies to things which happen in *sequence*.

CEREMONIAL *or* CEREMONIOUS

Both adjectives derive from *ceremony* but they have different meanings and applications.

Ceremonial means 'with the proper ceremony or ritual':

After the peace treaty was signed, there was a ceremonial exchange of pens.

By contrast, *ceremonious* conveys a note of criticism and means 'over-concerned with ceremony' and therefore 'pompous':

His ceremonious manner made it clear that we should feel privileged to meet him.

Embarrassment rating: ●○○ The chances are that the context will make the meaning clear, even if the wrong word is used.

How to avoid: *Ceremonial* tends to be applied to events or things like costumes; *ceremonious*, like pomp*ous*, is used about people and their behaviour.

CHAFE *or* CHAFF

Two slightly out-of-the-ordinary words where an additional 'f' can produce a difference in meaning.

To *chafe* – pronounced with a long 'a' – is to 'fret or wear by rubbing'. It can have a physical application (*chafed* skin) or a mental one. If a person *chafes* (at, against or under something) it means that he/she is resentful and uncomfortable on account of some external circumstance:

Wyndham had spent years chafing under the demands of the US pulp magazines he had written for under the name John Beynon. (Guardian)

As a noun *chaff* – pronounced with a short 'a' – has several meanings. It describes 'corn husks' (i.e., the useless part) and is widely used in the phrase 'sorting the wheat from the chaff'. *Chaff* is the metal foil scattered by fighter planes to deceive enemy radar. And, more generally, it describes 'anything which is worthless'.

As a verb, to *chaff* is to 'make fun of' (in a gentle way):

> . . . *cuddling his fragile mother and chaffing his once-feared father, now 85.* (Daily Telegraph)

Don't get the two confused. In this next sentence, the weights were apparently teasing the expert's thighs:

> ☒ ☒ *The unfortunate expert suffered chaffing* [should be **chafing**] *to his thighs from the weights.* (Independent)

Embarrassment rating: ●◐○○ Unintended humour may result if the wrong spelling is used, as above.

How to avoid: *Chafe* recalls other painful verbs with a long 'a' such as 'scrape', 'grate' and 'abrade'. Like some other words with a double-letter ending – 'dross', 'fluff' – *chaff* describes something of little value.

CHAOTIC *or* INCHOATE

Two words that look similar. The echo of 'chaos' in *inchoate* makes it look like a synonym for *chaotic* but the words do not mean the same.

Chaotic is obvious enough, having the meaning of 'very confused':

> *A tense calm reigns after the bloody, chaotic storm.* (Guardian)

Inchoate is a more literary word meaning 'just begun', 'not formed':

> *Sims, who was 30 years older, recognised his inchoate talent and encouraged him to work at his technique and stay out of trouble.* (Observer)

Although something which is newly started may also be jumbled, even *chaotic*, there is a distinction between the two words and the writer ought to be certain of the sense in which he/she means it. This example isn't clear:

> ☒ *This, though, was the fabled Sound of the Westway, in all its guttural, frenetic, inchoate* [does the writer mean **chaotic**?] *glory.* (Observer)

Embarrassment rating: ●○○, because people don't recognise the error in the first place. If there was a hit parade of pretentious words which are on the make, *inchoate* would be on it, not in the top 100 perhaps but not far outside it. The relative popularity of this obscure word is baffling to me.

How to avoid: Don't write *inchoate* at all. Use 'incipient' or 'embryonic' instead. If you have to say it, then it's pronounced with a hard '-ch-' (another reason why it is confused with *chaotic*).

CHILDISH *or* CHILDLIKE

Two words which obviously relate to childhood yet which aren't usually applied to children themselves. One is insulting, the other is a potential compliment. Which is which?

Childish is used about adults in a critical sense, and describes behaviour which is 'non-adult', 'petulant', 'spoilt' – all the things which adults are supposed to have grown out of. *Childish* is the antithesis of 'grown-up':

> *Even in his 30s he had childish tastes in food, preferring dishes that were bland or sweet.*

Childlike is also applied to adults but this time often in approval, as it describes not so much behaviour as responses such as surprise and delight, or qualities like simplicity and trust – things that allegedly come more easily to children. *Childlike* is the opposite of 'worldly', 'cynical':

> *. . . he attends most games and displays an almost childlike pleasure at the exciting match-day atmosphere at Stamford Bridge.* (Daily Telegraph)

Embarrassment rating: ●●○, if you mean to express approval and use *childish* in error for *childlike*. That said, plenty of people wouldn't be too pleased to be described as *childlike*, either.

How to avoid: Both words need careful handling. *Childish* is a particularly patronising term.

CHORD *or* CORD

Both words were originally to do with lines and strings, and were interchangeable. There's a distinction in meaning now, but some association between strings and music makes for uncertainty over which one to use in which context.

A *chord* refers to 'two or more musical notes sounded together', and is the spelling to use in sentences such as:

> *The opening chords of the symphony rang through the hall.*

For all non-musical senses, the *cord* spelling can be used. The 'thick string' for tying parcels; the umbilical *cord*; the vocal *cords* (never *chords*); the spinal *cord* (but sometimes spinal *chord*).

Embarrassment rating: ●○○ But any written reference to umbilical *chords* somehow suggests music composed for a birth, and vocal *chords* would be ambiguous (because it might refer to the cords in the throat or to a musical sound).

How to avoid: For anything connected to music, *chord* (as in *chor*al) is likely to be all right: use *cord* for everything else.

CHRONIC *or* ACUTE

These two words, both with unpleasant connotations, are frequently confused, particularly when applied to illness or disease.

Chronic means 'long-lasting'. In itself a neutral word, it is almost always linked to some ongoing problem, as in 'chronic poverty', 'chronic back pain'.

By contrast, *acute* means 'sharp', 'urgent' – an *acute* illness is one which occurs suddenly and lasts a short time but may be life-threatening. Although a *chronic* condition will almost certainly be an unpleasant one, it does not necessarily endanger the life of the sufferer. But the negative associations of the word – and the long-time slangy use of *chronic* to mean 'bad' ('a chronic film') – have given it a heavier, more serious meaning than its strict definition justifies. Even so, it's worth distinguishing between the two words in formal use.

Embarrassment rating: ●◐○, unless you are in a situation which demands precision, e.g. a doctor's surgery.

How to avoid: The connection between *chronic* and the passage of time is suggested by other 'chron-' words such as 'chronology', 'chronometer', etc.

CLAQUE *or* CLIQUE

This is not exactly a confusion but many people coming across *claque* must have wondered whether they're looking at a misprint for *clique*. And it's fair to say that a *claque* and a *clique* do have quite a lot in common.

Claque is a fairly rare word – although one much favoured by Simon Hoggart, the parliamentary sketch writer in the *Guardian* – and goes back to the 19th century when it described a 'group hired to applaud a theatre performance'. It fits easily in the theatrical world of politics:

Naturally this was because of the claque, instructed by the whips to whistle and cheer him and jeer at everyone else. (Guardian)

The more familiar *clique* is a 'small group of people', an 'exclusive circle'. The word is usually pejorative – but that may be because it tends to be used by those outside the magic circle. *Cliques* exist just about everywhere but they seem particularly prevalent in the arts and media and, of course, politics:

A clique of modernisers sets about making the party re-electable. (Observer)

Embarrassment rating: ●○○ Any misinterpretation here is not likely to lie with the user but the reader.

How to avoid: The theatrical origins of *claque*, and its associations with sycophantic supporters, are echoed by *clap* and *clapping*.

CLASSIC *or* CLASSICAL

Two terms which derive from the same source and confer status on whatever they describe. But, although there is a considerable overlap, the two words have a variety of differing applications. An item can be *classic* without being *classical*, and vice-versa.

Classic indicates that whatever is being described is an 'outstanding' example of its type or, at least, a 'highly representative' one: a book, film, song, dress, car etc. may be 'classic' – even a remark or a mistake can be so described, although not in a formal context. *Classic* is adjective or noun:

The miniskirt was a classic example of 1960s clothes design.

The Russian novel Dr Zhivago *is a 20th-century classic.*

The word tends to suggest not only that the object in question is good, the product of great skill, loving attention, etc., but also that a certain amount of time has gone by since its creation, *classic* status being achieved over a period rather than arrived at in a day. However, reference to an 'instant classic' is quite common, even if it is almost a contradiction in terms.

As a plural noun, the term *the classics* generally has a bit of dignity and weight; it is applied to works of art (most frequently literature and music created before 1900) which have lasted and achieved the status of intellectual and cultural touchstones. *Classics*, usually capitalised, refers to the literature and culture of ancient Greece and Rome, and more particularly to their study in school or university.

Classical is an adjective originally describing 'anything relating to the Roman and ancient Greek period' – history, literature, studies. But it is also used about more recent cultural products, particularly in music and architecture, at least until the early 19th century. In this sense it points towards a certain formality and order (here's the link with the Roman/Greek application) and is usually contrasted with the more exuberant term 'romantic'. Just to confuse things, though, in the field of music, almost anything which isn't obviously pop/folk/easy listening, etc. can be described as *classical*, whatever its date.

Embarrassment rating: ●○○ People don't use *classical* much, perhaps because of its somewhat specialist senses. Instead, everything can be referred to as *classic*, and this somehow covers last year's top sitcom, the latest TV costume drama, even a good joke. *Classic* is so handy as a word of approval that it has undoubtedly been diminished by overuse.

How to avoid: Avoid using the term *classical* about anything produced in the last two hundred years (with the exception of certain kinds of music). Use *classic* about whatever you like – since everyone else does.

CLIENT *or* CUSTOMER

This isn't so much a trap as a crisis of identity. Are we clients or customers? Which is it better to be?

Choosing or being labelled one of these two reveals an attitude. A *client* is (or sounds) slightly more upmarket than a *customer*, being a 'person who consults/employs a professional adviser'. Surgeons, lawyers and financial consultants have clients – as do prostitutes. With its faint overtone of refinement, the word is appropriate in these professional contexts. A *customer* was once merely 'someone who buys something', or a 'regular visitor to a shop'. It still means this, of course, but recently the *customer* has become a very exalted figure. Ever since the market-mad end of the 20th century, *customers* have been all the rage. Doctors used to treat patients, while the railways carried passengers and schools looked after children – now all they have is *customers* who expect the delivery of services.

Embarrassment rating: ●●●, if you refer to customers when talking to your solicitor or your hospital consultant. Clients, *please* . . .

How to avoid: Not a problem. The more you pay, the less likely you are to refer to – or be referred to as – a *customer*.

CLIMATIC *or* CLIMACTIC

Two adjectives with completely different meanings but similar pronunciations. It is easy to overlook the 'c' in *climactic*, in both speech and writing.

Climatic is the adjective from 'climate':

Climatic changes such as the earlier arrival of spring are a likely sign of global warming.

Climactic is the adjective from 'climax' (also see below) and means 'culminating', 'most exciting':

You end up rooting for all of them, making the obligatory climactic gig one of the most genuinely uplifting moments you'll see in a cinema all year. (The Times)

Embarrassment rating: ●◑○ There is some potential for ambiguity in a phrase like 'climatic experience', often heard in speech. Usually the speaker is talking not about the weather but about some highly memorable moment. It is the awkwardness of saying 'climac-tic' which causes the word to come out slurred.

How to avoid: *Climactic* – when said aloud and correctly – seems to rise to a peak in the middle, an echo of its meaning.

CLIMAX *or* CRESCENDO

The second of these two words is regularly used in the sense of the first, although this is not its primary dictionary meaning.

Climax means 'culmination' and applies to the end-point and/or the most exciting moments in music, books, films and other forms of story-telling – and sex. No difficulty with the definition of *climax*. It's *crescendo* that causes problems. In fact it is quite rare to find *crescendo* used in its correct sense of 'increasing loudness':

One of the marvellous things about Augusta is that you know when anyone big is coming because you hear this murmur, which grows in a crescendo of cheers . . . (quoted in the Daily Telegraph)

More usual is the application of *crescendo* to mean 'climax' or 'high point':

☒ *Takeover speculation reached a crescendo* [should be *climax*] *this weekend . . .* (Daily Telegraph)

(The plural of *crescendo* is *crescendos*.)

Embarrassment rating: ●◐○ There are some uses, or misuses, where people simply vote with their feet and nothing said by any careful user or pedant – if the two can be separated – is going to change things. The 'disinterested/uninterested' distinction in one such example. So is *climax/crescendo*. This 'mistake' is so well established that the newer meaning is driving out the proper one. Music specialists will continue to understand *crescendo* but for the rest of us there will soon be no single word to describe a growing noise.

How to avoid: Restrict the use of *crescendo* to a noise, musical or otherwise, which is actually getting louder.

CODA *or* CODICIL

These slightly similar terms refer to things which are added or come at the end. But they derive from different sources and have quite specialist and distinct uses.

A *coda* is a musical term describing a 'passage which brings a piece to a satisfactory end'. So it comes to apply to anything which makes a 'fitting conclusion':

I'm tempted to describe it as an admirable coda to a distinguished career. (Observer)

A *codicil* is primarily an 'addition to a will' (which may modify some earlier provision of that will) but it can also describe any 'supplement to a document':

The deceased later revoked this bequest to his brother in a codicil to the will, but this was not witnessed. (Observer)

Embarrassment rating: ●●○ Although these are 'specialist' terms in music and law, they are also in fairly wide circulation, so that an incorrect reference to, say, a 'musical codicil' will look ignorant.

How to avoid: *Coda* derives from the Latin *cauda* or 'tail'. *Codicil* also comes from Latin, ultimately from *codex*, one of whose meanings is a 'manuscript'. This may not be a great aid to memory but it's interesting all the same.

COLLUDE, CONNIVE *or* CONSPIRE

These words share the common idea of plotting, but they have different shades of meaning and care needs to be taken before applying them to anybody.

To *collude* is to 'conspire with', especially in fraud. One of the parties in a collusion is likely to be on the 'inside' and so betraying his/her employers or colleagues:

The . . . security fear is of the croupier colluding with a customer. (The Times)

To *connive*, meaning to 'plot', is a less critical term. It can suggest turning a blind eye to another's unofficial or illicit activities, or a slightly underhand working together, as here:

Your staff will always connive at presenting [a member of the Royal Family] as a dutiful grafter. (Observer)

Conspire, once again to 'plot', is the strongest of these three terms and tends to be restricted to criminal or treasonous contexts.

Embarrassment rating: ●◐○○ These are all words of condemnation. But *conniving* is relatively mild, while to *collude* or to *conspire* have distinctly dubious, not to say criminal, overtones.

How to avoid: The stronger the 'offence', the more justified is the use of *collude* or *conspire*. Remember that people connive *at* something but collude *in* it with someone, or they conspire *to do* it with someone.

COME *or* -CUM-

The words are pronounced the same. Hearing a phrase like 'owner-cum-manager', some people assume that the link word must be spelled as 'come'. It's a mistake.

Cum (the Latin for 'with') is used as a link word to show a double position or function: cook-cum-proprietor; café-cum-bar. Suggesting a slightly closer connection than the straightforward 'and', *cum* should be hyphenated with the words on either side of it:

*. . . her French publicist, who has accompanied her to London as
chaperone-cum-translator . . .* (Daily Telegraph)

Come cannot be substituted for *cum* – it doesn't mean anything in this
sentence:

☒ ☒ [Prime Cut] *Ritchie's superb, brutal thriller stars Lee Marvin as
Chicago mob enforcer Devlin, pitted against Gene Hackman's
Mary-Ann, a slaughterhouse owner-come-drug* [should be
owner-cum-drug] *baron.* (Guardian)

Embarrassment rating: ●●● This mistake may be one for the purists
and classicists but it is genuinely irritating because the word which is
used in error makes no sense in this context, and shows up the writer's
ignorance.

How to avoid: A moment's thought will show that 'come', when used
to join two nouns, can't mean anything. What is it that's coming and
where's it going?

COMMON *or* MUTUAL

**Two words which contain the ideas of sharing and exchange.
The confusion between them is an old chestnut of usage
dictionaries.**

The difference between *common* and *mutual* is perhaps more apparent
than real but it is nicely illustrated in:

*The common ground [which] Castleford, Wakefield and Featherstone
Rovers, the third party, share is mutual loathing . . .* (The Times)

Common means 'shared', 'held jointly', as in *common* knowledge.
Mutual describes something which is 'reciprocated'; in the example
above, a feeling of loathing which each of the three teams involved in
the Rugby League gives out and receives back from the other two. But
mutual can also be used in the sense of 'held in common', e.g. *mutual*
funds.

Embarrassment rating: ◐○○ There used to be a kind of nit-picking
pedantry – the kind that underlies some of this book, perhaps –
which would pick up on any confusion between *common* and
mutual. But it was Charles Dickens who called his novel *Our Mutual
Friend*, and what was good enough for him . . . Anyway, this is a
usage which has long found general acceptability. In fact, had Dickens
called the novel *Our Common Friend* the title would have been

ambiguous (Our Vulgar Friend?). So the pedants were never more than half-right.

How to avoid: If you really want *mutual* to mean 'reciprocated' it may be better to use the second word, otherwise *common* may be understood.

COMPARE *or* CONTRAST

Both terms suggest an examination of two or more items, but the underlying meaning of each indicates a difference of approach.

To *compare* is to 'put things side by side and look for similarities':

She compared their faces and could see many traces of the father in the son.

To *contrast* is to 'look for differences':

He contrasted the crude forgery with the genuine article.

(*Compare to* and *compare with* have different applications. *Compare to* means to 'liken': 'Shall I compare thee to a summer's day?' is the first line of a famous Shakespeare sonnet. *Compare with* has more the sense of to 'look for what is similar and different': *We compared last year's prices with this year's.*)

Embarrassment rating: ●○○ The words are used almost interchangeably but the careful users will want to point out whether they're looking for similarities or differences.

How to avoid: Everybody understands that a *contrast* contains the idea of balance or opposition (contrasting colours, contrasting viewpoints) whereas to talk of things being *comparable* suggests that not much separates them. This is a guide to the distinct applications of *compare* and *contrast*.

COMPELLING, COMPULSIVE *or* COMPULSORY

Three words deriving from *compel/compulsion*, which fit different contexts.

The adjectives *compelling* and *compulsive* are close in meaning when applied to experiences or processes: a *compelling* or *compulsive* book or TV programme is one that is 'irresistible' and so highly readable or viewable.

When applied to a person, *compulsive* is usually a pejorative term describing someone who is 'in the grip of strong drive to behave in a certain way': a *compulsive* thief, a *compulsive* gambler. This kind of *compulsion* comes from inside the individual.

By contrast, *compulsory* (which is never used to describe an individual) applies to something which is 'obligatory' and imposed from outside:

> *The reason that ties are in . . . is that so few of us have to wear them any more that we have started to see them as a fun thing rather than a boring compulsory thing.* (The Times)

Embarrassment rating: ●●○ if you confuse the first two when describing another person. Many of us would like to have *compelling* personalities but be less pleased if referred to as having *compulsive* ones.

How to avoid: If you are using *compulsive* about an individual, then the word must relate to some activity, and usually an undesirable one.

COMPLACENT *or* COMPLAISANT

The second word is not very often found, but where it is, it risks being confused with the first.

Complacent means 'pleased', 'satisfied with a situation as it is'. The word almost always contains the implication that something is wrong but is being overlooked by the *complacent* person:

> *The large scared woman had grown complacent and frequently left nappies unchanged until they were brimming o'er with pee.* (Daily Telegraph)

Complaisant means 'wanting to fall in with the wishes of others'. At one time it acquired a rather specialised use to describe husbands who ignored what their wives were up to, as in this eye-catching sentence:

> *As for Walston, an American sexual adventuress married to an extremely rich but complaisant husband, she was notorious for sleeping with other women's husbands, and later with Catholic priests.* (New Statesman)

The trouble with using *complaisant* in its primary sense of 'compliant' is that your readers may not be sure whether you meant to put *complacent*, since the distinction between the two words is quite fine:

> *A lying bullyboy, a complaisant management and over-generous payouts . . . bring a once-eminent institution to near collapse.* (The Times)

Embarrassment rating: ●○○, since many readers will probably interpret *complaisant* as an interesting variant on *complacent*.

How to avoid: *Complaisant* – with its overtones of conniving at sexual high jinks – is an interesting word but is probably better left aside in favour of 'compliant' or 'obliging'.

COMPLEMENT *or* COMPLIMENT

This is a very familiar pair of confusables in all its forms (including *complementary/complimentary*). The words have a one-letter difference but share the same pronunciation, and an underlying sense of something given or added.

As a noun *complement* is the 'number which will make complete' (as in a 'ship's complement') or an 'addition which makes for rightness or wholeness':

For the British, chips are the right complement to fried fish.

The verb *complement* describes the process of adding something to 'make complete':

Almond's tight bouffant perfectly complemented the stripped-down primal throb of the duo's music . . . (Guardian)

Compliment, whether noun or verb, is 'praise':

She complimented him on his skill in cooking.

The usual mistake is to use this word when the other (the 'e' one) is intended:

☒☒ *The first of two movies being shown to compliment [should be **complement**] the Wild West [season]* . . . (Independent)

But in the following example the writer meant *compliment* and used the other one:

☒☒ *. . . the ultimate Yorkshire complement [should be **compliment**]: "This one's not bad."* (Independent)

The confusion extends to the adjectival forms *complementary* and *complimentary*, whose meanings are connected to the noun and verb definitions given above.

Embarrassment rating: ●●○, because this is a common mistake. It will irritate, though.

How to avoid: *Complement* is connected to the idea of completeness: note the 'e's in the middle and end of each word. *Compliment* is praise: they share an 'i' in the middle.

COMPRISE *or* CONSIST

These two verbs have more or less the same sense, both being to do with the elements that make up a whole, but confusion comes over the way in which each fits into a sentence.

Both *comprise* and *consist* mean to 'include', to 'be formed of', but *consist* is always followed by 'of' or 'in':

The New Testament consists of 27 books.

He claimed that the answer to falling sales consisted in cutting prices.

Comprise cannot always be used in place of *consist of* but, where it is, it must stand alone, without 'of' or 'in':

The New Testament comprises 27 books.

'Comprised of' is frequently found but still wrong:

> ☒ *'Over half of the building is actually comprised* [should be *the building actually consists*] *of thatched roof.'* (Radio 4)

Embarrassment rating: ●●○ The almost invariable mistake is the one in the final example ('comprised of'), and this grates on many people.

How to avoid: If in doubt, avoid *comprise* altogether. It can usually be replaced with a simpler formula such as 'made up of' or 'include' or, alternatively, left out altogether (e.g. 'Over half the building is actually thatched roof.').

CONFIDENT *or* CONFIDANT(E)

These words are quite closely connected but there is sometimes confusion over the spelling and application of the second.

Confident means 'self-assured', 'trusting':

Despite his nerves, he put on a confident performance from the moment he stepped on stage.

A *confidant* is a 'person in whom secrets are confided' and therefore a trusted friend:

The Middlesbrough manager remains a confidant of Eriksson. (Guardian)

Confidante with a final 'e' is used when the person confided in is female.

Embarrassment rating: ●○○ Misspelling *confident* with an 'a' is a fairly basic error. More frequent is the failure to include (or to drop) the final 'e' in *confidant(e)*. The male/female difference is the same as for blond(e) and should be observed.

How to avoid: *Confidant(e)* is a noun and so will usually be preceded by 'a' or 'the'.

CONGENIAL *or* GENIAL

There's more than a shade of meaning between these two words and the careful user will pick the right one for the right context.

Congenial and *genial* both carry the general sense of 'friendly', but *congenial* tends to be applied to surroundings and atmospheres rather than to individuals. It also means 'sympathetic' or 'suitable', as in this example:

. . . the hour and the place were congenial to supernatural cogitations . . . when I asked him who or what might occupy the tunnels at night . . . (The Times)

Genial is used about people and means 'pleasant', 'cheerful':

He's a naturally genial man, good company, and will be the host at dinner and in the bar . . . (Guardian)

Embarrassment rating: ◑○○, since the two words can be swapped around at a pinch. However, it would be wrong to refer to a place as being *genial* to a particular activity.

How to avoid: Use *congenial* about place and atmosphere; use *genial* of people.

CONSEQUENT *or* CONSEQUENTIAL

Both of these adjectives derive from *consequence*, but can have distinct meanings which shouldn't be confused.

Consequent means simply 'following on from':

. . . the share price fell by some 16 per cent on the consequent profits warning. (Daily Telegraph)

Consequential can be used in the above sense of 'resulting from' but its more usual meaning is 'significant':

Their lack of menace around the Celtic box might not have been consequential had Thistle been more alert. (Daily Telegraph)

(*Consequential* is often found in its negative form of *inconsequential* where it always means 'insignificant', 'trivial'.)

Embarrassment rating: ●◐○ There is a real ambiguity if the wrong word is chosen. A 'consequent profits warning' (see first example) is different from one which is 'consequential'.

How to avoid: If the writer means *consequential*, it may be better to use a more familiar term like 'important' or 'significant' to avoid potential confusion.

CONTAGIOUS *or* INFECTIOUS

Both words originally described different ways in which disease is spread. The difference between them seems 'technical' since the end result is the same.

A *contagious* condition is spread 'by direct contact' – all sexually transmitted diseases, for example, are *contagious*. An *infectious* condition (e.g. flu or mumps) is 'carried by microbes through air or water'. When applied metaphorically to something which is 'quickly spreading' – enthusiasm, panic – either word can be used.

Embarrassment rating: ◐○○, unless you're a health professional, in which case you presumably need to be precise.

How to avoid: The similarity between *contagious* and *conta*ct helps to underline the means of transmission.

CONTEMPTIBLE *or* CONTEMPTUOUS

Both adjectives derive from *contempt* but have different applications which shouldn't be confused.

Contemptible means despicable, 'worthy of contempt':

The efforts of the accused to shift the blame from himself to others were contemptible, said the judge.

Contemptuous describes a person 'who shows contempt', is 'scornful':

And when she does finally produce an excuse it is so feeble as to seem almost contemptuous – she was late because she couldn't find a hair-dryer.
(Observer)

Embarrassment rating: ●●◐, even though it's quite easy to get these the wrong way round. There is a real – and insulting – difference between referring to a person as *contemptuous* or *contemptible*.

How to avoid: *Contemptuous* is descriptive, applying to a person's attitude towards others. Like its synonym 'scornful' it is often followed by 'of'('contemptuous of middlebrow culture'). *Contemptible*, a more judgemental word, works the other way round, applying to an individual and his/her actions or words.

CONTINUOUS *or* CONTINUAL

These words are close but not quite identical. Even those who are aware that there is a difference must pause to consider which way round it works.

Continuous means 'occurring without interruption':

> *We had continuous rain for 24 hours.*

Continual also indicates something 'lasting over a period but with breaks or interruptions' and so means 'repeated':

> *The council's budget is subject to continual cutbacks.*

(The same distinction applies to the adverbs *continuously* and *continually*.)

Embarrassment rating: ●○○, since the difference between these two is quite fine, and the same essential sense is conveyed. Nevertheless, a careful user will observe the distinction.

How to avoid: *Continual* means the same as repeated, and both words share an 'a'. *Continuous* is the same as unbroken: note the 'o' near the end of each word.

CONTRADICTION *or* PARADOX

There is an overlap of meaning between these two, but though all *paradoxes* have a contradictory element to them, not all *contradictions* are *paradoxes*.

A *contradiction* is a 'denial' in speech or an 'inconsistency' in a viewpoint:

> *Does anybody still believe there is a contradiction between liking art and committing foul deeds?* (Daily Telegraph)

If you contradict yourself you may be accused of fuzzy thinking, but to express a *paradox* suggests a more ingenious and agile state of mind since it is a 'statement which appears to be contradictory but which, when examined more closely, contains some truth'. A *contradiction* usually arises by accident while a *paradox* is the deliberate formulation of an unusual point of view:

This has much to do with [Audrey] Hepburn's on-screen persona – the paradox is that she radiates youth, yet seems older than her years. (Daily Telegraph)

Embarrassment rating: ●○○ But to term something a *paradox* is to give it a kind of intellectual status, while to call it a *contradiction* is to disparage it.

How to avoid: Reserve *paradox* for those situations which justify the word. A simple clash or contrast is not a *paradox*.

CORRESPONDENT *or* CO-RESPONDENT

It's important to get these two the right way round. Missing out the 'r' from the first word produces a quite different sense.

A *correspondent* is a 'letter-writer' or a 'journalist with a particular field of expertise' (e.g. an arts correspondent or war correspondent).

A *co-respondent* (sometimes spelled without a hyphen) is the 'man or woman cited in a divorce case as the third party' (i.e. the person the husband or wife has committed adultery with):

In cases based on adultery, most judges no longer insist that the petitioner should name the co-respondent – the third party. (Daily Telegraph)

Embarrassment rating: ●●◑ Some *correspondents* are no doubt also *co-respondents*, but the second term has a specific legal meaning which isn't exactly complimentary, even if it no longer carries the sense of condemnation it once did.

How to avoid: *Co-respondent* is pronounced with a long 'o', more easily realised when the word is hyphenated. Unless you're involved in such a case, the normal spelling will be the double '-rr-' one.

CORROSIVE *or* CORUSCATING

A pair of words whose meanings have blurred into each other although they are quite different. The confusion over *coruscating* probably arises from some blending of *corrosive* and 'excoriating' (which means 'severely critical').

Corrosive means 'eating away', and so gradually destroying. It can be used literally or metaphorically:

I now think infidelity is corrosive and I couldn't survive it.
(The Times)

Coruscating comes from 'coruscate' and means 'sparkling'. It may be used literally (e.g. of the effect of sunlight on water) but its most frequent application is metaphorical. Any public performance – on the football field, in the theatre or concert hall – can be *coruscating*:

> . . . *let us hope your career as a novelist is rather more coruscating than your time spent leading the good ship Tory.* (Guardian)

For a relatively obscure word *coruscating* is surprisingly popular, often because it is used in the wrong sense of 'harsh' or 'rugged'. *Coruscating* does seem to be incorrectly used in the following example, since a polemic is naturally associated with what is harsh rather than sparkling:

> ☒ The Constant Gardener, *a thriller which was . . . a coruscating* [should this be *corrosive* or *excoriating*?] *polemic against pharmaceutical companies and their impact on Africa.* (Guardian)

Embarrassment rating: ●●◐ If you could make money on the rise of a word, then a pound on *coruscating* a few years ago would have earned the price of a good meal by now. But you'd make more money betting on its misuse.

How to avoid: *Coruscating* has nothing to do with criticism or severity. It is about the bright surface of things (think coru*scating, skating*).

COUNCIL *or* COUNSEL

Two identical-sounding terms which describe very different things, although both are linked by ideas of direction and advice.

A *council* is an 'official group of people'; this is a noun only and is most often found in the context of local government:

> *It would be wrong to smear all Labour councils . . .* (Sun)

Someone who serves on such a *council* is a *councillor*.

Counsel is both a noun and a verb and carries the sense of 'advice or advising', often with a professional aspect to it:

> *A doctor for over 30 years, she could be relied on to give good counsel to newly qualified GPs.*

> *Their solicitor counselled them to let the matter drop.*

But the real growth area for this word relates to the professional *counsellors* who give therapeutic advice and help after any traumatic event, or who assist people more generally to overcome their problems (e.g. marriage guidance *counsellors*). The process is referred to as *counselling*.

Counsel also has the more specialised meaning of 'courtroom lawyer' (the US variant of *counsel* in this legal sense is *counselor*).

Embarrassment rating: ●●●, if someone tells you that they work as a *counsellor* and you ask them why they allowed that playing field to be built over.

In fact, all of us are much more likely to encounter *counsellors* these days than we are to meet our local *councillors*. Presumably we're better off as a result.

How to avoid: *Counsel* can be connected with *counsel*ling. The phrase '*ci*ty coun*ci*l' gives some helpful context and repeats the letters 'ci'.

CREDIBLE, CREDITABLE *or* CREDULOUS

Three words connected with ideas of belief and trust, but with quite different meanings.

Credible means 'believable':

> *He had some extraordinary things to say but his quiet manner made them credible.*

The adjective is very widely used now to suggest not so much that something exists (i.e. is not a fiction), but that it should be taken seriously, as in 'a credible fighting force'. (The associated noun is *credibility* with the sense of 'believability'.)

Creditable means 'worth praising', with the slight suggestion that whatever is to be praised has been achieved in difficult circumstances:

> *Despite her ankle injury, she put up a very creditable performance.*

(The noun equivalent is *credit* with the sense of 'honour', 'worth', and frequently with a financial application, as in *credit* limit, *credit* facilities, etc.)

Credulous means 'easily deceived', too 'ready to accept whatever people say':

> *He made a living selling suspect designer perfumes to credulous tourists.*

(The associated noun, not often used, is *credulousness*. *Credulity* has the same meaning and is more often found, especially in phrases such as 'strain/stretch someone's credulity'.)

Embarrassment rating: ●●○, since one of these words (*creditable*) confers a degree of praise; one is somewhere between favourable and neutral (*credible*); and the other (*credulous*) is a pejorative term. Putting one in error for another changes your meaning.

How to avoid: *Credible* usually applies to individuals, either to their stories or their capabilities (think of the opposite, 'incredible'); *creditable* describes actions and performances which are to someone's *credit*; *credulous* generally refers to a person's character but 'gullible' or 'naive' do the same job.

CRITERION *or* CRITERIA

Confusion very often arises over the singular and plural forms of this word, with *criteria* being taken for the singular (possibly by analogy with 'hysteria', 'dilemma', etc.).

A *criterion* is a 'standard for judging' or a 'test', suggesting a level you must reach in order to qualify for something:

> *The criterion for owing truly impressive sums is what you might call the Debtor Personality . . .* (Daily Telegraph)

The plural is *criteria* (never 'criterias'):

> *They are based on criteria including innovation . . . financial soundness and long-term investment value.* (Guardian)

The standard mistake is to treat *criteria* as a singular:

☒ ☒ *There's only one criteria in this situation.*

Embarrassment rating: ●●○ This is an error that shows up the ignorance of the user, and for someone who is alert to such things it will sound almost as jarring as 'we is . . . '.

How to avoid: The '-a' ending of *criteria* indicates the plural, just as it does in other unusual plural forms like 'stadia', 'phenomena' or 'referenda'.

CURRANT *or* CURRENT

These two words are entirely unrelated in meaning or grammar but they sound the same, with the second – and more usual – word pronounced as though it ends '-ant'.

As a noun a *current* is a 'stream of air or water'. As an adjective *current* means 'of the present time' (as in 'current affairs'). A *currant* is a 'small dried grape', a 'raisin'. The first spelling is sometimes found where the second should be used. In a chipper piece of rhyming slang the *Sun* newspaper is known as 'the Currant Bun', although not to this writer:

> ☒ ☒ . . . *the Sun's affectionate soubriquet, Current* [should be **Currant**] *Bun.* (Guardian)

Embarrassment rating: ●●○ It is a fairly elementary spelling error. I sometimes wonder whether the *Sun's* nickname is partly responsible through some association between 'current' affairs and a newspaper. But the error certainly predates the paper.

How to avoid: Current and stream both have an 'e'. Currant and *ra*isin both contain 'ra'.

D D **D** D D

DECRY *or* DESCRY

Two words similar in spelling and pronunciation, these verbs both have a literary feel and a relative rarity that lead to their being confused. The temptation is to use the second word incorrectly with the sense of the first. It is probably the '-cry' of *descry* which leads to a false association with the idea of 'crying out' against something.

Decry means to 'condemn':

> *Although Mr Minghella decried British negativity, he conceded that the outlook might be a spur to creativity.* (Independent)

To *descry* is to 'find out something by looking'. It can be used of literal vision but is also used metaphorically for an attempt to peer into the future:

> *Perhaps, too, in the future, the Brownies dimly descry how Europe could be their ultimate salvation . . .* (Daily Telegraph)

Descry may not be a very usual word but on its infrequent outings it is sometimes put in error for *decry*, as in the next example, where the writer was searching for a word to contrast with 'admire' and picked the wrong one:

> ❌❌ *You could admire the supporters' determination that their world must go on or you could descry* [should be ***decry***] *the lack of sensitivity in language.* (Daily Telegraph)

Embarrassment rating: ●●○ – since *descry* is a rare bit of vocabulary, anyone using it should know its meaning.

How to avoid: If you can *descry* something – i.e. make it out – you can probably *describe* it.

DE FACTO *or* DE JURE

This pair of Latin phrases is usually found together, as balanced as a pair of scales, but they are opposites and shouldn't be confused.

De facto means 'in fact', 'actually', and applies to the situation that exists without regard to what is rightful or what the law says about it. In contrast, *de jure* means 'by right', 'according to law'. So, in the example below, the writer states that Hitler and the rest were absolute rulers as a matter of fact and also because the laws of their respective countries said that they were:

> *For one thing, Hitler, Mussolini and Hirohito were all sovereign rulers, de jure as well as de facto.* (Daily Telegraph)

De facto is sometimes allowed out by itself. In the following example, the writer means that, whatever the libel laws say, in practice they do not operate:

> *In the US, there is virtually no legal protection for a public figure, especially a political one, from defamation. Libel laws are de facto defunct.* (Guardian)

Embarrassment rating: ●●● High if you get them the wrong way round, since any person who uses such 'specialist' terms should know better. In practice, it's probably the reader or listener who must pause for a moment to work out which definition belongs to which phrase.

How to avoid: *De facto* suggests the *fact*-based, actual state of affairs, while *de jure* echoes a set of other legal terms beginning 'jur-' ('jury', 'jurisdiction').

DEFECTIVE *or* DEFICIENT

There is a considerable overlap of meaning between these two but also a useful difference.

Defective means 'faulty', 'badly made', 'not working to full effect', and can apply to body parts ('defective genes') as well as gadgets or merchandise:

> *. . . my workstation as I now expect to find it – ie, with no chair, someone else's defective mouse and my phone facing the wrong way.* (Observer)

Deficient means 'falling short', 'lacking in some way'. The word is not necessarily critical, or not as critical as *defective*. However, it usually implies that something could be better done:

From locker room to court house, the Rusedski saga has exposed the ATP's anti-doping procedures as deficient. (Guardian)

Embarrassment rating: ○○○ Nil to very low, since the terms are used almost interchangeably.

How to avoid: It's hard to pin down the difference here, but *defective* tends to apply to an item or faculty which was working properly and is now faulty, while *deficient* describes a shortage or lack of something which was never there in the first place. Thus eyesight which fails with age is *defective*, while a diet which is lacking in iron may be *deficient*.

DEFER *or* DELAY

This is a shade-of-meaning distinction but one which is worth noting.

Defer and *delay*, both meaning to 'put off', can be used almost interchangeably but there is also a difference of emphasis:

Our visit was deferred can mean not only that the visit was delayed but that it was put off until a later and specified time, often as a result of a conscious decision on our part.

Our visit was delayed may mean that the visit was held up, often for reasons outside our control, and would simply take place later than scheduled.

Defer followed by 'to' also has the sense of 'submit', 'give way to':

The board was compelled to defer to the wishes of the majority shareholders.

Embarrassment rating: ○○○ But it would be odd to talk about *deferring* a visit to your granny.

How to avoid: *Defer* has a rather more formal ring to it even in the sense of 'delay', and should be restricted to 'official' arrangements.

DEFINITE *or* DEFINITIVE

It's tempting to use these words interchangeably although they carry quite distinct meanings: *definitive* is not simply a more emphatic form of *definite*.

Definite means 'exact', 'not vague':

Have you got any definite plans for the summer?

Definitive means 'decisive', 'final':

> . . . *he had excessively high hematocrit in his body – taken as a possible but not definitive indication of doping.* (Independent)

Definitive also carries the sense of 'setting a standard':

> *His version of* Macbeth *is likely to be the definitive one for a generation.*

Embarrassment rating: ●◐○ Ambiguity results if the wrong word is used. There is a difference between a *definite* plan (i.e. a clear one) and a *definitive* one (i.e. one which can't be changed or improved on).

How to avoid: *Definitive* is one stage down the road from *definite*, and the first word should only be used when the sense of 'concluding' or 'absolute' is required.

DEFUSE *or* DIFFUSE

A pair of words with totally different meanings but with the same '-fuse' ending, which could explain the more than occasional confusion. Perhaps it's far-fetched but there may also be some underground association between the idea of scattering (the meaning of *diffuse*) and the effect of a bomb if it is not *defused*.

Defuse can be used only as a verb and means, literally, to 'take the fuse out' (of a bomb) or, figuratively, to 'bring calm into a tense situation':

> *That's to say, making his life more comfortable, but also defusing his violent tendencies.* (The Times)

Diffuse as a verb means to 'scatter or spread through something, or over a large area':

> *Substances can diffuse into and out of cells if the cell membrane is permeable to them.*

but it mainly occurs as an adjective meaning 'spread over a wide area', or figuratively in the sense of 'imprecise':

> *Diffuse plotting and too much blood mar the opening.* (The Times)

The usual mistake is to put this second word where the first would be correct:

❌ ❌ *Cade attempts to diffuse* [should be ***defuse***] *the situation in his usual diplomatic fashion . . .* (Daily Telegraph)

The verbs *diffuse* and *defuse* are pronounced the same, with a z-sound for the *s*, while *diffuse* the adjective has a sibilant-sounding *s*, as in 'mousse'.

Embarrassment rating: ●●○, because the meanings are so different. If you *diffuse* tension you spread it rather than reduce it.

How to avoid: The sense of *defuse* is obviously contained in the word itself, de-fuse. *Diffuse* is a less usual word, more common in scientific contexts and not to be applied to tension, crises or other fraught situations.

DELIVERANCE *or* DELIVERY

Two related words which seem to have wandered in different directions, one connected to escape and the other to the arrival of the postman or a baby. How come?

Deliverance is a literary word meaning 'liberation', a setting free sometimes from a literal imprisonment but more often from a difficult or painful state of affairs. It is occasionally used as a euphemism for death, although not in the following example where it refers to life in a girls' grammar school in the 1950s:

They were . . . pitted against each other in a hell of eternal competition from which there seemed to be no deliverance. (Guardian)

Delivery also contains the idea of releasing or giving up, which turns into the notion of 'distribution'. *Delivery* is a bit of a buzzword at the moment, very popular in government handouts, company mission statements and other guff where it refers to the 'provision' of services. However, the more familiar use of the word applies to the supply of mail or giving birth.

Embarrassment rating: ●○○, although you might raise eyebrows if you talked about the *deliverance* of the mail. And the redneck film thriller from the 1970s would never have attracted audiences if it had been called *Delivery*.

How to avoid: *Delivery* is the standard word. There are not many everyday contexts where *deliverance* is required.

DEMUR *or* DEMURE

A verb and an adjective which look alike. They are not connected, although both have a suggestion of mildness about them.

A fairly unusual word, *demur* – pronounced to rhyme with 'purr' – means to 'disagree with'. It does not suggest a violent objection, and is often found with 'not' as if to indicate that the speaker didn't feel strongly enough to disagree:

While not demurring from the suggestion that alcohol is occasionally taken during such trips, my colleague Sir Ron Atkinson felt they were worthwhile. (Guardian)

Demure – rhyming with 'pure' – is an adjective which means 'modest', with the suggestion of primness:

. . . Victorian missionaries, shocked to find Herero [Namibian] women naked, introduced demure clothing matching their own. (Daily Telegraph)

Embarrassment rating: ●◐○ Nevertheless, these are different parts of speech as well as words with distinct meanings and they do not make sense when confused.

How to avoid: The rhymes suggested above for pronunciation – 'purr' and 'pure' – hint at the meaning of each word, since a person who *demurs* is keeping his/her voice down rather than noisily voicing disagreement, while a *demure* individual is presenting a respectable front.

DEPENDANT *or* DEPENDENT

The problem – or trick – with these two, one a noun, the other an adjective, comes in getting the ending right. Though spelled slightly differently they sound the same, hence the confusion. And the *independent* parallel is no help, since that word does not change according to what part of speech it is.

Dependant is a noun only and describes 'someone who depends on another for support' (usually financial):

She had four dependants, including her aged mother.

Dependent is an adjective meaning 'contingent', 'relying on':

The college place is dependent on his results.

It is incorrect to use the '-ant' spelling for this adjective:

☒☒ *They will inevitably become even more dependant* [should be **dependent**] *on drug company influence.* (Private Eye)

(*Independent* has only one spelling whether it is used as a noun or an adjective: *she stood as an independent in the election; an independent analysis.*)

Embarrassment rating: ●○○, because this is quite a frequent mistake and a forgivable one too. In any case, the meaning is not obscured.

How to avoid: *Dependant* and 'pendant' are both nouns. But in truth you either know this one or have to go to the dictionary each time. Sorry.

DEPRECATE *or* DEPRECIATE

Two very similar words, both carrying the idea of 'running down, placing a low value on'.

Deprecate is more forceful than *depreciate*, and means to 'disapprove strongly of', to 'protest against':

Churchill was right to deprecate the celebration of Dunkirk and to warn that "wars are not won by evacuations". (Daily Telegraph)

The adjective *self-deprecating* has the milder sense of 'self-disparaging', and suggests a modesty which is sometimes tactical:

The Oscar winner gave a self-deprecating speech in which he credited everyone but himself with his award.

To *depreciate* is to 'go down in value':

Most cars depreciate the moment they are driven out of the showroom.

The word can also carry the sense of 'run down', 'disparage' when a person is doing the *depreciating*:

No car salesman is likely to depreciate his own products.

Embarrassment rating: ◐○○ The meanings of these words run into each other in the sense of 'disparage'. However, *deprecate* still has value when the notion of 'protest' is needed.

How to avoid: *Deprecate* is literally to 'pray against', and the origin of the word indicates a more energetic response to a situation. *Depreciate* is the opposite of 'appreciate', and contains the idea of price or value.

DERISIVE *or* DERISORY

There's not much of a trap here since the two adjectives receive broadly the same definition in many dictionaries (i.e. 'scoffing'). However, there is a difference in their application.

Derisive means 'showing (humorous) contempt for':

> *The week's other new release,* Agent Cody Banks 2: Destination London, *tanked with $7 million and derisive reviews.* (The Times)

To describe something as *derisory* means that it is absurdly inadequate and can justifiably be treated with a dismissive laugh because it is 'worth deriding'. The adjective almost invariably occurs in a financial context to describe pay rises, football transfer offers, etc.:

> *Another factor was the derisory offer from Inter. They bid only £2 million.* (Daily Mirror)

Embarrassment rating: ●○○, but there is the possibility of confusion if the wrong word is used: a *derisive* remark is one that pokes fun at something, while a *derisory* remark is more likely to be a ridiculous one (i.e. one that shows up the speaker).

How to avoid: The user needs to consider where the derision is directed. If it is directed outwards then *derisive* is probably right; if it is reflected back, as it were, then *derisory* should be used. Remember also the virtual cliché a derisory offer, in which both words share an 'o'.

DESERT *or* DESSERT

Quite similar pronunciation and uncertainty over the doubling of 's' can cause confusion between this familiar pair.

When these two are mixed up, it is usually in their plural forms: *deserts/desserts*. Just to get things straight, the *desert* is a 'dry sandy place' and, collectively, they – the Sahara, the Kalahari, etc. – are *deserts*.

An altogether different word, with the same spelling but a different pronunciation stressing the second syllable, is *desert* with the meaning of 'what one deserves'. This term, usually in the plural, has a negative ring. To get one's *deserts*, almost invariably *just deserts*, is to receive one's 'comeuppance', the unpleasant consequences of unpleasant actions.

Dessert - also pronounced with the stress on the second syllable – is the 'last course in a meal' and so, metaphorically, anything which comes at the end. It is not difficult to get the two words, *deserts* and *desserts*, confused. In the following clipping what the film apparently received from its audience was a pudding:

╳╳ *At least Jim Jarmusch's existential western* Dead Man *got its just desserts* [should be *deserts*] *from the audience: glum faces and a sprinkling of shallow laughter.* (The Times)

Embarrassment rating: ●●◒ Although the words share the same sound they differ in spelling, and are a part of fairly basic vocabulary. That said, the mistake has comic value (see above).

How to avoid: The single 's' in the middle of deserve and deserts, and their associated meanings, help to avoid the error of confusing them with *desserts*.

DEVIANT *or* DEVIOUS

Both of these terms carry critical overtones when applied to people but anyone should think twice before applying the first of them.

Deviant means 'departing from what is normal'. When used as a noun, the word almost always has a sexual application, a *deviant* being one step short of a 'pervert', at least in tabloid-speak. The adjective is also generally restricted to a sexual context, though it doesn't convey such strong condemnation:

Apparently, 'senior figures from within rugby HQ' . . . thought there was something deviant about O'Driscoll's lifestyle, 'which is more in line with a pop star than an athlete'. (Observer)

Devious can mean 'winding' when describing such things as roads but a much more usual application is to people, where it means 'cunning':

She previously stalked a diabolically devious mystery killer in The Bone Collector. (The Times)

(The associated nouns are *deviance/deviancy* and *deviousness*.)

Embarrassment rating: ●●◒ Although both terms are pejorative, to describe someone as *devious* is much less damaging than to term them *deviant*.

How to avoid: Be wary of both expressions.

DIAGNOSIS *or* PROGNOSIS

This is one of those which-comes-first confusions. One word looks backwards, the other forwards.

Although *diagnosis* can be used more generally, the original meaning of the word refers to the 'identification of a medical condition through its symptoms':

The first thing that GPs learn about making a diagnosis is that bombarding the patient with closed questions is the worst way to go about it. (The Times)

The *prognosis* can only take place after the *diagnosis* since it is the 'forecast of the likely development' (of the disease or condition). Both words are often used outside a medical context, *diagnosis* to mean simply an 'analysis' and *prognosis* a 'prediction':

When a Thomas Hardy character says: 'You'll catch your death sitting there', you know it's not a figure of speech but a grave clinical prognosis. (Guardian)

Embarrassment rating: ●◐○ But there is more than a shade of difference here. The question 'What's your diagnosis?' asks for a summary of a situation or problem so far, while the question 'What's your prognosis?' is a request for an informed prediction based on a *diagnosis*.

How to avoid: A *prognosis* is a projection forward into the future.

DISCOMFIT *or* DISCOMFORT

These words have different roots in French and Latin, but they look alike and one often leads to another – if you're *discomfited* you'll probably feel some mental or physical *discomfort* as well. So it's quite hard to draw a line between them.

To *discomfit* (verb) is to 'disconcert', to 'embarrass', with the sense of being put on the spot:

Party political broadcasts started life as modest, unaffected television appeals delivered straight to the camera by discomfited politicians. (The Times)

(The associated noun is *discomfiture*.)

As a verb *discomfort* literally means to 'deprive of comfort', though in practice it is used in the same meaning as *discomfit*:

He [Michael Howard] slimmed down the shadow cabinet and successfully discomforted the Government . . . (Economist)

Despite the apparent merging of *discomfit* and *discomfort*, there's also a distinction that is worth maintaining, as shown by this example:

We all join in the fun, because we rightly like seeing those who govern us discomfited, and we know cycling is a discomfort. (The Times)

Embarrassment rating: ●○○, because this mistake tends to occur not so much with the user but with the listener or reader, who may assume that being *discomfited* is exactly the same as being *discomforted*. In practice, most people would use 'uncomfortable' when the latter is meant.

How to avoid: Use *discomfit* as a verb, and discomfort as a noun.

DISCREET *or* DISCRETE

These two words, originally derived from the same Latin word, are pronounced identically and also share the idea of 'keeping apart'. But they have acquired quite different meanings.

Discreet is used almost always in the sense of 'being able to keep secrets or confidences' and therefore 'careful or tactful':

Doctors are expected to be discreet in their treatment of patients.

This word shouldn't be confused with *discrete* which means 'separate' and tends to be applied to abstract rather than concrete things:

. . . it's hard to understand why psychiatrists still cling to the idea that madness and sanity are discrete. (Observer)

The frequent confusion between these two may be made worse by the fact that the noun from *discreet*, 'discretion', looks uncommonly as if it's derived from *discrete*.

Embarrassment rating: ●◑○ Any misunderstanding is likely to be for the reader who wonders whether *discrete* is a misprint for *discreet*, since there are contexts in which either word would make sense (e.g. 'a discrete approach to a problem'.)

How to avoid: *Discreet* is the more usual word and tends to be applied to people; *discrete* rather applies to ideas, categories, etc. and is found in more technical or impersonal contexts.

DISCRIMINATING *or* DISCRIMINATORY

Both of these words derive from *discriminate*, but the meaning of one is positive, the other negative.

As an adjective, *discriminating* is usually complimentary since it describes a person who is capable of 'showing good judgement' (often in relation to food and drink):

She showed a discriminating palate when it came to choosing the wine for each course.

Discriminatory is generally negative since it carries the sense of 'prejudiced' (because a particular group is being picked out or *discriminated* against on grounds of race, gender, etc.):

An advertisement showing cigarettes dripping fatty goo on smokers has been condemned by pro-smoking groups as discriminatory. (The Times)

(The noun *discrimination* contains both the positive and negative overtones of the words above – but these days it's generally applied in the second, 'bad' sense.)

Embarrassment rating: ●●◐, if you want to compliment someone and describe their attitude as *discriminatory*. In fact, simply to refer to a person as *discriminating* is, in these sensitive times, likely to be misunderstood unless you connect it to a word like 'taste' or 'values'.

How to avoid: The positive overtones of *discriminating* might be reinforced by association with one of its meanings, 'penetrating', while *discriminatory* recalls 'accusatory'.

DISINTERESTED *or* UNINTERESTED

Two words which sound similar and which everyday use has made into equivalents. But precise definitions and careful usage say otherwise.

To take the one with the obvious meaning first: *uninterested* means 'bored by', 'not attracted to':

Few newspaper readers are uninterested in the private lives of public figures, though some pretend to be.

The original meaning of *disinterested* is 'neutral', 'impartial'. Correctly, this is the sense in which it's used here:

Then I was reminded of my childhood. It was a time when politicians were all deemed to be disinterested public servants. (Guardian)

But for some time now *disinterested* has been used to mean what *uninterested* means (i.e. 'bored by'), and this switch of use gets dictionary support and is apparently quite acceptable in some of the quality papers:

> . . . *[claims] that Mr Bush had failed America in the war against al-Qaeda by initially being disinterested in terrorism* . . . (The Times)

This newer meaning is likely to drive out the older one – indeed it is well on the way to doing so. When that day comes it will no longer be possible to be simultaneously *interested* and *disinterested*, as a judge or a football referee ought to be (that is, paying attention to proceedings but not showing a bias towards one side or the other), because it will sound like a contradiction in terms. Correct usage wants to preserve the distinction between the two words and quite a few people continue to observe it, as the *Guardian* quotation above shows. It's a difference of meaning that still has a bit of life left in it.

The twist to this tale is that the 'newer', disputed meaning of *disinterested* is the earliest recorded meaning of the word – so usage is in effect coming full circle.

(As a noun, *disinterest* can mean both 'impartiality' and 'lack of concern with' but it tends to be used in the second sense.)

Embarrassment rating: ●○○ Low, unfortunately, because the 'misuse' of *disinterested* is so widespread. This is one of the real minor battlegrounds of English usage and it's not only the purists and pedants who would say that there is a clear distinction between the two words.

How to avoid: I can't think of any way to help here. If you are sensitive to English and want to preserve valuable distinctions of meaning then you will not talk about being *disinterested* in the sense of *uninterested*. If you're not bothered you won't care. So why are you reading this book?

DISTIL *or* INSTIL

Two words, with identical endings and with vague 'chemical' overtones, whose meanings may sometimes be confused.

To *distil* (spelled with a double 'll' in the US) is to 'produce in concentrated form'. The word describes a chemical process for producing spirits, perfumes, etc. but is frequently applied to any attempt to reach the essence of a situation:

Confucius says, a man going nowhere is certain to reach his destination . . . the old Chinese sage managed to distil West Brom's existentialist dilemma in a single sentence. (Daily Telegraph)

To *instil* is to 'introduce slowly or drop by drop':

. . . our [doctors'] training is designed to instil in us the crazy notion that we can make things better . . . (The Times)

(The related nouns are *distillation* and *instilment*.)

Embarrassment rating: ●◐○○ Errors could be comical – to say that such-and-such was 'distilled' in someone would mean that they were being used to brew alcohol.

How to avoid: To *instil* contains the idea of *inst*alling some quality or principle within a group or person. It generally relates to people. By contrast, the process of *distillation* normally applies to a 'product' which is being reduced to its purified essence.

DISTINCT, DISTINCTIVE *or* DISTINGUISHED

These adjectives, containing the idea of something 'standing out', tend to run into one another but they have separate functions.

Distinct means 'standing out', 'noticeable':

There's a distinct smell of gas in the kitchen.

To describe something as *distinctive* suggests that it is 'typical or characteristic' of a person or place:

Foie gras is one of the distinctive products of south-west France.

Distinguished means 'eminent', 'worthy of respect':

After a distinguished period as Foreign Secretary, he retired to write novels.

Embarrassment rating: ●◐○○ These words should not be swapped around, something it is quite easy to do with the first two. The difference could be shown by a reference to someone's *distinctive* habit of slurring their words so that their speech was not *distinct*.

How to avoid: *Distinct* goes with words like 'advantage', 'possibility', 'impression', and 'feeling': you can replace it with 'definite' in a sentence. For *distinctive*, substitute 'typical' or 'characteristic'.

DOMINANT *or* DOMINEERING

Both of these similar-sounding words are to do with control but the first can be more or less neutral while the second always implies a criticism.

Dominant is 'leading', 'commanding', and can be applied to people, countries, styles, etc.

The story of the individual quest . . . has become the dominant theme for Western entertainment as celebrated by Hollywood. (Observer)

Domineering, almost always used about individuals, means 'overbearing', 'bullying':

Nobody knows what causes a stammer. In Arnold Bennett's case, his mother thought it came from dropping him on his head at age three, but most observers think it came from a domineering father. (Observer)

(The associated verbs are *dominate* and *domineer*.)

Embarrassment rating: ●●○ Rather as with the 'masterly'/'masterful' distinction, although to a greater degree, one of these terms is always pejorative.

How to avoid: *Domineering* can only be applied to people and their manner. *Dominant* is more simply descriptive and neutral: think of *dominant* genes.

DOWNSTAGE *or* UPSTAGE

One of those 'which-way-round-is-it?' differences, with the added complication that the 'down-'/'up-' prefixes may suggest the opposite meanings to the correct ones.

Downstage describes the 'area of the stage closest to the audience' while *upstage* is the 'area farthest away from the audience'. To *upstage* someone, inside or outside the theatre, is to 'draw attention away from that person to oneself' (since an actor moving upstage may force the other actors to turn towards him, so putting their backs to the audience).

Embarrassment rating: ○○○, unless you're part of the theatre world or into am-dram.

How to avoid: Keep in mind the image of a stage that is raked, that is, tilted so that the part further from the audience is higher (or *upstage*) and the area nearer the audience lower (or *downstage*).

DRAFT *or* DRAUGHT

These words are very easily confused. They are pronounced the same, and both are connected to different senses of 'draw'.

Draft has the sense of 'something drawn'. As a noun it is a 'first version' of something like a plan or document, and as a verb it means to 'produce a rough, early version':

He drafted the outline of his speech on the back of an envelope.

This kind of *draft* involves words, and its producer would be a *draftsman* – this second sense and spelling is not often found.

By contrast, a *draughtsman* is 'someone who works with designs or pictures'. The word *draught* is more concerned with the 'act of drawing' and is the spelling used to describe 'beer which is drawn from the cask', or the 'current of air' which is drawn through a partly open door.

(US English, sensibly, has only one spelling: everything is *draft*. One of the American senses of *draft* is 'compel [someone] to do military service', the British equivalent being 'call up', although the use of the term has faded with the disappearance of National Service.)

Embarrassment rating: ●◑○ Even if mistakes are made the meaning is usually clear, although to talk of *draft* beer would suggest a proposed beer which hadn't yet been brewed, while reference to a writer producing a first *draught* conjures up an odd image . . .

How to avoid: *Drafting* is only to do with words and plans: think of the 'f' in fair copy. The current-of-air sense of draught might be remembered through their shared 'u'. And regular drinkers (also with a 'u') are likely to know their *draught* ales.

DUAL *or* DUEL

Two identically pronounced words which are quite easily confused, perhaps suggested by the idea of the 'two' sides involved in a *duel*.

Dual is an adjective meaning 'twofold': *dual* controls, a *dual* personality:

The briefcase, however, serves a dual purpose. It holds documents. But right now, as he walks towards me, it is also acting as a sort of fig leaf.
(The Times)

Duel is a noun or verb indicating an 'arranged fight between two individuals'. In the days of pistols-at-dawn, a *duel* would be fought over some abstract concern like honour or sometimes a woman. But in a less romantic age a *duel* is simply a 'contest between two sides'.

Embarrassment rating: ●●○, since these words are part of everyday vocabulary and any mistake – as in an erroneous reference to 'duel carriageway' – looks like straightforward carelessness.

How to avoid: A *duel* is always connected to a quarrel of some kind and their shared endings will help in getting the spelling right.

DUE TO *or* OWING TO

The difference between these two phrases signalling an explanation is an old favourite in reference books. If, like me, you can never quite remember what the difference is, you might like to be reminded once again. If not, skip this page.

Due to, meaning 'on account of', should be used only in an adjectival sense, so that it is actually qualifying a noun:

The outbreak of food poisoning was probably due to the shellfish.

(*due to* qualifies 'outbreak')

It is, in traditional terms, wrong to put *due to* when the phrase applies to a complete clause:

☒ *The guide warns that some streets are losing their character due to chain pubs, cafes and restaurants.* (Independent)

(Grammatically, *due to* qualifies 'streets', but it is being used to apply to the whole clause *some streets are losing their character*. This part of the sentence ought to read: *some streets are losing their character owing to chain pubs* . . . An alternative phrasing would be: *the loss of character in some streets is due to chain pubs* . . .)

The different applications of *due to/owing to* are not observed by many people, and this is a case where 'declining' standards may be justified – or even celebrated.

Embarrassment rating: ○○○ Although this fiddly distinction may have been a favourite in some usage books, in my view it's not worth preserving.

How to avoid: The difference between the two phrases can be observed by following the guidelines above. Better still would be to do away with the explanatory use of *due to/owing to* altogether. They sound clunking and bureaucratic. Most of the time *because of* can be used, and this not only produces simpler English – in the example given earlier, *some streets are losing their character because of chain pubs* – but also avoids the problem of whether to put *due to* or *owing to*.

EEEEEEE

EATABLE *or* EDIBLE

Some people get fussed about the distinction between these two but in my opinion this is not a battle worth joining. Although there's a shade of difference, both words are largely neutral and don't carry the positive overtones of 'nutritious' or 'tasty'.

If something is *edible* then it's 'safe to eat', that is, it won't poison you:

Many kinds of mushroom are not edible.

If *eatable* then it is 'fit to eat', even quite good – but the word does not convey much enthusiasm and you wouldn't use it as a compliment on someone's cooking. The adjectives are used almost interchangeably:

"It's all very well trying to impose quality standards but these strawberries were perfectly edible." (*quoted in the* Sun)

(the producer presumably wanted them to be *eatable* as well)

Embarrassment rating: ◑○○, if you describe something as *edible* when you mean *eatable*.

How to avoid: The distinction between the two can perhaps be more clearly seen in their opposites. The negative form *inedible* – routinely applying, say, to certain types of mushroom or berry and meaning 'not suitable for eating' – indicates the neutral quality of *edible*. The negative *uneatable* tends rather to pass judgement on food that is badly prepared or that tastes unpleasant.

ECONOMIC *or* ECONOMICAL

These two terms are frequently used as if they amounted to the same thing but there is a gap between their meanings.

Economic means 'relating to the economy', and can be used on several levels from the global or the national down to the personal:

. . . the Debtor Personality, which is essentially an unwillingness to allow

your personal growth to be contained by mere economic constraints.
(Daily Telegraph)

Economical is an altogether more homely term, and when applied to an individual means 'careful with money' (with a hint of stinginess); when used about products it suggests that the consumer is getting value for money:

This is an economical car: it averages 50 mpg.

Economical can also suggest 'sparing', 'small in quantity' (an *economical* portion).

Embarrassment rating: ●◑○ *Economic* is often found where *economical* would be more accurate (as in, an *economic* car) and the sense is usually clear. But there would be potential confusion, for example, in a mistaken reference to an *economic/al* speech since the talk could either be about economics or simply be a brief one.

How to avoid: *Economic* is connected to *economics*, famously termed the 'dismal science' in the 19th century. *Economical* is related to the 'thrift' sense of *economy*, and like 'frugal' ends in 'al'.

EERIE *or* EYRIE

Any confusion between these two arises because of uncertainty over their spelling rather than meaning.

The adjective *eerie* (sometimes *eery*) describes something which is 'strange', 'unsettling'. The word can have supernatural overtones but it generally seems to be used as a synonym for 'weird':

Tim Henman followed up against Lleyton Hewitt with a performance that was so quiet it bordered on the eerie. (Daily Telegraph)

An *eyrie* – which has variant spellings such as *eyry* and *aerie* – is the 'nest of an eagle' (or any bird of prey) but is more commonly used to describe 'any high and secure place':

From this lofty glass-plated eyrie the London streets look surreally calm in the early autumn sun. (Daily Telegraph)

Embarrassment rating: ●◑○ Putting one word where the other is meant will probably not impede meaning but it is an error.

How to avoid: Some of the alternatives to the *eyrie* spelling are *aerie*, *aery* and *ayrie* (pronounced as 'airy'), all of them suggesting the lofty associations of the word. The doubled letter at the start of *eerie* is matched by the doubled letters in o*dd* and unse*tt*ling, two of its synonyms.

EFFECTIVE, EFFECTUAL *or* EFFICACIOUS

These words are very close – all having the sense of 'producing a result' – but they appear in slightly different contexts.

Effective tends to be used of people and things in the sense of 'having an impact', 'producing the desired result':

> *Cigarette companies recently agreed to put more effective warnings on the packets.*

Effectual is a much less usual word meaning essentially the same (and more frequently found in its negative form of *ineffectual*):

> *The new warnings on tobacco products were effectual in reducing sales.*

Efficacious also means 'capable of producing the intended result', but its use is almost entirely confined to medicines and remedies. There's a slightly humorous overtone to the word, probably the result of its being applied in the past to tonics or dubious cures:

> *. . . but what more efficacious balm for his [cricketer Neil Fairbrother's] troubles than a century in the Roses match at Headingley* (Daily Telegraph)

Embarrassment rating: ◐○○ Almost nil if the first two are changed round since the distinction between them is quite hard to make. As indicated above, *efficacious* does not sound appropriate in most contexts where the other words would appear naturally.

How to avoid: As *effectual* is restricted to more formal contexts stick to *effective*. And *efficacious* is best avoided, unless you want to use it for humorous effect.

E.G. *or* I.E.

The common abbreviations *e.g.* and *i.e.* (almost always appearing in lower case, and sometimes without full stops) are short for Latin phrases and are occasionally confused, through a misunderstanding of their individual functions.

The abbreviation *e.g.* (*exempli gratia* – 'for example') introduces an example, one or two out of several:

American lawyers (e.g. John Grisham and Scott Turow) wrote some of the most successful crime novels of the 1990s.

In contrast *i.e.* (*id est* - 'that is') introduces an explanation or amplification of a previous statement:

Each bird is easily divided into four. First, gently pull the leg (i.e. drumstick and thigh) away from the body . . . (Sunday Telegraph)

and is also used (sometimes comically) as an alternative way of expressing something:

Mitrevski is a Christmas present for Portsmouth, until such time that Chelsea require his services, i.e. never. (Guardian)

It's not always easy to tell but there are contexts where one abbreviation seems to be wrongly employed for the other. The use of *i.e.* in the following sentence implies that there are only two big football clubs:

☒ *Chris Coleman has warned the big clubs – i.e.* [?should be *e.g.*] *Manchester United and Arsenal – against trying to sign Louis Saha.* (Guardian)

Embarrassment rating: ●○○, although there is a small potential for confusion if the writer doesn't make clear whether a statement is meant to provide one or more possibilities/examples (*e.g.*) or whether it is explanatory/inclusive (*i.e.*).

How to avoid: Both of these Latin abbreviations are widely used. They occur frequently in this book. If in doubt over which to use, substitute 'for example' or 'that is'/'by which I mean' to determine which more accurately reflects your meaning and then go back to *e.g.* or *i.e.* The English expressions could always be employed in the first place, of course.

ELDER *or* OLDER

People sense vaguely that there is some difference between these almost identical terms but are not sure what it is.

Of these two adjectives in the comparative form (the superlatives are *eldest* and *oldest*), *older* can be used in almost any context (an *older* person, an *older* car) while *elder* should be restricted to people, generally within a family framework (my *elder* sister). *Elder* also has the noun sense of 'someone who should be looked up to', on account of their years of experience, as in 'elders and betters' (although it's hard to imagine this phrase being used now without a trace of irony).

Embarrassment rating: ○○○, since this is a confusion that is likely to be ironed out before speaking or writing. Anyone uncertain about whether *elder* is 'right' would instinctively plump for the equally correct *older*.

How to avoid: Avoid using *elder* about things.

ELECTRIC, ELECTRICAL *or* ELECTRIFYING

Only one of these words is usually applied in a literal sense, but which?

All these terms derive from 'electricity' but *electric* is used in a figurative sense to mean 'exciting' or 'startling' (an *electric* performance; an *electric* intervention in a debate) as well as in its literal application (*electric* light). *Electrical* simply means 'related to electricity' and is applied to supplies, faults, etc. (an *electrical* breakdown). The adjective *electrifying* is almost always used in the figurative sense of *electric* but carries an even stronger charge: 'astonishing'.

Embarrassment rating: ●◐○, if a careless choice of word leaves the sense uncertain. An *electric* interruption could be taken to mean an exciting break or intervention in proceedings, while an *electrical* interruption would always describe a period when the power is off.

How to avoid: If you intend to refer to supplies of electricity, use *electrical*. When describing events, atmospheres, etc. the other two words are appropriate.

ELEGY *or* EULOGY

Two words that sound similar and which, in their origins, describe speeches or poems delivered on significant occasions.

An *elegy* was originally a 'song or poem of mourning'. Now it tends to be used of anything which takes a nostalgic or melancholy look back at the past:

Harry even manages to make a reference to insurance sound like an elegy for a bygone age . . . (Daily Telegraph)

A *eulogy* can also be delivered at a funeral since it means a 'speech of praise', but it is frequently found in lighter contexts:

> *The channel is asking viewers to send in two photographs of themselves and their shed along with a 150-word eulogy describing why they consider their shed to be the best.* (The Times)

(The associated adjectives are *elegiac* – often employed to describe pictures, music, moods, etc., and meaning no more than 'pleasantly sad' – and *eulogistic*.)

Embarrassment rating: ●○○ As suggested by the examples, these words have largely lost their old, formal associations. Nor are the boundaries clear, since it is possible for an *elegy* to contain elements of the *eulogy* (for example, a nostalgic speech which praised past times). Even so, there is a difference between the two terms which should be observed.

How to avoid: You are more likely to be called upon to give a eulogy than an elegy; the word *elegy* can be reserved for literary efforts. A *eulogy* is generally more upbeat.

ELICIT *or* ILLICIT

These words may be confused because they sound almost identical but in fact they have nothing to do with each other.

The verb *elicit* means to 'evoke' or 'draw out':

> *This brings us to the real reason why the death of someone famous elicits such powerful responses.* (The Times)

The adjective *illicit* means 'not allowed', 'unlawful'. The word carries a stealthy overtone, but is less forceful than 'illegal':

> *. . . illicit [video] copies of Disney productions are swelling the coffers of drug barons . . .* (Guardian)

Embarrassment rating: ●●● The two words are different parts of speech and using one in place of the other not only breaks rules of grammar but makes no sense.

How to avoid: Although *illicit* is not as strong as *ill*egal, there is an overlap – in sense and spelling – between the words. *Elicit* and *e*voke mean more or less the same.

ELOQUENCE *or* LOQUACITY

Each of these terms is connected to speech, one in a positive way, the other negative.

Eloquence is 'persuasive, flowing speech':

> *. . . in speeches that fused an economic message with an often electrifying eloquence . . .* (The Times)

Loquacity is 'talkativeness'. It tends to be used in a pejorative sense:

> *The loud loquacity that made him and Watson so irritating to colleagues in Cambridge is undimmed.* (Daily Telegraph)

(The related adjectives are *loquacious* and *eloquent*. This second word can apply to other things apart from speech – a gesture can be *eloquent* [i.e. 'expressive'].)

Embarrassment rating: ●●○, if describing someone as *loquacious* when you intend the more complimentary *eloquent*.

How to avoid: *Eloquence* in speech is likely to entail elegance in speech as well. *Loquacious* can be a slightly indirect way of saying 'talkative', 'chatty', etc. and it may be preferable to use the more familiar words.

EMINENT, IMMINENT *or* IMMANENT

The first two words are close in pronunciation, the last two even more so. The first carries the idea of importance, the second implies urgency, so some confusion is perhaps natural. The last word is quite rare but is sometimes confused with the second.

Eminent means 'conspicuous', 'distinguished', and is usually applied to people:

> *The company required an eminent chairman to raise its public profile.*

Imminent means 'about to happen'; it is applied to events, almost always in a threatening context:

> *Raised voices and tense expressions showed an argument was imminent.*

The two words should not be confused:

> ☒ ☒ *My views would hardly receive so much attention from such imminent [should be eminent] people if I had not made the original mistake.* (The Times)

Immanent is a fairly rare adjective with a specialist religious/ philosophical meaning of 'pervading', 'inherent'.

(The noun forms are *eminence*, *imminence* and *immanence*, respectively.)

Embarrassment rating: ●●○, because the mistake looks like simple carelessness even though the reader will probably be able to work out what is meant.

How to avoid: *Eminent* should be confined to people, and *imminent* to events. *Immanent* is really a piece of specialist vocabulary.

EMOTIONAL *or* EMOTIVE

Both words are obviously connected to *emotion*, but have different applications.

Emotional tends to be used in the sense of 'excitable' or 'moody'. The word sometimes has a slightly critical edge to it. Years ago *Private Eye* adopted the phrase 'tired and emotional' for 'drunk' to avoid being sued by Members of Parliament and others. But *emotional* primarily means 'related to the emotions' (as opposed to the head), as here:

Love, on the other hand, strikes me as the emotional equivalent of hollandaise sauce. (The Times)

Emotive means 'intended to stir the emotions'. It's usually applied to language and sometimes to images which set out to manipulate an audience by triggering certain responses:

The highly emotive advertisement suggested that the Massachusetts Governor was so soft on criminals that he happily released such men from jail. (The Times)

Embarrassment rating: ●◐○, since an *emotional* speech is not the same as an *emotive* one. But my feeling is that both of these adjectives are slightly tainted. *Emotional*, rarely used in a neutral, descriptive sense, carries a dismissive note as in 'an emotional person'. And to characterise anything as *emotive* is to suggest that you are aware of, and probably resent, some attempt at manipulation.

How to avoid: *Emotive* cannot be used of people, but only of words and images, topics, subjects, and so on.

EMPATHY *or* SYMPATHY

Both nouns are to do with feeling, and probably because they describe somewhat amorphous reactions tend to blur into each other. However they have fairly different applications which are worth preserving.

Empathy is 'imaginative identification with someone else' and his or her situation, whether that situation is a good or bad one:

He [John Edwards] has shown a real flair for the 'I feel your pain' empathy that Bill Clinton made his own. (The Times)

Sympathy also involves the attempt to see things from the perspective of another person and carries the additional sense of 'compassion':

As we'd only recently been burgled ourselves I had sympathy for the neighbours when their house was broken into.

(The related verbs are *empathise* and *sympathise*.)

Embarrassment rating: ○○○ It's generally seen as a good thing to show either empathy or sympathy, and the person on the receiving end probably won't be quibbling over which it is.

How to avoid: *Sympathy* is the more familiar and somehow the 'warmer' term – tea and sympathy, anyone? – while *empathy* seems less spontaneous. Indeed, much education and training now involves 'empathy exercises', suggesting a slightly artificial quality to the feeling.

EMULATE *or* IMITATE

Both of these terms are to do with 'copying' and are sometimes used interchangeably. But their associations are quite different and worth noting.

To *emulate* is to 'imitate' but it carries more positive overtones than the second word because the idea of rivalry is often involved rather than mere copying. Therefore to *emulate* is also to 'try to equal or outdo'. However, in the example below, *imitate* might have been more accurate since it refers to viewers' home-grown attempts to perform hospital-style operations:

*Medical organisations believe there could be merit in television operations but there are concerns that viewers might emulate [?should be **imitate**]*

procedures, as has occurred with drama series such as Casualty.
(The Times)

To *imitate* is simply to 'copy'. The word frequently has negative associations – imitations are much more often described as poor than good.

Embarrassment rating: ●◑○, since one term is generally complimentary while the other is not. Unless one is talking about deliberate mimicry, to suggest that someone is *imitating* another person in behaviour, achievements, etc. is not to praise them. But to *emulate* has more of a follow-in-the-footsteps-of sense to it and doesn't imply the loss of personality which is involved in imitation.

How to avoid: *Emulate* should be reserved for positive, approving contexts.

ENDEMIC, EPIDEMIC *or* PANDEMIC

Three terms which are widely linked to outbreaks (of disease) and their spread. The differences between them are sometimes blurred.

Endemic, an adjective, means 'widely found among a certain group or in a certain area', and although often referring to disease it can extend to other topics:

Poverty and prostitution were endemic in Victorian London.

Epidemic is a noun or adjective describing an 'outbreak' – usually of a disease (though one could talk of 'an *epidemic* of panic'). A characteristic of an *epidemic* is that it is relatively short-lived, unlike something *endemic*, which is likely to be there for good:

The school was hit by an epidemic of flu after Christmas.

Pandemic (noun and adjective) is an *epidemic* on a grand scale: something 'affecting a whole people', even on a global scale:

Keeping up with the Joneses has been thoroughly rebranded as Status Anxiety – a vast pandemic that afflicts the entire civilised world.
(Daily Telegraph)

Embarrassment rating: ●●○ To refer to a condition as *endemic* when *epidemic* is meant, or vice versa, could cause confusion.

How to avoid: Something which is *endemic* has to be en*dur*ed, since it is a localised, long-lasting condition or illness which is very difficult to eradicate. By contrast, an *epidemic* strikes suddenly.

ENORMITY *or* ENORMOUSNESS

Two words both deriving from *enormous* and suggesting size, although the principal meaning of the first word is connected to crimes of great magnitude. (The Latin root of *enormous* indicates something which has deviated from the rule or norm.)

The first word in this pair is definitely the more widely used of the two, whatever the context. Strictly speaking, there is a distinction, since the noun *enormity* characterises 'extreme wickedness' or an 'outrage':

. . . the enormity of Hitler's crimes had been exposed . . . (The Times)

In recent years the word has also been employed in the sense of 'vastness' (i.e. *enormousness*), although quite a lot of people dislike the usage. This sense, relating purely to size, may eventually push out the original meaning of 'outrage', and then we shall be one word poorer. For the moment, though, there's something odd about a phrase like this:

☒ *The enormity of the universe . . .* (Guardian)

Here the first response of some readers could be to wonder what crime the universe has committed.

The preference for *enormity*, when what is really meant is *enormousness*, may have something to do with the slightly cumbersome quality of the longer word, and there are contexts when the two senses do seem to blur together:

Yossarian choked on his toast and eggs at the enormity of his error . . . (Joseph Heller, *Catch-22*)

Embarrassment rating: ●○○, because *enormity* is so frequently used to describe something of great size (and there is some dictionary support for this sense).

How to avoid: Careful users will still want to differentiate between the two words. The link between *enormity* and crimina*lity* may be helpful, while the lumbering length of *enormousness* seems to hint at the meaning of that word.

ENQUIRY *or* INQUIRY

The different spellings of this word may be appropriate in particular contexts.

Inquiry tends to be used for an official investigation, where the word is usually capitalised: *the Greater Manchester Police Inquiry; the Hutton Inquiry*. This version of the word, in lower case, may also be used in the less threatening sense of merely 'asking for information':

He said yesterday that he had received numerous inquiries in response to the advertisement . . . (The Times)

but the general preference is to use the other spelling in such contexts as 'enquiries welcomed'.

(Most dictionaries simply list 'enquiry' as a variant spelling of 'inquiry'. US usage favours 'inquiry'.)

Embarrassment rating: ○○○, although one of the key clues in an Agatha Christie mystery (*A Murder is Announced*) is based on the inquiry/enquiry difference. It is usage which prefers the 'i' form of the word to be applied to official investigations, and there would be a possible ambiguity in referring, say, to the 'Hutton enquiry', since this could relate to a single question in a larger process.

How to avoid: *Inquiry* will do across the board but memorise the phrase 'official inquiry' (both words have two 'i's').

ENVELOP *or* ENVELOPE

Confusion arises over the spelling of these two, with a tendency to use the more familiar second word in all contexts. Moreover this tendency has caused further confusion: the verb 'develop' is often misspelled as 'develope'.

To *envelop* is a verb meaning to 'cover' or 'wrap round'. It is not spelled with an 'e' at the end, and the stress falls in the middle of the word:

Whatever the reason, it's become the second controversy to envelop her this year. (Observer)

Envelope, with the stress falling on the beginning of the word, is a noun only and describes the 'thing which does the covering':

He had to nerve himself to open the envelope from the Inland Revenue.

Embarrassment rating: ●◐○ The mistake only occurs in the present tense of the word, i.e. *envelop/envelops*, since the past is spelled *enveloped*. But to substitute by mistake the *envelope* version in the *Observer* quote above would convey the odd image of someone being wrapped up prior to posting.

How to avoid: Knowing whether the noun or verb use is intended will keep the spellings distinct. The change in stress between the two forms is also a help. It helps to recall that *envelopes* are for *ope*ning.

EQUABLE *or* EQUITABLE

Both of these adjectives contain ideas of balance and evenness, but they are found in different areas.

The adjective *equable* means 'even', 'without extremes'. Frequently applied to the weather, where it means much the same as 'temperate', it also describes character:

> *He had such an equable temperament that it was impossible to pick a quarrel or an argument with him.*

Equitable means 'just', 'following the principles of fairness':

> *Last year Kenya called for the treaty to be revised, but all efforts to negotiate a more equitable arrangement have failed.* (The Times)

Embarrassment rating: ●●○ It would be an error, for example, to talk about an 'equitable climate'.

How to avoid: *Equable* is used only of individuals (and the weather); like 'peaceable', 'tractable', and 'biddable', all descriptions of easy-going people, it has three syllables. The longer word *equitable* is more abstract and applies to decisions, judgements and arrangements.

EROTIC *or* PORNOGRAPHIC

This isn't a confusion so much as a matter of definition . . .

. . . or rather a question of point of view since the definition of both words is essentially 'arousing sexual desire'. *Pornographic* carries the additional sense of 'obscene'. But the goalposts – or the bedposts – are constantly changing in this field, and what was yesterday's *pornography* becomes today's *eroticism*.

Embarrassment rating: ◐○○, since the two terms are frequently mixed up. The claim of *eroticism* is a definite selling point since the term still has a fig leaf of respectability. *Pornographic* has lost some of its old stigma but is still associated with sleaze and exploitation.

How to avoid: Upmarket and expensive, with the merest hint of art: that's *erotic*. Cheap and artless: that's *pornographic*.

ESCAPEE, ESCAPER, ESCAPIST *or* ESCAPOLOGIST

The four words characterise the individual who seeks to get out of somewhere uncomfortable or confining, but each of them crops up in a different context.

An *escapee* is 'one who escapes'. The word almost always has a literal application to describe the person who gets out of a jail, a POW camp and so on. An alternative form is *escaper*.

An *escapist* is a 'person who is looking to escape from reality'. This word – most usually found as an adjective describing books, films and so on – doesn't necessarily carry a negative charge. But someone who gravitates towards *escapist* material all the time may not be in a healthy state of mind:

> . . . *he argues that the flood of books about fairies and angels and Incas and crystals is a symptom of escapist despair by people who feel impotent to improve their lives* . . . (Guardian)

An *escapologist* is a 'person who repeatedly gets out of tricky situations'. Originally used about those showmen and magicians who made their living out of escaping from 'impossible' situations (involving chains, padlocks, barrels flung into rivers, and the rest), it's now applied to politicians and, well, politicians:

> *Let us be in no doubt: last week belonged to the prime minister. The great escapologist has wriggled out again.* (Sunday Telegraph)

(The related abstract nouns are *escapism* and *escapology*.)

Embarrassment rating: ●◐○, since these terms carry distinct meanings. *Escapist* reading is quite different from *escapologist* reading (if such a genre exists).

How to avoid: The straightforward *escapee* will do for one who gets out of physical confinement. The *escapist* may be confined in some sense as well, but his or her escape will be inwards to the realms of fantasy. The -ology/-ologist endings to *escapology/escapologist* indicate that this is a kind of profession or a field of study.

ESPECIAL *or* SPECIAL

The adjectives *especial* and *special*, and the adverb forms (*especially*, *specially*), are used almost interchangeably although there is a useful distinction between them.

Especial and *especially*, meaning 'principal', 'very much', intensify whatever word they are linked with: an *especial* friend; an *especially* happy day.

    Special is very often used in the sense of *especial* (a *special* friend, occasion, etc.) but it carries the additional sense of 'specific' or 'confined to a particular subject':

    I had a special reason for wanting to see you today.

Special can also be a noun: today's *specials* (on a menu).

    (*Especial* should not be used in the sense of 'specific' shown above.)

Embarrassment rating: ◑○○ In speech the distinction between the two words hardly registers. And most people would not observe it in writing. Nevertheless there is, in strict English, a difference in meaning between 'The warning applied especially to him' (i.e. to him above everybody else) and 'The warning applied specially to him' (i.e. specifically to him).

How to avoid: The association between *special* and *specific* makes this sense easy to remember.

ESTIMATE *or* GUESSTIMATE

What's the difference between an *estimate* and a *guesstimate*? See below for the answer.

An *estimate* is a 'rough calculation' (notoriously rough in the case of builders' estimates and the like) or an 'attempt to judge the worth of anything'. A *guesstimate* is supposedly better than a 'guess' but less accurate than an 'estimate'. It's a car crash of a word that should be taken to the scrapyard. Most of the time those who use it are really saying, 'I can't be bothered to make the basic calculations that would entitle me to call this an estimate but on the other hand I wouldn't like you to think I'm only guessing'. *Guesstimate* fits their bill perfectly. But if you are guessing, then say so. If you're estimating, then say that instead. Don't sit on the fence:

    The only available guesstimates of how much a bailout would cost are little more than back-of-the-envelope calculations. (Daily Telegraph)

(Even back-of-the-envelope calculations would justify calling this an *estimate*.)

Embarrassment rating: ●●● Embarrassment should be high for anyone using *guesstimate* but this word seems to be built into some people's vocabulary. I've even heard reference to a 'best guesstimate', as though there were degrees of difference for the wretched thing.

How to avoid: Just say no to *guesstimate*.

EUPHEMISM *or* EUPHUISM

The unusual spelling of both these words means the second is sometimes mistakenly used when the first is meant.

A *euphemism* is a 'word or phrase which expresses a potentially offensive fact or truth in a more palatable way' – and that's an elaborate definition for an activity which all of us practise every day. *Euphemisms* tend to cluster around the embarrassing or threatening aspects of life: sex, death, bodily functions ('sleep with', 'pass on', 'spend a penny'). But even an innocent act like asking to 'borrow' sugar from a neighbour – do people still do that? – could be called a euphemism since what's usually meant is 'have'. More often, however, a *euphemism* is designed to blur the truth and can come close to being a lie:

> As a species lions are singularly unsuited to what is known as "sustainable utilisation", a euphemism among conservationists for hunting.
> (Guardian)

By contrast, *euphuism*, sometimes used in error for *euphemism*, has a very restricted application since it defines a 'high-flown, extravagant style of writing' which was in vogue at the end of the 16th century.

Embarrassment rating: ●●○, since to put *euphuism* in place of *euphemism* makes no sense.

How to avoid: *Euphuism* is such a rare term that its usage is pretty well restricted to academic specialists. By contrast, *euphemism* and its adjective *euphemistic* are quite often found since they describe words and turns of phrase which we use all the time. If in doubt over the spelling, check the dictionary!

EVERY DAY or EVERYDAY

These two are not identical and the distinction between them – one which is plainer in writing than in speech – should be kept.

Every day means just that, 'occurring daily':

Looking back, it seemed as though the sun shone every day that summer.

Everyday (one word) means 'ordinary' – since something that happens every day soon becomes usual:

The benefits of the everyday application of superconductivity in the medical, industrial and scientific fields are incalculable. (Guardian)

Embarrassment rating: ●○○ The temptation is to write the two words as a single unit – as in, erroneously, 'Everyday he had a new idea'. The meaning will probably be clear but it remains a mistake.

How to avoid: The two-word version is actually more usual than the one-word version. If in doubt, ask yourself whether 'ordinary' can be substituted. If it can, put *everyday*. If not, then it's *every day*.

EVERY ONE or EVERYONE

As with the previous distinction between 'every day' and 'everyday', this one is more obvious in writing than in speaking, where the words naturally run together.

Every one is chiefly used of things:

Dozens of used cars – every one a bargain!

Everyone is only used of people:

Everyone was shocked by the news.

Every one can be used of people in a more emphatic or specific context:

There were quite a few people in the room and every one was shocked by the news.

Embarrassment rating: ●◑○ But using the single-word spelling to apply to objects looks odd.

How to avoid: *Everyone* can only be used of people.

EVIDENCE or EVINCE

Two similar-sounding words which involve ideas of displaying or proving.

Evidence is mainly found in its noun use (the *evidence* in the case) but it can also be used as a verb with the sense of to 'make evident', to 'show':

It had been a poor year for the company, as evidenced by the figures.

Some people don't like – all right, I don't like – this verb use of *evidence*. It sounds awkward and a simple word like 'show' will do a better job.

Evince means to 'show clearly', and is used of people rather than figures, data, etc.:

He never evinced much interest in investment or business transactions . . . (The Times)

Embarrassment rating: ○○○, although substituting *evidence* for *evince*, as in 'He never evidenced much interest . . . ', sounds cumbersome.

How to avoid: More straightforward terms such as 'demonstrate' or 'show' are often preferable to these two terms.

EXALTED *or* EXULTANT

A similar look to these two words, together with the idea of being at a kind of peak, may cause confusion.

Exalted (adjective) means 'high', 'dignified':

Despite his exalted position, the President never lost touch with his roots.

Exultant (adjective) means 'triumphant':

. . . having slipped the plaster cast from his broken arm as an exultant sign that he could be back in time for Cheltenham himself. (Guardian)

(The associated verbs are *exalt* and *exult*, while the noun forms are *exaltation* and *exultation*.)

Embarrassment rating: ●●○ These are both fairly formal terms, especially *exalt*, and to confuse them is to convey the wrong meaning.

How to avoid: Of the two, *exultant* (or *exulting*) is the more usual and its connection with triumph can be remembered by their shared 'u's.

EXCEPTIONAL *or* EXCEPTIONABLE

Both of these adjectives derive from the noun *exception*, which has the double meaning of 'something excluded' and an 'objection', and this is what causes the confusion. The second word is sometimes used for the first, perhaps because people think it sounds like an intensified form of *exceptional*.

Exceptional means 'outstanding', 'excluded from the normal run of things':

> *That summer was exceptional for its low rainfall.*

Exceptionable means 'objectionable' (i.e. it describes something to which *exception* could be taken):

> *Williams may be guilty of impoliteness . . . but there was nothing exceptionable about the sentiment.* (Guardian)

Embarrassment rating: ●◑○○ Because the two words are occasionally confused, there may be an ambiguity for some listeners/readers in sentences such as: *It took an exceptionable amount of time for the luggage to arrive.* (Were you irritated about the time the luggage took – or merely surprised?)

How to avoid: Only use *exceptionable* when referring to something to which one can object – that is, the word should appear in a negative context. The context for *exceptional* is usually positive.

EXHAUSTED, EXHAUSTING *or* EXHAUSTIVE

Because of its shared root in the verb *exhaust*, the third of these terms is sometimes confused with the second one.

Exhausted is simply 'very tired':

> *Working for six months without a break left her totally exhausted.*

Exhausting means 'very tiring':

> *She found it exhausting to go for so long without a holiday.*

Exhaustive means 'very thorough':

> *When she came back she gave us an exhaustive account of her holidays.*

Embarrassment rating: ●◑○○ There is a faint connection between *exhaustive* and *exhausting*, in that a study, discussion, etc. which is *exhaustive* may also be *exhausting* for the participants. For this reason it's necessary to be clear about which word to use.

How to avoid: *Exhausted* applies principally to living things (although one can talk of supplies, etc. being *exhausted*, i.e. used up). *Exhausting* describes the experience which has caused exhaustion. *Exhaustive* tends to be used of abstract things such as investigations, lists and inquiries: like 'comprehensive', another word meaning all-inclusive, it ends in '–ive'.

EXHIBITER, EXHIBITIONER *or* EXHIBITIONIST

Quite different, these three, although ideas of 'showing off' link the first and last.

The term for a person who shows pictures, works, etc. at art exhibitions is an *exhibiter*. An *exhibitioner* is a 'university student awarded an exhibition' (i.e. a grant of money, usually made in recognition of academic achievement – this is an older and specialist meaning of *exhibition*). An *exhibitionist* is a 'person who likes showing off'. It also describes those people who expose themselves sexually in public. In this sense *exhibitionist* is a unisex term – although the slang equivalent, 'flasher', is generally applied only to men.

Embarrassment rating: ●●● if you mix up the painter or the student with the *exhibitionist* in the sexual sense. Of course it's quite possible that these people are *exhibitionists* in the more innocent meaning of 'show-offs'.

How to avoid: Be careful over the endings of these terms: the '-ist' one may give offence!

EXHORT *or* EXTORT

Two words, similar in shape and sound, which both carry overtones of force.

To *exhort* is to 'encourage' or 'urge' and there is usually a faintly bullying overtone to the word:

A slightly alarming poster in Tube stations exhorts travellers to read a book about "Britain's first Iron Lady". (Independent)

To *extort* is to 'obtain something (usually money) by violence or the threat of it':

The protection gang extorted money from half the clubs in the city.

(The noun forms are, respectively, *exhortation* and *extortion*: the latter also has a related adjective form *extortionate*, meaning 'outrageously expensive'.)

Embarrassment rating: ●●○ It may not be particularly enjoyable to be on the receiving end of an *exhortation* but it's preferable to being the victim of *extortion*.

How to avoid: People are *exhorted*, while money or some other illegal gain is *extorted*. An individual can't be the direct object of *extort* (i.e. one cannot *extort* somebody, only something). Keep in mind the adjective *extortionate*, which should help to clarify things.

EXPLICIT *or* IMPLICIT

These adjectives are both applied to the meaning of something but in opposite senses.

Explicit is 'frank', 'clear':

The notice gave an explicit warning that shoplifters would be prosecuted.

(*Explicit* is also the shorthand term for sexually frank language or action in the media. As such, it can operate as a warning or – more often, surely? – as an inducement to watch and listen.)

Implicit means 'suggested', 'not openly stated':

Downing Street's implicit dream of a grand league table not just for every school but for every teacher and every pupil . . . (The Times)

(*Implicit* also carries the sense of 'absolute', 'unquestioning': *implicit* trust.)

Embarrassment rating: ●●◑, since the wrong choice of word conveys a meaning opposite to the one intended.

How to avoid: Most people are familiar with *explicit*, if only through warnings on videos and CDs. The more subtle associations of *implicit* are suggested by one of its synonyms, *impli*ed.

EXTEMPORE *or* IMPROMPTU

Two words from Latin which are frequently used interchangeably although there are subtle differences of emphasis and application between them.

Extempore describes a speech, performance, etc. which is done 'off the cuff', 'without the help of notes' but not necessarily without any preparation:

. . . she [Mary Queen of Scots] had given an extempore Latin oration in the Louvre at the age of 13 on the education of women . . . (Daily Telegraph)

Impromptu also applies to performances with the sense of 'unprepared', but it carries the additional meaning of 'makeshift' and can describe arrangements, structures and so on:

Around the city impromptu car dealerships have sprung up on roadsides offering everything from old bangers to second-hand BMWs. (Guardian)

Embarrassment rating: ●○○ In most contexts involving speech or performance the two terms can be swapped around. But it would be incorrect to use *extempore* in the *Guardian* quote above.

How to avoid: *Impromptu* will generally do, but if you mean to imply that the speaker or performer knew what was coming – as Mary Queen of Scots surely did (see first quote) – then use *extempore*.

F

FACTIOUS *or* FRACTIOUS

These words not only look very similar but both contain the idea of 'troublesome'.

Factious – from 'faction', describing a small group (usually within a larger one) that has its own agenda – means 'inclined to form factions', 'trouble-seeking':

> *While the House [of Representatives] is . . . disparate and factious, the Senate is seen as a lofty, almost Olympian body in which petty sniping is set aside.* (Daily Telegraph)

Fractious means 'tetchy', 'quarrelsome'. The word is generally applied to children. In some ways it's the junior version of *factious*:

> *When the children get back from an outing, tired, fractious and hungry, it is essential to remove them to a safe place while you cook lunch.* (Guardian)

Embarrassment rating: ●●○ Neither word is complimentary but to call an adult *fractious* verges on the patronising.

How to avoid: It takes a faction to be *factious* and the word is not easily applicable to an individual. *Fractious* is best reserved for children – think fractions and small units!

FAINT *or* FEINT

Both words are pronounced the same. Any confusion is sometimes attributed to the fact that printers refer to the *faint* lines printed on some stationery as *feint*, although this term seems too specialised to have affected general usage.

As a verb *faint* means to 'lose consciousness briefly'; as an adjective it means 'not distinct', 'weak'. The word shouldn't be confused with *feint* (noun and verb) which describes a 'deceptive move made during a fight/battle to trick one's opponent' – usually to conceal the direction from which the real blow is coming:

Even after allied units burst across his frontier . . . Saddam decided that the attack was a feint and refused to order a counter-offensive.
(Daily Telegraph)

Embarrassment rating: ●●○, since there is a possible ambiguity in a statement such as 'The boxer then fainted'. If the fight continues, however, the reader will know that the 'feinted' spelling was intended.

How to avoid: The *faint* spelling is already familiar. *Feint* is connected to 'feign' and 'feigning', with the French origin of the words accounting for the slightly unusual '-ei-' spelling.

FAIR *or* FARE

The biggest traps sometimes lie in the simplest words. This is a pair of confusables, like 'bail/bale', with a raft of meanings attached.

Fair as a noun describes a 'market for business or pleasure'(antiques *fair*, trade *fair*, fun*fair*). As an adjective, *fair* has a range of meanings from 'bright' (a *fair* day) to 'just' (a *fair* exchange) to the very English 'not bad' (*fair* marks). As a verb *fare* means to 'travel' or 'get on' – not much found now except in slightly quaint expressions like 'How are you faring?' As a noun a *fare* is the 'price of a journey' (train *fare*) or 'food/provisions', although this second sense seems restricted to supermarket advertising and the hospitality industry. Only a local hostelry actually talks about putting *fare* on the table, as in *The farm also offers a tea room with traditional fare . . .*

Embarrassment rating: ●○○ Any mistake will emerge only in writing and the meaning is unlikely to be affected.

How to avoid: Except when it carries the noun sense of 'market', *fair* is an adjective, and so will always be found describing something or somebody. By contrast, *fare* usually occurs in its noun form (bus *fare*) and so can stand alone.

FANCIFUL, IMAGINARY *or* IMAGINATIVE

Three words associated with the imagination but with widely differing meanings.

'Fancy' in its old sense is connected to the 'imagination', since it was regarded as a kind of younger brother, a bit wilder and more frivolous.

This historical sense has pretty well disappeared but the adjective *fanciful* occupies ground somewhere between imaginative and silly; best defined perhaps as 'unrealistic':

> But it would be fanciful to claim that [the Lottery] has to compete with betting shops or casinos, whose customers are rather different.
> (Daily Telegraph)

Imaginary means 'having no basis in reality', 'illusory':

> Middle Earth was Tolkien's imaginary landscape in Lord of the Rings.

Imaginative means 'showing imagination' in a creative sense:

> Using only a couple of chairs the group staged an imaginative reconstruction of the trial.

Embarrassment rating: ●●●, if the second and third are confused, something which is quite easy to do. There is a large gap between characterising someone as *imaginative* (i.e. having an active imagination – not always a compliment) and calling them *imaginary* (which would imply that they don't exist). The word *fanciful*, whether applied to people or to ideas, is usually pejorative.

How to avoid: There's no short cut to memory here. Simply take care over which word is meant.

FARTHER *or* FURTHER

Is there any difference between these two variant words or can they be used interchangeably?

Farther means the same as *further*, and is preferred by some people when physical distance is the topic because it looks as though it is the comparative form of 'far':

> We overtook them a few miles farther on.

The more generally found *further* could be substituted in the sentence above, and it is this spelling which should be used when the sense of 'extra', 'to a greater degree' is required:

> Inflation rose further than expected last month.

Embarrassment rating: ●●○, if the *farther* spelling is used in certain contexts like 'until *further* notice'. The other word would be wrong here.

How to avoid: Since *further* is acceptable in all contexts, stick to this spelling if in doubt.

FAUN or FAWN

There is a link between these identically pronounced words in that both can refer to shy, perhaps skittish creatures. This is the probable reason for a confusion over spelling.

Faun has only one meaning: it describes a 'mythological creature with a man's body and a goat's legs, horns and a tail'. It – or he – should not be confused with *fawn*, a 'young deer', even though in a sense both *fauns* and *fawns* are woodland creatures. But since the faun is male as well as imaginary, the following reference to Audrey Hepburn is particularly inappropriate:

> ☒ ☒ *She is often described as looking like a cat or a faun* [should be *fawn*] . . . (Guardian)

Fawn is also a colour ('yellowish-brown') and, as a verb followed by 'over', means to 'flatter or show affection' – always used pejoratively:

> *There is a thinly veiled vein of social snobbery in the way that magazines endlessly fawn over girls who raid their grandmothers' closets, when all of said grandmothers seem to dress entirely in Yves Saint Laurent couture.* (Guardian)

Embarrassment rating: ●○○, since the usual mistake of putting *faun* for *fawn* is quite likely to pass unnoticed. But, if understood, it conjures up the wrong image.

How to avoid: *Fawn* has a range of meanings and is the spelling which will almost always be the right one. Only use *faun* if you are dealing in mythology.

FAZE or PHASE

These two are often confused – and they shouldn't be! *Faze* **'looks' like a new word although in fact it is found as early as the 19th century in the US, and it is perhaps people's unfamiliarity with the written form that causes them to substitute** *phase/phased.*

To *faze* (it only appears as a verb and in the participle form *fazed*) is to 'shake up', to 'worry'.

> *He saw off the world's bankers in 1991 when they tried to put him out of business, so a few City institutions . . . will not faze him.* (Observer)

Phase is a noun and a verb. As a noun, it describes a 'stage in the development of a person, organisation, etc.':

Most teenagers go through a phase when they find their parents terminally embarrassing.

As a verb, *phase* is usually coupled with 'in' or 'out', and describes a slow process in which something new appears or something old vanishes:

Any charge would be phased in over a number of years and consultations would take place before they were introduced, she added. (Guardian)

Embarrassment rating: ●●◐, when the second sense/spelling is used for the first, as in the erroneous 'I wasn't phased'.

How to avoid: *Phase* and its associated sense of 'stage' both have five letters. You cannot use the word about people but only of processes, changes, etc. *Faze* only applies to individuals and has (appropriate) echoes of 'daze' and 'amaze'.

FEMININE, EFFEMINATE *or* EFFETE

Almost everyone is aware of the difference between the first two words, but many assume mistakenly that *effete* – probably because of the similarity of sound and the contexts in which the word often appears – means the same as *effeminate*.

Feminine means 'characteristic of women' and although used principally of women (obviously!) it can describe an attribute which a man might have: a *feminine* voice; a *feminine* sensitivity. *Effeminate*, only used of men, means 'woman-like' and so 'unmanly' – it's a pejorative term:

Today, he can hold forth about bedtime stories and potty training without the risk of being thought effeminate. (Daily Telegraph)

Effete has nothing to do with *effeminate* but, by a rather complicated process, moves from meaning 'worn out' (originally through childbirth) to 'barren' to 'degenerate'. In fact, the usual application of the word is lighter than its serious history suggests and *effete* winds up meaning something between 'useless' and 'frivolous':

And there is something pleasingly effete about the existence of three artisan chocolate-makers within a few hundred metres of each other. (The Times)

Embarrassment rating: ●◐○ To be described as *effete* is often disparaging (although not in the example above) but it is nowhere near as insulting as *effeminate*. Even if *effete* packs less of a punch than it appears to, you may still be misunderstood.

How to avoid: Of these three words, only *feminine* is a word of unqualified approval – and that in particular contexts. The other two need careful handling.

FERAL *or* FEROCIOUS

There are fashions in words and it's my impression that *feral* has been growing more popular recently. There is some overlap of meaning with *ferocious* but the two words are not synonymous.

Feral means 'wild', 'not (or no longer) domesticated'. It can be applied to people and occasionally to someone's appearance (a *feral* child is one who has been 'brought up' by animals, Romulus-and-Remus style – although the expression is sometimes used about an extreme case of a child who has been allowed to run wild). But the usual context is animal life – cats, pigeons and so on:

One student, Alysia, told of her holiday fun: she goes hunting for feral pigs with her nine dogs. (Guardian)

Though the adjective *ferocious* can mean 'cruel', it is more often found in the sense of 'intense':

Roy Disney, the nephew of the company founder, has also launched a ferocious campaign against Mr Eisner and is seeking to have his re-election to the board blocked next week. (Guardian)

Embarrassment rating: ●●○ *Ferocious* might be a word of approval on the battlefield or in the cut-and-thrust world of the boardroom, but to characterise someone's behaviour as *feral* would generally be perceived as insulting as well as inaccurate.

How to avoid: Stick to *ferocious*. Anything which is *feral* is closely connected to the wild (note the shared 'l') in the real sense of that term.

FEWER *or* LESS

These words are frequently swapped for each other in speech and writing but formal English makes a distinction between them.

Both of these adjectival comparatives (*few/fewer; little/less*) indicate a smaller number or quantity. *Fewer* should be used when referring to a number of objects or people (i.e. with a plural noun):

There were fewer swimmers in the pool today.

Less should be applied to any singular item or unit:

Diet experts advise us to put less salt on our food.

Not many people would think to use *fewer* in the above sentence but it is quite common to find the mistake made the other way round, that is, *less* employed with plural nouns:

☒ *There are less openings for graduates in this area.*

Not only is *fewer openings* grammatically correct but it sounds better as well.

Embarrassment rating: ●◑○○ As indicated above, this tends to be a one-way mistake, with *less* being erroneously put for *fewer*.

How to avoid: *Fewer* indicates a smaller number, *less* a smaller amount, so it helps to step back one degree from the comparative and substitute *few* and *little* in the original sentence: you can say *few* openings but not *little* openings, and *little* salt but not *few* salt.

FIANCÉ *or* FIANCÉE

Both words are now slightly formal terms for people who are engaged to be married and the ending is an indication of gender.

A *fiancé* is the 'husband-to-be'; a *fiancée* is the 'wife-to-be'. The first spelling is sometimes used for both sexes but the difference should be observed. (Each word takes an accent over the first 'e'.)

Embarrassment rating: ●◑○○ The context will almost always make clear which way round the word applies (e.g. 'He is her fiancé'), but it is a courtesy to get the spelling right.

How to avoid: *Fiancé* applies to the shorter word, man, while the longer *fiancée* applies to the woman.

FLAIR *or* FLARE

A pair of words that are quite often confused, perhaps because of an underlying idea of something standing out or being distinct.

Flair is a noun indicating a 'natural ability' in something (a *flair* for languages), while *flare* as a verb means to 'blaze out' or, as a noun, denotes a 'sudden light' (generally some kind of warning signal). It's this second spelling – *flares* – that describes the trousers of the 1970s, the decade when taste took a back seat. If the two words are confused it's usually because the second is used in error when the first is meant:

⊠ ⊠ *He had a particular flare* [should be *flair*] *for recruiting new members* . . . (The Times)

Embarrassment rating: ●◐○ As with many mistakes of this kind, the usual error, evoking an image of someone waving a torch, has a humorous value.

How to avoid: A *flair* is a natural ability or aptitude – all the nouns contain 'i's. And the association between *flare* and gl*are* should help to keep that spelling straight.

FLAMMABLE, INFLAMMABLE *or* INFLAMMATORY

Ideas of 'going up in flames' underlie all three words but they have different uses. The first two words are interchangeable since the 'in-' prefix on the second does not turn it into a negative. The last term cannot be used in place of the other two.

The first two adjectives mean the same thing, 'capable of being (easily) set on fire'. The story goes that *flammable* was 'invented' because the 'in-' prefix on *inflammable* gave it the appearance of a negative (along the lines of 'visible/invisible'), thus suggesting that the object described could <u>not</u> be set on fire. Is there any recorded case of someone dropping a match on an item labelled *inflammable* and being surprised when it went up in flames? Nevertheless, *flammable* is the preferred alternative now.

Inflammatory should not be applied to the fire-raising properties of a substance but rather means 'rousing strong feelings'. It normally describes comments or articles that, intentionally or otherwise, spark a protest:

. . . *he is also unusual in offering a fan's perspective of the game that is expressed without the bias of the usual supporter, or the inflammatory rhetoric of the media.* (Guardian)

Embarrassment rating: ●●◐, if reference is made, say, to an *inflammatory* fabric since this is an incorrect usage. Similarly for an *inflammable* remark.

How to avoid: *(In)flammable* is literal. *Inflammatory* can only be applied to things like words that <u>cannot</u> be set on fire.

FLAUNT *or* FLOUT

These similar-sounding verbs are easily confusable, perhaps because there's a sense of cocking-a-snook in both or because of some association between *flout* and 'flounce'. Yet they have different meanings.

To *flaunt* is to 'make a public exhibition of', to 'show off':

> *The glamour girl of the Fifties flaunted her 36D-23–35 figure in low-cut tops . . .* (Sun)

To *flout* is to 'treat something with contempt'; it's generally used when laws, rules, conventions are being disregarded – in a very public way:

> *'They flouted the law just to get publicity.'* (*quoted in the* Sun)

The two terms are quite often confused:

> ☒ ☒ *[the Commonwealth] has drawn up a formal mechanism for suspending and even expelling nations that flaunt* [should be *flout*] *its values.* (The Times)

Embarrassment rating: ●●○ Although there is an association of ideas between these two – in that a person who is *flouting* the rules may also choose to *flaunt* the fact – they are words with quite distinct meanings.

How to avoid: *Flout* is the more abrupt word, and the curtness of the single syllable does convey something of the contempt or couldn't-care-less-ness which lies behind the word. The association of *flaunt* with display might be remembered through the shared 'a'; likewise the shared 'ou' in *flout* and flounce.

FLOTSAM *or* JETSAM

These two generally appear together, but there is a small difference in their original sea-going definitions even though the product ends up in the same place. So it is one of those 'which-way-round-is-it?' differences.

Flotsam describes 'any items lost during a shipwreck and later found floating in the water'. *Jetsam* applies to 'items which are deliberately thrown overboard' (e.g. to lighten the ship). The pair almost always have a metaphorical application now. *Flotsam* quite often appears by itself, sometimes with a glance at its nautical roots:

> *. . . the American public and much of the rest of the world believed that after Saddam's regime sank, a vast flotsam of weapons of mass destruction would bob to the surface.* (Guardian)

but *jetsam* is almost invariably coupled with *flotsam*:

> *. . . her own office is free of any of the flotsam and jetsam that bogs down mere mortals.* (Guardian)

Embarrassment rating: ◑○○, I imagine, unless you're talking to a literal-minded sea dog or an amateur yachtsperson.

How to avoid: *Flotsam* is what is found *float*ing in the water; *jetsam* is what has been intentionally *eject*ed overboard.

FLOUNDER *or* FOUNDER

These two verbs, very similar in sound and with associated meanings, are often misused.

To *flounder* is to 'struggle', to 'stumble':

> *Without his notes he was floundering for something to say.*

To *founder* means to 'fall in ruins', to 'sink', and might be seen as the next (and last) stage after *floundering*. The verb is sometimes applied to horses, who might *founder* on the home straight, but most often to ships and, in a figurative sense, to people's schemes:

> *It was a great idea but it foundered because he couldn't persuade the others to share his vision.*

In the next example the first word is used where the second is meant (because the plans didn't work at all):

> ☒☒ *To his disappointment, plans to bring the production to London foundered* [should be *foundered*]. (The Times)

Embarrassment rating: ●●○ The writer or speaker's meaning is genuinely obscured if the wrong word is chosen here. To say that someone's hopes *floundered* is quite different from saying that they *foundered*; in the first case there is still some remote chance of success, in the second there isn't.

How to avoid: A fish out of water will *flounder*, that is, it will thrash about and struggle. There is no connection between the word origins of the fish known as the flounder and the verb to *flounder*, but the association may help to suggest the meaning of that word. But if something *founders* it falls to ruin – or to its *found*ations.

FLU *or* FLUE

The second word is sometimes mistakenly used in place of the first, perhaps because of uncertainty over how to abbreviate *influenza*. The informal adjective 'fluey', as in 'feeling a bit fluey', probably compounds the spelling problem.

Flu is the familiar and shortened form of 'influenza' (from an Italian word for 'influence' and following the old idea that diseases were the result of the malign effect of the 'stars'):

> *Ullrich's preparation has been delayed by an attack of flu.* (Guardian)

A *flue* is a 'pipe for carrying away hot air, smoke and so on':

> *He visits the woman whose £8,000 conservatory was built over a boiler flue.* (Guardian)

The two words are occasionally confused, with the result that people appear to suffer from a chimney disease:

> ☒☒ *Withdrawal symptoms included nausea, flue-*[should be *flu-*] *like symptoms, anxiety and sweating.* (Guardian)

Embarrassment rating: ●◐○ Overall meaning is unlikely to be affected but, if taken literally, any reference to 'flue symptoms' is absurd.

How to avoid: Spell out *influenza* in full if uncertain over the right way to abbreviate it. The four-letter *flue* with an 'e' is a chimney.

FOOLISH *or* FOOLHARDY

Both deriving from 'fool', these words carry distinct shades of meaning.

Foolish is applied to anybody or anything which the speaker or writer considers 'unwise or stupid':

> *. . . it's not foolish modernity to talk about Christianity as a brand.* (Guardian)

Foolhardy also means 'unwise' but with an overtone of 'impetuous' (i.e. foolish + hardy). There's sometimes a touch of admiration in the word when it carries the sense of 'risk-taking':

The truly foolhardy can even stay the night in an arctic sleeping bag on an iceblock bed. (Guardian)

Embarrassment rating: ●○○ As with some other word pairs, the distinction between these two tends to reflect the attitude of the user.

How to avoid: Even if *foolhardy* is less damning than *foolish*, it is in general a pejorative term.

FORBEAR *or* FOREBEAR

Two words not always distinct in their spelling but with no connection in meaning.

To *forbear* (with the stress falling on the second syllable) is to 'abstain', to 'hold back from'. The word is really for formal use, especially in its past tense form of *forbore*:

He was severely criticised in the report but forbore from making a public response.

A *forebear* (which can also be spelled *forbear* but with the stress falling on the first syllable, regardless of spelling) is an 'ancestor', usually from several generations back.

If the Greeks are guilty of anything, it is hubris, a failing their classical forebears identified and gave its name. (Guardian)

Embarrassment rating: ●○○ The words are different parts of speech – *forbear* a verb, *forebear* a noun – so mistakes over meaning are unlikely.

How to avoid: Your *forebears* are those who have gone be*fore* you. But the *forbear* spelling will always be correct, whichever word you are using.

FORBIDDING *or* FOREBODING

These words are different but they are both connected with the idea of threat, which is probably what causes any confusion.

Forbidding is an adjective with the sense of 'sinister', 'threatening' (usually in the appearance of people, buildings or places):

The Valley of the Kings feels forbidding; it exudes a sense of something immense. (Daily Telegraph)

Foreboding is a noun which describes a 'feeling of unease':

> . . . *the Somerset hamlet creates a sense of foreboding, because it appears to be the birthplace of what some have called a new 'Motorists' Resistance Army'*. (Daily Telegraph)

Foreboding should not be used as an adjective in place of *forbidding*, as it is here:

> ❌❌ *a ramshackle house with . . . a foreboding* [?should be *forbidding*] *pair of zinc-covered barn doors . . .* (Daily Telegraph)

(If what the writer meant was that the barn doors gave him a sense of *foreboding*, 'ominous' would have been better choice of word.)

Embarrassment rating: ●○○, although there is a small ambiguity of meaning if *foreboding* is inaccurately used as an adjective (as in the last example above). More important, such a use simply sounds grammatically wrong.

How to avoid: *Foreboding* cannot be applied descriptively to anything; it is a feeling in its own right. Check whether you can precede it by 'a sense of' to keep yourself on the right track.

FORCEFUL, FORCIBLE *or* FORCED

Like many sets of adjectives which derive from a single noun, in this case *force*, the meanings of the individual words carry distinct shades of meaning.

Forceful, meaning 'with force' or 'vigorous', tends to be used about a person's character, attitude or words:

> *[He] was a man of forceful personality and strong opinions.* (Daily Telegraph)

Forcible can also be found in this sense of 'imposing' (a *forceful/forcible* speaker), but it more usually has a physical context and means 'employing force' – one step away from 'violent':

> *The police made a forcible removal of the demonstrators from the scene.*

Forced has a variety of meanings from 'strained' (a *forced* smile) to 'rapidly ripened' (*forced* fruit) and 'compelled' (*forced* removal).

Embarrassment rating: ●○○, since *forceful* and *forcible* are often interchangeable. But not always. There is a difference between, say, a *forceful* entry, which would be one that impressed spectators, and a *forcible* entry, which would probably do some damage to the door.

How to avoid: *Forceful* is more to do with manner; *forcible* and, sometimes, *forced* carry the suggestion of physical coercion.

FOREGO *or* FORGO

As with a number of word pairs beginning 'for-/fore-', it is easy to get confused over which form to use.

To *forego* is to 'go in front of'. It is hardly ever – or never? – used except in the forms of *foregoing* and *foregone* (the *foregoing* points in an argument, a *foregone* conclusion).

To *forgo*, which has the alternative spelling *forego*, is to 'do without something':

> *When his parents were away, he was obliged to forego his usual tasty Tuscan food for the cooking of an English aunt . . .* (Guardian)

Embarrassment rating: ●○○ Even though it would be incorrect to refer to, say, a 'forgone conclusion', the meaning remains clear. The error would probably pass unnoticed.

How to avoid: The *foregone/foregoing* spelling can be remembered by splitting it into its component parts: going be*fore*.

FOR EVER *or* FOREVER

As with 'every day/everyday' and 'every one/everyone', there is a slight and useful distinction between these two forms.

The one-word spelling can be used all the time – *forever*, one might say. But when 'eternally' is meant then the two-word *for ever* is preferred by some people:

> *The universe won't last for ever, you know.*

In the sense of 'continually', 'all the time', the one-word form should be used:

> *It's forever raining round these parts.*

Embarrassment rating: ○○○

How to avoid: *Forever* is always right. But, if you are looking at an unending future, then the two-word form may be preferred.

FORMALLY *or* FORMERLY

The near-identical pronunciation of these two can cause problems over spelling.

Formally means 'in the proper style', 'officially':

The recent National People's Congress meeting formally adopted laws protecting private property rights . . . (Independent)

Formerly means 'at an earlier time':

. . . the money set aside for good causes . . . is now being spent on projects that would formerly have been paid for out of general taxation. (Daily Telegraph)

Embarrassment rating: ●◐○ In speech it is hard to tell these words apart, and only the context may indicate which is meant. On paper, if the wrong term is used, there could be an ambiguity in a reference to ' . . . formally/formerly adopted laws . . . '.

How to avoid: *Formal* and *former* are easy enough to distinguish, so it is a question of tacking the adverbial '-ly' ending onto the word of choice.

FORTH *or* FOURTH

A simple pair, but it is surprisingly easy to miss out the 'u' in *fourth* and so produce the wrong word.

Forth is an old word meaning 'forward' or 'outward'. It appears as a prefix in words such as *forth*coming or *forth*right, but is not used by itself now except in the phrase 'and so forth' or in jokey variants on the Biblical 'Go forth and multiply'. This spelling is sometimes used by mistake for *fourth*, referring to the number 4. (Incidentally, the river in Scotland is the Forth and its estuary is the Firth of Forth.)

Embarrassment rating: ●●○ These are simple words. Also, there's a real difference between the sentences 'He came forth' and 'He came fourth'. Was he emerging from somewhere or was he coming behind the third runner in a race?

How to avoid: The derivation of *fourth* from *four* is a helpful indicator of spelling.

FORTUITOUS *or* FORTUNATE

Fortuitous has gradually been encroaching on the territory of *fortunate*, and it is frequently used in the sense of the second word although its primary meaning is different.

Strictly speaking, *fortuitous* means 'occurring by chance':

They were just talking about him when he made a fortuitous appearance at the door.

while *fortunate* is 'lucky':

Given the nature of her offence, she was fortunate to receive only a suspended sentence.

But the similarity between the two words means that *fortuitous* is generally used to suggest an element of (good) luck combined with chance:

The timing of the Beatles' arrival [in America] in February 1964 was fortuitous. Coming just three months after the assassination of President Kennedy, their melodic songs and youthful optimism offered relief to a nation cast in deep gloom. (The Times)

Embarrassment rating: ●○○, since this application of *fortuitous* is so well dug in that it is close to standard use. This is fine as long as the listener or reader is on the same wavelength as the user; if they're not, there is potential confusion in a statement like 'Her arrival was fortuitous'. (Was it by chance or was it lucky?)

How to avoid: *Fortunate* is straightforward, but if you really mean that some event is accidental (rather than lucky) then it may be safer to avoid *fortuitous* altogether in favour of 'by chance' or 'accidental'. Note that people can be described as *fortunate* while events, arrivals, etc. are *fortuitous*.

FULSOME *or* HEARTFELT

These two are near opposites, yet the first word is sometimes used as if it meant the same as the second. It doesn't.

Fulsome is a tricky word to interpret because it oftens occurs in an ambiguous context. Meaning 'sickeningly admiring', it suggests hypocrisy, smarminess, as here:

Whatever fulsome reassurances about BBC independence drop from the lips of Tony Blair, Tessa Jowell, Alastair Campbell . . . (Observer)

But when *fulsome* is applied to, say, 'praise' or 'apology', it's not always clear whether the writer intends it in the (mistaken) sense of *abundant*, probably suggested by the 'ful-' prefix. If you want to convey sincerity then *heartfelt* is a better word, as it means what it says, i.e. 'deeply felt':

*And when he claimed that Tory opposition to the bill was "principled",
Labour MPs at last had an excuse for heartfelt, scornful, pipe-clearing
laughter.* (Guardian)

Embarrassment rating: ●●○ To talk, say, of *fulsome* praise is not really complimentary, although it is sometimes taken to be.

How to avoid: '*Fulsome* apology' and '*fulsome* praise' are virtually clichés nowadays. That said, it's occasionally better to choose another word altogether rather than risk being misunderstood. Hence, 'insincere' or 'superficial' may be preferable to *fulsome*.

GGGGGGG

GALLING *or* GRUELLING

A slight overlap in meaning and a similarity in sound sometimes cause these two to be confused.

Something which is *galling* is 'irritating':

> It's galling to know that when you emerge from your cubicle in your hot new miniskirt, some 9ft model is stepping out in Milan with her ankle-length tweed skirt. (Guardian)

Gruelling means 'punishing', 'very tiring', and is applied to an experience or course which entails great physical or psychological stress:

> We . . . have a right to know whether the person to whom we have entrusted the gruelling task of running the country is capable of doing so. (The Times)

Embarrassment rating: ●●○, because if the words are switched around an unintended meaning emerges.

How to avoid: *Galling* has nothing to do with the gall bladder or gallstones but derives from 'gall', an old word describing a sore place or swelling – hence it has come to mean 'irritating' (although not in a physical context). By contrast, *gruelling* – which is connected to 'gruel', the prison and boarding-school fare of the bad old days – frequently has a physical application.

GAMBIT, GAMUT *or* GAUNTLET

These terms are sometimes confused, the first and second probably on account of their similar sound and specialised uses and the second and third because they are often associated with the word 'run'.

A *gambit* is an 'opening move', originally in chess (where the term applied to the deliberate sacrifice of a piece to gain an advantage).

Now the term is extended to any 'thought-out manoeuvre which begins a game, negotiation, etc.'.

The team's intimidating gambit was to utter a series of war cries before each match.

(Incidentally, to talk about an *opening gambit* is a redundant repetition – all *gambits* are opening ones, by definition.)

Gamut means 'range', 'the full spectrum':

Sir Edward Lutyens's fluent drawings run the full gamut, from monumental projects to cosy, intimate spaces. (Independent)

The first word is quite often found, incorrectly, where the second is meant:

☒☒ ' . . . *a whole range of things, a whole gambit* [should be *gamut*] *of ideas . . . '* (Radio 4)

A *gauntlet* was originally an 'armoured glove', something thrown down by a knight as a formal challenge. Confusingly, in the familiar phrase 'run the gauntlet' – meaning to 'undergo a punishing process' – the *gauntlet* has nothing to do with a glove but is a mangled derivation from a Swedish word describing a course down a path! Whatever the source of the term, the phrase 'run the gamut' is absolutely distinct from 'run the gauntlet'.

Embarrassment rating: ●●◐, since different meanings are conveyed by each word.

How to avoid: A *gambit* is the first move in a *game* which may be bitterly contested. A *gamut* describes a full spectrum – note the shared 'u's.

GAMBLE *or* GAMBOL

Confusion between these two is a spelling error, not one of sense: pronunciation is no help here.

To *gamble* is to 'risk' or to 'play for money':

Some come to gamble high stakes, occasionally for as much as a car, but most are simply looking for a spectacle. (The Times)

To *gambol* is to 'leap around playfully':

Our pets need to be allowed to frolic, gambol, tussle, canter and generally scamper about. (Guardian)

(The past tense forms of each word are *gambled* and *gambolled*.)

Embarrassment rating: ●●◐ A red-face mistake if you refer to sheep gambling . . .

How to avoid: Only people *gamble*; I suppose they might *gambol* too if they won something but in general the second word is restricted to the behaviour of animals.

GARNER *or* GARNISH

These similar-sounding words are occasionally confused, perhaps through some indirect link between ideas of food and harvest.

Connected to granary (a storehouse for grain), *garner* means to 'gather up':

Gee and Levy have garnered particular critical acclaim for their novels, The Flood *and* Small Island. (Guardian)

To *garnish* is to 'decorate'. The word, which is verb or noun, is most often found in recipes, descriptions of dishes, etc. and refers to the small additions intended to make a meal look good and taste better:

[He] is said to have sent back his grouse because it came garnished with parsley. (Guardian)

The similarity in sound between the two words can cause confusion, as here:

☒ ☒ *He emailed the photos to some global chiropractic website, garnishing* [should be **garnering**] *international accolades for himself while incensing his wife.* (Guardian)

Embarrassment rating: ●●○ *Garnish* has become quite a standard word on menus (salad *garnish*, etc.), so it makes the confusion with *garner*, as above, less excusable.

How to avoid: *Garner* and 'gather' are near rhymes; while a d*ish* will have a *garnish*.

GEEZER *or* GEYSER

Identical pronunciation sometimes causes confusion here.

Geezer is a slang term for a 'man' (previously an old one). It's not for formal English, of course, and in recent times it has widened its meaning to include younger men, especially diamond geezers and the dodgy variety:

Cloughie, however, is one old geezer who could be tempted out of retirement if the right job came along. (Guardian)

There are things that can be done with an acoustic guitar and a voice that I find more interesting than standing on stage with four geezers in leather jackets. (*Guitarist Johnny Marr, quoted in the* Guardian)

A *geyser* is a 'hot spring, of water, mud or steam':

The volcano has been restless since 1991, with increased numbers of earthquakes, rising lake temperatures and geysers of boiling mud. (Guardian)

Embarrassment rating: ●●○, if any reference is made in writing to someone being an old *geyser*. Also moderate if you were to describe *geezers* as being among the attractions of Yellowstone Park. This is one of those red-face mistakes.

How to avoid: There is no handy way of separating the two words. *Geezer*, however, is very informal, and anyone confident or relaxed enough to be writing slang should know how to spell it. The 's' in the middle of *geyser* links to the first letters of its definition, *s*pouting *s*pring.

GOURMAND *or* GOURMET

As with those other French terms also connected with good living, 'bon vivant' and 'bon viveur' (see earlier entry), there is widespread uncertainty over the distinction between a *gourmand* and a *gourmet*.

Being called a *gourmand* is not a compliment since it means a 'glutton', a greedy eater who doesn't mind what goes down as long as he/she gets enough of it. What the writer of the following sentence presumably meant was *gourmet*, since a straightforward *gourmand* wouldn't be much use for the Michelin guide:

☒ *He was also something of a gourmand* [?should be **gourmet**] *and once confessed that if he had to pick another career it would be as a food critic for the Michelin Restaurant guide.* (Daily Telegraph)

A *gourmet* is a 'person with refined tastes in food and drink'. The word is also an adjective meaning 'refined', as here:

Most cookbooks now cater for after-work foodies who want to produce a gourmet meal in 30 minutes flat. (Daily Telegraph)

Embarrassment rating: ●●○, if you use *gourmand* in place of *gourmet* and if the reader's or listener's French is better than yours. Of course you may actually intend to say *gourmand* . . .

How to avoid: . . . but if you actually mean *gourmand*, then why not say 'glutton' and avoid ambiguity? *Gourmet* should be reserved for those people or dining experiences that deserve it. Like other words denoting quality – 'classic' springs to mind – it has become devalued through indiscriminate application.

GRAND *or* GRANDIOSE

These two look alike but more separates them than unites them.

The difference between the adjectives is that *grand* should be applied to something which is authentically 'splendid', while *grandiose* suggests that what is described is somehow 'inflated' or 'false'. A *grand* building is large and very imposing, a *grand* scheme is ambitious and conceived on a great scale. *Grandiose* ideas, by contrast, are hollow; they sound good but will never amount to anything.

   (*Grand* also has some currency as a colloquial term of approval, like 'brilliant', 'great', etc., although the term is dated now.)

Embarrassment rating: ●●○, since to term something *grandiose* is to imply criticism while to call it *grand* is usually a straightforward compliment.

How to avoid: Anything which is *grandiose* has something fal*se* about it.

GRILL *or* GRILLE

This is an easy trap to fall into. Both words describe metallic, perforated frames, and the frequent appearance of *grilled* (as in *grilled* meat) encourages the error of using the second where the first is intended.

A *grill* is a 'metal frame used in cooking':

   I walked in, almost expecting to be met by the smell of overcooked cabbage or toast burning on the gas grill. (Guardian)

A *grille* is a 'metal screen in front of a window or car radiator':

   . . . there was no sign of life behind the ornamental metal grilles which enclose the shuttered windows . . . (Guardian)

(*Grill* is sometimes used in this sense of window lattice but *grille* should never be used for the cooking frame.)

Embarrassment rating: ●○○, since the mistake is easily made and the meaning won't generally be obscured. 'He looked at the grille' could be ambiguous, however, if the wrong spelling is used.

How to avoid: A *grille* with an 'e' is for the *eye* to look through; the other *grill* is for cooking on.

GRISLY *or* GRIZZLY

Identical pronunciation, as well as the hint of an unpleasant experience which hangs behind both words, probably accounts for the mix-up between these two.

Grisly is an adjective meaning 'terrible', 'gruesome':

The latest grisly find – a large thigh bone and some smaller leg bones – was only two years ago when a kitchen was re-tiled. (Daily Telegraph)

Grizzly means 'of a grey colour' (the same as 'grizzled'). In its noun use it stands for the grizzly bear (whose scientific name is *Ursus horribilis*), usually just referred to as the 'grizzly'. This is the spelling which is often confused with the first word.

The right use is:

. . . our own Phil Collins, whining and yowling away as if he had a grizzly's teeth in his left buttock. (Guardian)

The wrong use is:

☒☒ *The Government should ban smoking in public places and make tobacco warnings even more grizzly* [should be *grisly*]. (Observer)

Embarrassment rating: ●●● This is quite a common confusion but the distinction between the two words is easy to observe, and the result of getting it wrong (usually by putting the second word for the first) is comic, since it inevitably conjures up images of a rampaging bear.

How to avoid: In the run of things, one is more likely to have *grisly* experiences than to have experiences with a *grizzly*. In other words, the *grisly* spelling is the 'normal' one. The link between *grizzled* and *grizzly* may help to fix the bear's spelling.

HANGED *or* HUNG

These are the past tense forms of the verb to *hang*. There's a
tendency to use *hung* for everything and everybody. *Hanged* should
be used in one context, however.

In general things should be *hung*. Pictures on walls, coats on racks,
meat in the butcher's; *hung* can apply even to people when they are
clinging on to something:

He hung from the window sill by his fingertips.

The single exception is in the context of capital punishment, when the
individual is *hanged*. The wrong form of the word is often used:

☒☒ *He was arrested immediately, found guilty of 'moral insanity' and
hung* [should be *hanged*]. (Big Issue)

Embarrassment rating: ●◐○ This is a common error but correct
usage demands that a person who is executed with a noose is *hanged*.

How to avoid: The profession of hangman, now fortunately gone, or
the old game of 'hangman' indicates the right version of the word
when you are referring to the ultimate punishment, i.e. *hanged*.

HAVE *or* OF

Of is sometimes wrongly used for *have* in writing. This is a phonetic
mistake, that is, one that occurs because of pronunciation.

Instead of *He should have been there* or its shortened form *He should've
been there* people sometimes write

☒☒ *He should of been there.*

The mistake comes about because of the similarity in sound
between the two words, particularly when *have* is shortened to *'ve*.
This confusion is always wrong; in fact, *of* makes no sense in this
context.

Embarrassment rating: ●●● This is an error that shows simple ignorance.

How to avoid: *Of* can never follow directly after would/should/could or may/might. In any case, the – *'ve* abbreviation should only be used in fairly informal writing.

HEROIN *or* HEROINE

That final 'e' makes all the difference, and the slip is easily made (see below).

Heroin is the 'drug which is a morphine derivative', while *heroine* is the female equivalent of 'hero', a 'woman who shows heroic qualities' or the 'central woman character either in real life or in a story, film, etc.' (e.g. Jane Eyre, Cleopatra). Although there's a tendency now to use a single term to apply to both men and women in some artistic contexts – actor, poet – the hero/heroine distinction tends to be observed. It is even more important to preserve the heroin/heroine difference:

    ❌❌ *Charles Saatchi has angered the parents of a dead heroine* [should be **heroin**] *addict by buying and exhibiting a macabre portrait of her . . .* (The Times)

Embarrassment rating: ●●●, because the mistake looks like carelessness, which it is.

How to avoid: Just be on the alert. It might help to recall that '-ine' is the ending of 'feminine' as well as *heroine*.

HISTORIC *or* HISTORICAL

Both of these terms derive from *history* but they carry fairly distinct meanings. How to tell them apart?

Historic indicates that the event, person, battle, etc. so described was 'important', 'history-making'. Although it's quite usual to see current events referred to as *historic* – as in 'Yesterday's historic meeting between the two leaders . . . ' – it's probably better to let history itself have the last word on what's really important. In other words, wait a bit before using the term:

The first testing of an atomic bomb, at Los Alamos in July 1945, was a historic moment for humankind.

Historical is an adjective meaning 'relating to history', and attaching it to a noun says nothing about the significance of that noun. It's a 'neutral' word:

Recent historical research has tended to investigate the lives of 'ordinary' people rather than those of rulers and generals.

Embarrassment rating: ●◑○○ There is quite a gap of meaning between a 'historic event' and a 'historical event', and it is not only careful users of English who will want to observe the difference.

How to avoid: *Historic* is a word which implies judgement, since by definition it describes something significant. But, as I've suggested above, *historical* is an essentially neutral term, describing anything which occurred in the (distant) past.

HOARD *or* HORDE

These two have the same sound and share overlapping ideas of mass and quantity.

A *hoard* is a 'hidden store' of something, usually valuable and put by for use in the future:

Rumours of a hoard of Nazi treasure at the bottom of the lake circulated for many years.

Horde describes a 'large number':

There were hordes of people in Oxford Street for the sales.

The first word is wrongly used here instead of the second:

⊠⊠ *. . . someone who can fight the hungry hoards* [should be **hordes**] *of other people who are going to apply for this job!* (recruitment advertisement)

Embarrassment rating: ●◑○○ It is quite tricky to discriminate between these two and there's nothing in the 'shape' of either word to give guidance.

How to avoid: *Hoard* is frequently associated with treasure, and the words share an 'a'. *Hordes* tend to be fairly horrible too.

HUMILIATION *or* HUMILITY

The difference between these two words is considerable, but they look as though they might be related and confusion is possible.

Humiliation is 'shame' or 'treatment which hurts a person's self-respect'. The *humiliation* may be intended or unintended, and the application of the word ranges from a sense of real grievance to a feeling that you haven't been handled quite as respectfully as you'd like:

In fact, no amount of indignity and humiliation will drive away the Ikea customer, whose children will queue for 40 minutes for a quick play in a pit filled with plastic balls, as long, that is, as the price is right. (Daily Telegraph)

Humility is 'modesty', the 'capacity of being humble'. Fairly or not, it is sometimes presented as a slightly suspect quality, and associated with hypocrisy. But there are genuinely humble individuals:

The gold standard for Tory repentance is provided by another former Defence Minister, John Profumo, whose humility has been proved over 40 years of quiet charitable work. (Observer)

Embarrassment rating: ●●◐, since one demonstrates *humility* by choice but *humiliation* is something imposed on one.

How to avoid: *Humility* is a quality that comes from within the individual who demonstrates it by his/her words, behaviour, etc. *Humiliation* is externally produced and felt by the individual as a painful experience.

I

ILLEGIBLE *or* UNREADABLE

These two words both convey the idea of 'hard to read' but they have two different senses which are reflected in their definitions.

Illegible refers to the physical appearance of handwriting or print and means 'hard or impossible to read'. *Unreadable* can be used in this sense too although its principal application is to the quality of someone's writing, where it means 'so poor as to be not worth reading'.

Embarrassment rating: ●◐○ Both words are pejorative, although most writers would much rather be accused of producing an *illegible* script than an *unreadable* one. Although I suppose that if it were *illegible*, how could you tell if it was also *unreadable*?

How to avoid: *Illegible* should be reserved for handwriting. When using *unreadable*, it may be necessary to specify which sense of the word you mean, since a book could be hard to read through bad printing, for example, as much as through shoddy writing.

IMPLY *or* INFER

This is a very familiar pair of confusables. People – or at least those who care – have long complained about the misuse of *infer* to mean *imply*.

Properly used, these verbs have a complementary quality. To *imply* something is to 'hint' or 'suggest' it without its being openly stated:

> *The remuneration committee was still looking at this issue, the company said, implying that a severance pay-off has not been ruled out.*
> (Guardian)

To *infer* is to 'draw conclusions from the evidence', and suggests skill at understanding hints and working out implications:

The 21 Grams of the [film] title . . . is apparently the weight a body loses when it dies, from which we might infer it is the precise weight of the human soul. (Guardian)

In this way one person will *infer* what another has *implied*, or (in noun terms) *inferences* will be drawn from *implications*.

Infer is sometimes used as though it meant *imply* – as in the erroneous 'I don't like your tone of voice. What are you inferring?' This usage gets some dictionary support, but it is wrong by the standards of correct English.

Embarrassment rating: ●◑○ As I've said, this is a pretty common error and sheer weight of numbers may eventually result in *infer* being used only in its wrong sense (rather as with 'disinterested/ uninterested'). However, this is a distinction worth defending because, when used properly, *infer* is a useful and natural opposite to *imply*.

How to avoid: This is a hard distinction to memorise. How about: when you *infer* something you take *in* information; when you *imply* something, you send it *out*.

INDIGNITY *or* INDIGNATION

This is one of those 'two-sides-of-the same-coin' differences. It's a question of knowing which face you're looking at.

An *indignity* is something that is inflicted or endured, an 'insult' or 'humiliation':

. . . the appalling televised indignities they suffer – meagre rations, round-the-clock discomfort and insects down the trousers . . .
(Daily Telegraph)

while *indignation* is what the sufferer may feel about it afterwards, a sense of 'justified anger'. *Indignation* can be expressed on behalf of others and the unfair treatment they have received, as well as being felt for one's own sake:

The chairman reacted with indignation to the suggestion that he was personally profiting from the scheme.

(The adjective relating to *indignation* is *indignant*, while the adjective most nearly linked with *indignity* is *undignified*.)

Embarrassment rating: ●●◑ An erroneous reference to, say, 'enduring an indignation' is a blunder.

How to avoid: *Indignity* is both an abstract feeling (of insult or shame) and the situation or punishment which led to it. *Indignation* refers only to the feeling or emo*tion* which has been provoked by the *indignity*.

INDUSTRIAL *or* INDUSTRIOUS

Both of these adjectives derive from 'industry' but they have acquired distinct meanings.

Industrial is used of objects, places, processes, etc. and means 'connected with industry or the manufacture of goods':

Industrial output remained high in the second quarter of the year.

Industrious is used only of individuals or groups of people and means 'diligent', 'hard-working':

Their defence foolishly started playing the ball around in their own penalty area only for the industrious Warrington to win the ball . . .
(Daily Telegraph)

Embarrassment rating: ●◐○ I suspect this is not a frequent confusion, if only because *industrious* has fallen from favour as a word of approval – it has a slightly patronising air.

How to avoid: *Industrious* means busy – note the shared '-us-'. *Industrial* is a plain, descriptive term to do with manufacture.

INFORMANT *or* INFORMER

Although both of these nouns describe a 'person who passes over information', they are used in different circumstances, one of which is more positive than the other.

An *informant* is a 'source' (who may be acting out of a sense of public duty to blow the whistle on wrongdoing, for example) and the stress is on the data he/she passes over:

One of the most intriguing aspects of the infamous Andrew Gilligan broadcast about the government dossier was his description of his anonymous informant. (Guardian)

The term *informer*, also describing a 'source', tends to be restricted to the person who names names, especially in police contexts:

[The Mafia] pulverised by the damage done to it by informers and the arrest in the early 90s of the 'boss of bosses' . . . (Guardian)

Embarrassment rating: ●◐○ Even so, the sentence 'I have my informants', sometimes used humorously, would be quite different if rephrased as 'I have my informers'.

How to avoid: It depends which camp you're in. Journalists and people avid for gossip are fed stories and leads by *informants*. The police are assisted by *informers*, aka 'grasses'.

INGENIOUS *or* INGENUOUS

Two words with a single-letter difference. They look as though they should be related but they are near-opposites.

Ingenious means 'clever', particularly in the context of finding solutions for problems or thinking up new methods:

Car manufacturers have spent millions devising ingenious ways to protect their cars against salt water and other elements. (car advertisement)

Ingenuous means 'artless', 'simple' – usually too much so, as it's not innocence so much as gullibility that is suggested:

When he spoke about money it was with an ingenuous enthusiasm that offended no one.

(This adjective is more frequently found in its negative form: *disingenuous*. This indicates a <u>devious</u> person or plan or remark which is masked by the pretence of straighforwardness: ' . . . *and to wear such an attention-getting accessory [as sunglasses] under the guise of wishing to deflect notice seemed disingenuous* . . . ' [*quoted in* The Times])

Embarrassment rating: ●●◐, if these two are confused. An *ingenious* plan and an *ingenuous* one are very different things.

How to avoid: This may be one to memorise, unless the link between 'ingenue' and *ingenuous* is likely to stick.

INHUMAN *or* INHUMANE

Both adjectives convey strong condemnation, and many people use them interchangeably. However, there is a distinction.

Inhuman, meaning 'brutal', 'barbarous', is the harsher of the two, and can describe an individual without any redeeming (human) features. More generally, it characterises people's behaviour towards each other, with the implication of being less than, not worthy of, a human being:

Memorial services recalled the inhuman treatment of concentration camp inmates.

Inhumane has the sense of 'cruel', 'lacking in qualities of kindness and sympathy', and is the opposite of 'humane'. It can be used about the way individuals or animals are treated:

Protesters claimed that the veal calves were transported in cramped and inhumane conditions.

Embarrassment rating: ●●○ Although both terms are condemnatory, *inhuman* is considerably stronger.

How to avoid: These remain loaded words and anyone using them should take care to discriminate between them. *Inhumane* is perhaps a more 'everyday' word than *inhuman*; thinking of their opposites, 'human' and 'humane', may help.

INNOVATION *or* INVENTION

These two are closely connected but in no way mean the same thing.

An *innovation* is the 'introduction of something fresh' – not as radical as an *invention*, it's usually the development or refinement of an existing idea or system:

CCTV coverage is extensive, but the real innovations are the movement sensors under each [car] bay. (Guardian)

By contrast, an *invention* is a 'new device or discovery':

Marconi is generally credited with the invention of wireless telegraphy.

Invention is also used in the sense of fiction – a 'deceit or lie'.

Embarrassment rating: ●○○ But historical accuracy demands that some people are credited with *inventions*, others with *innovations*, even if the distinction is often blurred.

How to avoid: *Invention* derives from a Latin root which means to 'come upon' – as if the discovery was lying hidden until the right person came along. To *innovate*, by contrast, has more to do with 'making new'; the idea of 'novel' and 'novelty' underlie it and share the same root. Like renovation, it describes an improvement to an existing system.

INNUENDO *or* INSINUATION

Both words describe something not openly stated but implied, and both have tacky associations.

An *innuendo* is an 'indirect remark', very frequently one with sexual overtones – it's often the equivalent of the French phrase 'double entendre', any remark with a nudge-nudge component:

> *The message is, 'In football girls really are on top' – those last two words picked out in pink, wink, wink. No sexual innuendo intended, says the FA.* (Guardian)

An *insinuation* is more general, being any 'hint carrying an unpleasant suggestion':

> *Mr Norman's comments about being better off ditching the vinaigrette and using Hellman's . . . amounted to an insinuation that his restaurant was buying in ready-made mayonnaise.* (Daily Telegraph)

(To *insinuate* is to 'hint' but also to 'work (oneself) gradually into a place' – an organisation, a person's good books – by stealth.)

Embarrassment rating: ●○○ Both words have slightly unpleasant connotations, and to make *innuendos* (plural also *innuendoes*) is probably on a par with making *insinuations*.

How to avoid: *Insinuation* will do for any indirect remark that aims to undermine another's reputation for honesty. *Innuendo* is generally found in a sexual context.

INOCULATE *or* VACCINATE

Two 'medical' terms that may appear to have distinct meanings but can, in fact, be used interchangeably in most contexts.

To *inoculate* is to 'protect against disease' by infecting someone with a mild form of that disease, so ensuring future immunity. To *vaccinate* was originally to 'protect against smallpox by using the cowpox virus' (*vacca* is Latin for 'cow'). The word is now interchangeable with *inoculate* and applies to providing comparable protection from any disease. The only time *inoculate* should be preferred is in a metaphorical sense (e.g. if describing someone as 'inoculated against racism').

Embarrassment rating: ○○○, since one can be used for the other.

How to avoid: See above.

INSIDIOUS *or* INVIDIOUS

These two adjectives have nothing in common except for eight letters out of nine and their negative associations – it's enough to cause the occasional confusion.

Insidious points to a kind of slow-burning malice, and means 'cunning'. It can be applied to people but is more often used to describe words, attitudes, effects:

Just as irritating was the insidious stereotyping throughout the article. I was portrayed as a 'girl' in a 'tight white Lycra dress' who had 'giggled' when introduced to Gower. (Guardian)

Invidious means 'causing bad feeling' or 'provoking envy'. Often qualifying 'position' or 'distinction', it should not be used as a synonym for 'difficult'. In the example below the word is correctly applied to describe a policy which is likely to provoke resentment:

. . . the record companies remain in the invidious position of trying to eradicate piracy and protect sales of their physical product while also encouraging legal downloads. (Guardian)

Embarrassment rating: ●◐○ The mistake may not be noticed, since there is a tenuous link between the two words: for example, an *insidious* remark may produce *invidious* results. And I have a feeling that for many the words are vaguely synonymous, with the general sense of 'nasty'. However, the original meanings and the distinctions are worth observing.

How to avoid: There is indeed something snake-like about *insidious* behaviour, as well as a hissing quality to the word. And whatever is *invidious* causes envy among other negative reactions.

INTENSE *or* INTENSIVE

There is some overlap between these two words and they can be found in the same context (*intense/intensive* questioning) but they also have distinct meanings.

Intense means 'strong' or 'characterised by extreme emotion':

What should have been one of the most intense Super League clashes of the season was reduced to near farce yesterday . . .
(Daily Telegraph)

While *intense* can be used about people, *intensive* – meaning 'thorough', 'without relief or let-up' – characterises things like research and investigation:

An intensive search of the crime scene, involving twenty officers, produced few results.

Embarrassment rating: ●◐○, since the two words do shade into each other.

How to avoid: *Intensive* means much the same as comprehen*sive*. Any use of *intense* should also suggest 'extreme'.

INTERMENT *or* INTERNMENT

Care needs to be taken over these words with their one-letter difference. Any confusion may be enhanced by notions of being 'shut away', common to both.

Interment is 'burial', almost always used literally:

The cemetery development was prompted by his father, who suggested he would like to be buried there. But the honour of first interment eventually went to Mr Taylor's aunt Evelyn. (Guardian)

Internment is 'confinement' (in a prison or camp). The word usually describes the pre-emptive treatment meted out to those regarded as potential troublemakers, spies, terrorists, etc. – that is, they are locked up as a 'precaution' and without the benefit of trial:

. . . one of the nastiest episodes in Britain's own wartime narrative: the mass . . . internment of some 27,000 'enemy aliens' during 1940, on the infamous instruction of Prime Minister Winston Churchill to 'collar the lot'. (Observer)

(The associated verbs are *inter* and *intern*. In the US and elsewhere, *intern* is also a noun meaning a 'trainee doctor in a hospital' or a 'person getting experience in any profession'.)

Embarrassment rating: ●●◐, although mistakes are perhaps more likely with the verb forms. 'He was interred yesterday' is a very different statement from 'He was interned yesterday'.

How to avoid: Careful pronunciation stresses the 'n' in *intern/ internment*, and is a guide to the spelling and meaning. Also, there is a noun 'internee', but no such equivalent exists for *inter*.

INVEIGH *or* INVEIGLE

Two slightly unusual words which are sometimes confused, perhaps because of their similar spellings.

To *inveigh* (pronounced to rhyme with 'say' and always followed by 'against') is to 'attack strongly', usually in speech:

> *His function, like theirs, is to climb the stairs to the pulpit on Sunday mornings and inveigh against sin.* (Guardian)

To *inveigle* (pronounced to rhyme with 'bagel') is to 'tempt' or 'coax'. The word carries the hint of something underhand:

> *Inveigle, bribe or bully friends or relatives to babysit once in a while so you can sneak out . . . with your husband.* (The Times)

Embarrassment rating: ●●○ These may not be everyday terms but the wrong word conveys a meaning quite different from the one intended.

How to avoid: *Inveigh* must be followed by 'against'; *inveigle* takes a direct object (i.e. is followed by the person or group you are trying to tempt).

ITS *or* IT'S

This is one of the commonest and most basic mistakes in written English. It's the apostrophe which causes the problem, of course.

It's is the contracted or shortened form of *it is* or *it has*:

> *It's a warm day.*

> *It's been raining all day.*

Its, without an apostrophe, is the possessive form of the pronoun *it*:

> *The cat flicked its tail.*

Here is a selection of mistakes, going both ways. The following should read *its*, with no apostrophe:

> ☒☒ . . . *unlike common-or-garden spring mattresses which will sag with age latex will hold it's* [should be *its*] *shape . . .* (advertisement)

> ☒☒ *Unlike other films on this event, Kasdan and Costner's gives the gunfight it's* [should be *its*] *factual 30 seconds.* (Independent)

Getting it wrong the other way round (i.e. leaving out the apostrophe when it ought to be included) may be less usual but the mistake is still found too often:

☒ ☒ *... Arnold Schwarzenegger finds his memory has been erased – so its* [should be *it's*] *off to Mars in the hope of piecing together his past.* (Independent)

☒ ☒ *Staff without windows say they do not know whether its* [should be *it's*] *dark outside, if its* [should be *it's*] *raining, sunny, hot or cold ...* (Sun)

But, just to show that it is possible to do it properly, the following example gets both spellings right in the right places:

But to its followers, it's the old story of demonising black subculture before exploiting its commercial fallout. (Guardian)

Embarrassment rating: ●●● This may be a very frequent error but that does not make it any more excusable. It's easy enough to find the correct form (see below), and the failure to get it right indicates a poor grasp of the basics of written English.

How to avoid: If uncertain over which form to use – whether *it's* or *its* – try substituting the full-length *it is* or *it has* in the sentence. As long as the phrase or sentence still makes sense (*It is* a warm day; *It has* been raining all day), then you can safely use the contracted form of the two words (*It's* ..). If, however, the sentence does *not* make sense (the cat flicked *it is* tail), then you are using the possessive form of *it* and must not include the apostrophe: write *its*.

J J J J J J J J J J J

JUNCTION *or* JUNCTURE

Both words mean a 'joining or union' but occur in different contexts.

Junction tends to have a physical application, describing the point where roads or railway lines or electric wires meet. *Juncture* is a coming together in time rather than space, and suggests a 'critical point' in some process:

> At that juncture Townsend and Princess Margaret were able to announce their love to each other – but not to the world. (The Times)

Embarrassment rating: ●●○ The words don't sound right if swapped around. To put *junction* in the *Times* sentence above would suggest a royal version of the famous love-in-a-railway-station film *Brief Encounter*. Conversely, one can't talk of an electric *juncture*.

How to avoid: The *junction* association with trains, electricity, etc. is familiar to everyone. If the sentence is about time, rather than place, then *juncture* can be used. The term shouldn't be applied to just any old event – where a simple 'now' or 'then' would do – but be reserved for a significant moment.

KKKK**K**KKK

KNELL *or* KNOLL

This isn't much of a trap perhaps but it may sometimes be assumed that *knoll* is the past tense form of *knell* (possibly under the influence of a bell *toll*ing). It isn't. Read on for enlightenment.

A *knell* describes the 'sound of a tolling bell' – particularly at a funeral. In fact the word is almost always used figuratively and prefaced with 'death':

> *Days after the United States said it would scrap the space shuttle, the death knell has been sounded for the Hubble space telescope.* (Daily Telegraph)

The verb is also *knell* (past tense *knelled*).

A *knoll* is a 'small hill'. I'd take a small bet that at least one in every four uses of this fairly uncommon word is in the phrase 'grassy knoll' – a reference to the roadside area in Dallas from where a gunman (other than Lee Harvey Oswald) is supposed by conspiracy buffs to have taken a shot at President Kennedy.

Embarrassment rating: ●○○ Most mistakes here are probably to do with correct spelling of *knell/knoll* rather than confusion over meanings.

How to avoid: *Knell* goes with b*ell*. *Knoll* goes with hill*ock*.

LAMA *or* LLAMA

It is surely the exotic source of these words – one from Tibetan, the other from Spanish via a Peruvian language – that sometimes causes confusion. There is nothing in them to hint at the meaning and so guide the spelling.

The *lama* with one 'l' is a 'Buddhist monk in Tibet':

Readers of Cosmopolitan who seek the serenity of a Buddhist lama but can't be fagged to put in hours of meditation each day for years can expect to be disappointed. (Daily Telegraph)

The *llama* with two 'l's is a 'four-legged beast of burden', the South American equivalent of the camel (in fact camels and llamas are related):

It's not often that you're offered a dried llama foetus – unless you're in La Paz, that is. (Daily Telegraph)

Don't confuse the man with the animal – for one thing, they come from opposite sides of the world:

⊠ ⊠ *They get a pleasant glow from name-dropping the Dalai Llama* [should be *Lama*]. (Daily Telegraph)

Embarrassment rating: ●◐○ People will know what you mean even if they detect the mistake. Amusing rather than embarrassing.

How to avoid: *Lama* and 'monk' have the same number of letters. So do the *llama* and the 'camel', its distant relation. Alternatively, both *llama* and 'woolly' have a double 'l'.

LARVA *or* LAVA

Both of these are slightly specialist terms, not in everyday vocabulary. That, and their identical pronunciation, probably accounts for the occasional confusion. Which one has the 'r'?

A *larva* (plural *larvae*) is an 'animal, usually an insect, in the earliest stages of its development':

> *The [eel] eggs hatch quickly into minute larvae, and over the next two to three years a proportion are borne on the great ocean currents to Europe, growing as they go.* (Guardian)

Lava is 'molten rock from a volcano'. The word is often applied metaphorically:

> *. . . the latest proposals from Alistair Darling, the transport secretary, have produced a molten lava stream of editorial protest.* (Guardian)

(Don't get the two mixed up: another *Guardian* article once told readers where they could buy 'larva lamps'.)

Embarrassment rating: ●◑○, since the meaning is likely to remain clear even when a mistake is made. For anyone aware of the correct spellings, however, the wrong choice of word will provide a moment's amusement.

How to avoid: The *larva* is the animal in its immature form – note the shared 'r's. *Lava* is (molten) rock – both have four letters.

LAST *or* LATTER

Is there any difference between these two or can they be used interchangeably?

Last applies to anything coming at the end of a sequence (the *last* word, her *last* book) and means 'final', 'most recent'. *Latter*, when properly used, should apply to the 'second of two items', and only two:

> *In strictly football terms, the momentary idiocy of Gary Neville is as bad, in my opinion, as Eric Cantona's infamous boot-in-the-chest in January 1995: the latter a breach of civil law, off the pitch when provoked, the former a triple corruption of sporting morals.* (Daily Telegraph)

It's best to use *latter* to contrast with *former*, as in this example. Be careful with *latter* anyway. A different wording may often be preferable since, if the reader has to go back and check what your particular *latter* is referring to, the flow of the sentence is broken.

Embarrassment rating: ◑○○ *Last* and *latter* are not quite interchangeable but this is a fine distinction.

How to avoid: There are sometimes stylistic reasons for avoiding *latter*. It's one of those words with a vaguely impressive ring, but anyone using it should ask whether a simpler alternative is available.

LATITUDE *or* LONGITUDE

This is one of those 'which-way-round-is-it?' confusions. Everyone is familiar with these imaginary lines which parcel up the globe, but which one runs from side to side and which from pole to pole?

Latitude is the 'angular distance from the equator, measured to the north or south' (so that Wellington, New Zealand is 41.17 degrees South while Wellington in Somerset, England is 50.59 degrees North). *Latitude* has the additional meanings of 'range' or 'freedom'.

Longitude uses the meridian, any one of the great and imaginary circles running from pole to pole, with the meridian line through Greenwich taken as the starting point. *Longitude* is therefore the 'angular distance between a particular place and the Greenwich meridian, measured to the east and west'. (Paris, Texas is 95.33 degrees West while Paris, France is 2.20 degrees East.)

Embarrassment rating: ●◑○, except for geography teachers or those who like messing about in boats – and presumably they already know the difference.

How to avoid: Lines of *longitude* run from pole to pole, and the two words contain an 'o' as the second letter. Getting this one right automatically defines *latitude*.

LAY *or* LIE

There aren't that many English confusables which one can honestly claim as nightmarish, but this is one of them. Not only do these basic words relate to the same sort of action – being put down/ putting oneself down – but the past tense form of one is the same as the present tense form of the other. The confusion is built in and even careful users are likely to have problems with this pair.

To *lay* is to 'put down' and is a transitive verb (i.e. one which is generally followed by an object):

Lay your sleeping head, my love . . . (first line of poem by W. H. Auden)

To *lie* is to 'be at rest on a horizontal surface' and is an intransitive verb (one which is not followed by a direct object):

He told the dog to lie down at once.

Confusion mostly arises from the fact that the past tense of *lie* is *lay*:

The dog lay down and went to sleep straightaway.

while the past tense of *lay* is *laid*:

They laid the picnic food out on the rug.

The past participle form (i.e. the one used after 'has' or 'had') is *lain* for *lie*:

The farmhouse has lain empty for almost two years now.

and *laid* for *lay*:

The soldiers had laid thousands of mines in the course of the war.

Mistakes like those in the following examples are quite frequent:

   ⊠ ⊠ *The coffin had laid in the chapel overnight . . .* (Independent)
       (should be **The coffin had lain . . .** because after 'has' or 'had' *lie*
       changes to *lain*.)

   ⊠ ⊠ *Take a rug to lay on and a sheet to shield you from prying eyes.* (Sun)
       (should be *a rug to lie on* – unless you're a chicken
       contemplating the production of eggs.)

  To *lie* in the sense of 'not tell the truth' takes a different (and regular) past tense/past participle: *He lied in claiming he was elsewhere at the time.*

Embarrassment rating: ●◐○ Although this is a tricky pair to sort out, it can be done with a little care.

How to avoid: Before using *lie* or *lay*, ask yourself which of the two you mean. Then work out whether it refers to an action in the present or past, and follow the *lie-lay-lain* or the *lay-laid* pattern. This is also one of those differences where a sensitive ear to the sound of a sentence can help.

LEACH *or* LEECH

There is a connection between the sense of these identically pronounced words, but also a distinction which should be observed.

To *leach* (only a verb) is to 'filter in or out':

But the summer glut of tourists and the huge irrigation of the 'growing' industry have caused underground aquifers to drop and salt water to leach in. (Observer)

To *leech* is to 'suck the blood out of', to 'drain', from the noun *leech*, a 'blood-sucking worm'. (The word was once used in a slightly disparaging sense to mean a doctor – presumably because of the medical use of leeches in blood-letting rather than the fees which doctors charged.) *Leech* is frequently used to describe any parasitic individual or organisation:

> . . . *the Mafia is an apolitical leech on any ideology that indulges or fears it enough to give it space.* (Observer)

Although there is a link between the ideas of 'filtering' and 'draining', where the sense of 'leaking out' is meant the correct term is *leach* rather than *leech*:

> ☒ . . . *we fear news of [defence] cuts will be leeched* [should be **leached**] *out discreetly over the coming months.* (Daily Telegraph)

Embarrassment rating: ●◐○, since the sense is not generally impaired by an error and there is an overlap of meaning between the verb forms. The *leech* spelling for the worm should be observed, however.

How to avoid: The association of meaning between *lea*k and *leach* is a spelling indicator.

LESSEE *or* LESSOR

This pair of 'legalistic' terms is quite easy to confuse. But at some time many of us will find ourselves on one side or other of the fence, and it's best to know which is which.

The *lessee* is the 'person to whom a lease is granted' (usually in property) while a *lessor* is the 'person who grants the lease'. A 'leaseholder' is the same as a *lessee* and a 'letter' (i.e. a person who lets) is the equivalent of *lessor*.

Embarrassment rating: ●●◐, especially if you're professionally involved in the property business.

How to avoid: As with other terms such as 'addressee' or 'detainee', the double '-ee' of *lessee* indicates that this is someone on the receiving end of a process.

LIBEL *or* SLANDER

These two are often used interchangeably, although there is a difference between them not so much of meaning but of application.

Both nouns and verbs, *libel* and *slander* refer to a 'defamatory accusation' or mean to 'defame'. *Libel* is used about anything written or presented in permanent form, including material on the Internet:

Drudge initially gained his celebrity by libelling me [on a website] on the day I began work in the Clinton White House in August 1997, reporting as fact that I was hiding police records of domestic violence. (Guardian)

Slander tends to be reserved for spoken comments:

Sixteen North Africans . . . are suing the Spanish prime minister . . . for slander after he . . . wrongly claimed they were proof of a dangerous alliance between Saddam Hussein and Osama bin Laden. (Guardian)

Embarrassment rating: ●○○, since the two terms are frequently used for each other. The careful user, though, will want to distinguish between defamatory comments made in print and those which are spoken.

How to avoid: The association between *libel* and anything written is suggested by their shared 'i'. *Slander* is more to do with speech.

LIBERTARIAN *or* LIBERTINE

These two words derive from 'liberty' so it's perhaps appropriate that they have moved off in different directions. One describes a political or ideological position while the other characterises a person who pursues sexual pleasure. Which is which?

A *libertarian* is a 'person who believes in the maximum possible amount of freedom for himself/herself and others'. This usually entails freedom under the law but includes the right to pursue behaviour that might be self-destructive. The word is often associated with a particular branch of right-wing thinking, as here:

Given his first-hand experience and neo-conservative ideology, you might imagine that Mr Limbaugh would adopt the libertarian's argument to legalise drugs and let the market decide. (The Times)

A *libertine* is a 'person who leads a dissolute life, especially in sexual matters'. The term is a bit dated now and conjures up images of rakish

18th-century aristocrats. However, it can still be applied to someone who's impatient with rules and pursues pleasure in a very single-minded way, even in the innocent field of gardening:

> *The proper gardener is no conservative; neither is she a socialist, sowing the common harvest. She is an anarchist, and a libertine.* (Guardian)

Embarrassment rating: ●●○ *Libertines* must be be *libertarians* by definition, I suppose, although the formula doesn't work the other way round. A *libertarian* might well be offended to be called a *libertine*. But the second word is not often found now.

How to avoid: In practice, *libertarian* is the only expression in general use and even then it's a somewhat specialised term.

LICENCE *or* LICENSE

This is a distinction that only emerges when the words are written. The 'c/s' difference applies to various words and is more fully discussed in the 'advice/advise' entry.

The noun form is *licence* :

> *TV licence; driver's licence; off-licence*

while the verb is *license*:

> *'Are you licensed to drive this vehicle, sir?'*

Embarrassment rating: ●○○ It's quite likely the error will not be noticed, and the sense remain clear. It's still a mistake, though . . .

How to avoid: The 'c' spelling goes with the noun form; the 's' with the verb (see 'advice/advise').

LIGHTNING *or* LIGHTENING

Pronunciation tends to overlook the 'e' in the second word and spelling follows suit. The difference between the two is further blurred by their common root in 'light'.

Lightning, as an adjective, applies to anything which is 'moving very fast', and as a noun is the accompaniment of thunder, a 'burst of light in the sky':

> *He was struck by lightning on the set.* (Guardian)

This spelling is sometimes confused with *lightening*, meaning 'making lighter' (applied to reducing a burden or to changing a colour):

. . . a few blond streaks hither thither, a little lightening around the fringe, y'know . . . (Guardian)

Embarrassment rating: ●◐○ The meaning will generally be clear, although there is a difference between the sentence 'There was some lightning in the sky' and 'There was some lightening in the sky'. And I don't imagine many people would take up a hairdresser's offer to provide a little lightning round the fringe . . .

How to avoid: Careful pronunciation will keep the words distinct, and so help with the spelling. *Lightning* has two syllables, *lightening* (like 'brightening') has three.

LIMP, LIMPID *or* LUCID

Limpid **looks as though it must be connected to** *limp*. **It isn't. Its proper association is with** *lucid*.

Limp means 'drooping', 'lacking firmness and authority':

[The film] needs an actor with the presence of a Richard Burton to carry off the limp and clichéd dialogue. (Daily Telegraph)

Limpid has nothing to do with the previous word but, if anything, is a near-opposite since it means 'very clear', 'transparent'. Frequently applied to music performances – often those at the piano, for some reason – it can also be used in more literal contexts:

Rachel Hunter . . . fixes me with her limpid blue eyes and starts telling me all about women's knickers. (Daily Telegraph)

Lucid has the same sense of 'very clear' and therefore 'easy to understand'. The context here is normally language, books, explanations:

. . . finally there is a book which explains in non-romantic, lucid terms, better than anything else I have read, why the French are as they are. (Daily Telegraph)

Embarrassment rating: ●●●, if one confuses *limp* with *limpid*, since the words are not only unconnected but have opposed meanings.

How to avoid: The similarity of meaning between *limpid* and *lucid* is suggested by their rhyming ends.

LIVID *or* LURID

Both of these similar-sounding adjectives have connections with colour but are most widely used in other contexts. I suspect that their meanings remain a bit hazy, however.

Livid is 'dark', 'leaden':

> *His cheeks are livid with bruises, although these turn out to be the result, not of the accident, but of dental treatment . . .* (Observer)

but it's most frequently used to mean 'extremely angry' (presumably because of the colour of an angry face). *Lurid* has been used about a range of colour tones, from pale yellow to purple. In another sense it is also a favourite tabloid expression, generally applied now to news stories which have a 'sensational' quality, often but not exclusively sexual:

> *At its peak, tens of thousands would await the latest lurid tales of alien autopsies and flying saucers spying on sleepy market towns.* (Observer)

Embarrassment rating: ●●○, since the two words don't make much sense if swapped around in some contexts ('I was *lurid* with him'; 'a *livid* story'). However, it would be possible to refer to a stormy sky or someone's complexion as being either *livid* or *lurid*.

How to avoid: When the words are used metaphorically (i.e. *livid* to mean 'angry', *lurid* to mean 'sensational') they need to be kept distinct.

LO(A)TH *or* LOATHE

Both of these words convey an idea of hostility to something but they are different parts of speech, and used in different contexts.

Lo(a)th – with or, occasionally, without the middle *a* – is an adjective indicating reluctance, being 'unwilling'. It's a slightly literary and dated expression but still useful:

> *I'd be loath to get involved in their quarrels.*

Loathe is a verb meaning to 'regard with disgust':

> *She loathed his insinuating, flattering manner.*

(Although the definition almost suggests revulsion, the word is often used to signify simple dislike, as in *I loathe the taste of beetroot*.)

Embarrassment rating: ●●○, since the terms are distinct – for example, one can be *lo(a)th* to do something without in any way *loathing* it.

How to avoid: Correct pronunciation is a guide to spelling: *lo(a)th* to rhyme with 'both'; *loathe* with 'clothe'.

LOSE, LOOSE *or* LOOSEN

In their verb forms these words are occasionally confused, particularly the first two because of the doubling of the 'o'.

To *lose* or 'mislay' has one 'o' :

The maze of streets in the old part of town made it easy to lose one's way.

To *loose* is to 'set free', 'cast off':

We loosed the dinghy from its moorings.

To *loosen* is to 'make looser', to 'untighten', either literally or figuratively:

A few drinks certainly loosened his tongue.

(The past tense forms are *lost, loosed* and *loosened*, respectively.)

Embarrassment rating: ●●◐ since this is a fairly basic spelling error.

How to avoid: *Lost* and *lose* both share a single 'o' spelling – a useful guide to which meaning you are dealing with.

LUSTFUL *or* LUSTY

Although both of these adjectives derive from *lust*, the meaning of one is essentially innocent.

Lustful is only connected to sex. It means full of 'lust', 'sensual', and hints at something passionate and perhaps forbidden:

Boredom at work could be manifested by lustful dreams about a colleague . . . (Daily Telegraph)

Lusty, however, is a cheerful adjective with a range of applications. In the sense of 'vigorous' it can describe anything from a baby's cries to a batsman's strokes:

With four fours and three lusty sixes he again exposed New Zealand's woeful inability . . . (Daily Telegraph)

Even when *lusty* enters the sexual stakes the word has a jauntiness to it which is lacking in the altogether more biblical-sounding *lustful*:

'No sex please, we're British' was never true. We've always been a lusty lot. (Daily Mirror)

Embarrassment rating: ●●○ if you were to describe someone's performance – on the cricket field, say – as *lustful* when you really meant *lusty*. However, I suspect this is a slip that is rarely made.

How to avoid: Of all the seven deadly sins, lust has probably been the one taken most lightly, even in more religious ages. So either term now could be interpreted as a compliment. Even so, the distinction is worth observing.

LUXURIANT *or* LUXURIOUS

Both adjectives derive from *luxury* but have distinct meanings which shouldn't be confused.

Luxuriant describes anything which is 'produced in abundant quantities' or is 'lush' – its use is generally restricted to natural growth (hair, foliage, etc.):

Seventy-three, but with the luxuriant dark hair of a rather younger man . . . (The Times)

Luxurious conveys notions 'of great comfort', expense and (sometimes) flashiness:

The house has the self-made man's stamp of being rather too meticulously luxurious to rank as a true grandee's residence. (The Times)

Embarrassment rating: ●◐○ But it would be an error to describe vegetation as *luxurious*.

How to avoid: Roughly speaking, anything which is natural can be characterised as *luxuriant* while items (or surroundings) which are man-made are *luxurious*.

MACHO, MANLY *or* MANNISH

All of these terms relate to masculinity but they apply in quite different contexts.

To take the second word first, *manly* means 'brave', 'fitting for a man'. It isn't used much now, perhaps because it has stiff-upper-lip, Victorian overtones. *Masculine* would be the modern equivalent. *Macho* – from the Spanish word for 'male' – is a rough contemporary version but carries a suggestion of swaggering masculinity which the Victorians would certainly not have approved of:

> *The International Conference was a fairly macho negotiating forum, with a great deal of banging of fists on tables and ripe language . . .*
> (Independent)

(*Macho* should be pronounced 'matcho', not 'macko'; the noun is *machismo*.)

Mannish can be applied to women who are considered insufficiently feminine – and for this reason it may sometimes be code for 'gay' or 'lesbian'.

Embarrassment rating: ●●◐ Most men would be pleased to be thought of as *manly/macho*, but would not be so chuffed with the description of *mannish*.

How to avoid: *Mannish*, like 'childish' and 'womanish', carries negative overtones.

MAJORITY *or* MOST OF

Both of these very ordinary expressions describe the greater part of something, and there is a tendency to use the first in all circumstances even when the second would be better English.

Majority is a noun meaning 'the greater number':

The majority of the people in the poll favoured the death penalty.

Majority should not be used to mean 'the larger part' of something which cannot be split up into individual elements. When referring to a single unit, *most of* should be used, or another expression such as 'the greater part of':

I was on tenterhooks for the most of the film.

Embarrassment rating: ●◐○ It's quite common to hear references to 'the majority of the film', but this is better avoided.

How to avoid: Only use *majority* when talking numbers or percentages.

MALEVOLENT, MALICIOUS *or* MALIGNANT

Rather as with the words associated with 'benevolent' (see entry for this), the opposite expressions to do with *malevolent* have shades of meaning which fit them for particular contexts.

Malevolent and *malicious* apply to individuals and their words or actions, in the sense of 'ill-disposed', 'wishing harm to'. *Malevolent* is also used of animals. *Malicious* is perhaps less strong; a *malicious* remark (i.e. one that shows *malice*) may be nothing more than 'spiteful' while a *malevolent* one suggests something darker and more deep-rooted. *Malignant* contains these meanings but, as indicated by its frequent application to cancerous tumours, it carries the more intense sense of 'causing harm or evil to'.

Embarrassment rating: ●◐○ There are some situations in which the words may be interchangeable: for example, a person's action might be *malevolent*, *malicious* or *malignant* depending on how they are interpreted.

How to avoid: There's not much to avoid here but the careful user will pick the appropriate term.

MANTEL *or* MANTLE

A switch-around of the last two letters produces a different word. When the two are confused it's usually because the second, more familiar spelling is put in place of the first.

A *mantel* (usually *mantelpiece*) is the 'shelf above a fireplace'. A *mantle* is a 'cloak or covering', but the word is very often applied metaphorically to mean 'status', 'authority'. In particular the handing over of a *mantle* suggests the symbolic moment when power changes hands:

> *The brief exchange is a defining moment, denoting the passing of the action star mantle from 56-year-old Schwarzenegger to the 31-year-old Rock.*
> (Daily Telegraph)

Embarrassment rating: ●◑○ The only context in which *mantel* occurs now is when it forms part of *mantelpiece*, and some dictionaries show *mantlepiece* ('-le') as an acceptable alternative spelling.

How to avoid: A *mantel* is a kind of sh*el*f: note the shared 'el' in that order.

MASTERFUL *or* MASTERLY

These two terms deriving from 'master' have an overlap of meaning but can carry different emphases.

The adjective *masterly* means 'highly skilled', 'brilliantly accomplished', and is most often used when a performance of some kind is being praised:

> *Many will never forget his masterly appearances on TV, smoking the pipe that became his symbol . . .* (The Times)

Masterful is often used to mean the same thing, but it carries overtones of 'bullying', of aggressive assertion, even if this is intended in a complimentary way:

> *'My camera is often low,' Newton explained, 'because I like the illusion of looking up. I like superwomen, physically strong and masterful.'*
> (Daily Telegraph)

Sometimes it's not clear whether a writer means *masterful* in this second sense (of 'domineering') or is using it as a synonym for the more complimentary *masterly*, although when applied to performances, films, etc., rather than people, the sense is usually 'highly accomplished':

> *James Stewart laid his amiable all-American guy persona on the line in Hitchcock's masterful thriller-cum-psychodrama [Vertigo] . . .*
> (Independent)

Embarrassment rating: ◑○○ These two are often used interchangeably, but there are circumstances in which *masterful* is pejorative and it's as well to be aware of this.

How to avoid: A careful user will tend to apply *masterly* to performances, works, etc. It's worth noting also that some people object to *masterly* as being an inherently sexist term.

MAY *or* MIGHT

There is a growing tendency to use *may* in all circumstances, even where *might* would be correct.

May is the present tense form: *We think he may ring.* (But we don't know yet whether he's going to.)

Might is the past tense: *We thought he might ring.* (Either he did ring or he didn't, but the sentence implies that we know one way or the other.)

It would be incorrect to put: ☒☒ *We thought he may ring.* (This doesn't make sense, since the question of whether he rang or not is left hanging in the air, even though the past tense 'thought' indicates that we already know the answer.)

Very generally speaking, *may* should be used when talking about a present or future possibility, and *might* when talking about the past. The following sentence, for example, would read better with *might* since it refers to the past:

☒ *Without the Beatles there may* [should be ***might***] *have been a Bob Dylan, but Brian Wilson would not have written the Beach Boys'* Good Vibrations. (The Times)

However, things are a little more complicated since there are occasions when *might* can be used to refer to future possibilities as in *He might ring.* (This phrasing suggests greater doubt on the user's part than *may* would do.)

Conversely, *may* followed by 'have' can be used about the past when the speaker or writer is unsure of the situation:

He may have rung; I haven't checked the answerphone.

Might followed by 'have' signifies that something is less likely or no longer possible:

He might have rung if he hadn't been unexpectedly called away.

(In addition, *might have*, used colloquially, can express disappointment or frustration: *He might have rung!*)

Embarrassment rating: ●◐○, since the use of *may* when *might* is required is a very common error. I have a feeling that many people have given up on this one, if they were ever aware of the difference in the first place, and simply grab for *may* whatever the context. All the same, careful users will distinguish between the two.

How to avoid: Quite hard. It takes a bit of thought. As a very rough rule, be wary of using *may* about something that has already occurred.

MAY BE *or* MAYBE

As with other pairs such as 'all ready/already', the two-word version of *may be* is hardly distinguished in pronunciation from the single word. But when a mistake is made in writing, the wrong meaning results.

May be is a combination of two verbs and is used when talking about a possibility:

   He hasn't answered but it may be that he didn't get my letter.

Maybe (one word) means 'perhaps':

   He hasn't answered but maybe he didn't get my letter.

It's quite usual to find this second version used where the first one would be correct:

   ☒☒ *If having . . . a chef to cook your food would put a spring in your step keep reading – this maybe* [should be *may be*] *your lucky week.* (Metro)

Embarrassment rating: ●●○ Even though the writer's meaning won't really be impaired, since both *may be* and *maybe* contain the notion of possibility, this remains a basic error.

How to avoid: If 'perhaps' can be substituted without changing any other word in the sentence then the form/spelling required is *maybe*. Otherwise it's *may be*. Try this test on the first two examples above.

MEDIA *or* MEDIUM

There is not a confusion over meaning here but uncertainty over the singular or plural forms of the word.

Media, a collective term for 'means of communication such as television or newspapers', is the plural form of *medium*. As a plural it should take the appropriate verb form:

   The media are influential in shaping people's opinions.

The tendency is to treat the word as a singular noun (an 'it' rather than a 'they'):

So why does [strictly, should be *do*] *the media disagree?* (Independent)

. . . what the media, for better or worse, has [strictly, should be *have*] *done for royalty . . .* (The Times)

Strictly speaking, this is incorrect, but it is apparent that *media* is on its way to becoming a collective noun which can take singular or plural as the writer wishes, particularly when (as in the examples above) the *media* is/are seen as a single homogenous lump.

Embarrassment rating: ●○○, although some people still object if *media* takes the singular.

How to avoid: This is a matter of choice. My preference, though, is for the *media* to be followed by 'are', 'have', 'do', etc.

MEDICAL *or* MEDICINAL

Both of these words are obviously connected to health and sickness but they have slightly different applications.

Medical means 'relating to the practice of medicine' (*medical* student, *medical* insurance) and, as a noun, describes a 'physical examination to check a person's health/fitness':

Beckham, whose lopsidedness emerged during his medical for Real Madrid, is not alone. (Daily Telegraph)

The adjective *medicinal* means 'used in medicine' and so 'helping to cure'. Very often the word has a slightly jokey overtone since it's applied to drinks which are taken for their alcoholic value rather than their supposed 'curative' properties:

His father is an alcoholic, addicted to a medicinal concoction of cornflower syrup and turpenhydrate. (Spectator)

Embarrassment rating: ●○○ *Medical* tends to be the standard term.

How to avoid: *Medical* treatment is the more general term, covering anything from a visit to the doctor to a session with an osteopath; *medicinal* treatment tends to describe the actual remedies taken for prevention or cure, such as plants or their properties.

MERETRICIOUS *or* MERITORIOUS

These two quite similar sounding words have almost opposite meanings, and the echo of 'merit' in the first word may mislead.

Meretricious has an interesting history since it derives from the Latin word *meretrix* meaning 'prostitute', and indeed its primary sense is 'relating to prostitution'. Never used in this sense now, as far as I can see, it has come to mean 'flashy but without substance':

> *Already this year we have had* Cold Creek Manor, *a meretricious slice of Hollywood slumming from a should-know-better director . . .*
> (The Times)

Meritorious means 'worth praising':

> *Being healthy is not meritorious in itself.* (The Times)

Embarrassment rating: ●●◐ in the slightly unlikely event that these two are confused, since a *meretricious* action would be very different from a *meritorious* one.

How to avoid: *Meretricious* contains almost all of *trick* in its centre and this hints at its meaning, while the beginning of *meritorious* indicates the sense of this word too.

METAL *or* METTLE

The two are sometimes confused not only because of their identical pronunciation but because ideas of strength and toughness are common to both. Both words/spellings, in fact, have the same origin.

Metal describes 'any of the elementary substances such as gold or iron'. This spelling is sometimes used when *mettle* is meant. The confusion isn't surprising since both words are pronounced the same, and *mettle* carries the metallic-sounding idea of 'hardness', 'spirit'. When people are 'on their mettle' they are put in a situation in which they have to prove themselves:

> *England rugby's men of mettle put on the sort of glistening collective tap dance that takes the breath away.* (Guardian)

Embarrassment rating: ●●◐, since this falls into the category of fairly elementary errors. The mistake, say, of writing about a team's being put on its 'metal' creates an odd image if taken literally.

How to avoid: If associated with verbs such as 'prove', 'show', 'test', the *mettle* sense/spelling is almost certain to be the correct one.

METEOR *or* METEORITE

These two words refer to the same object but in a 'before and after' sense.

A *meteor* is a 'small object which turns to a fireball when it enters the earth's atmosphere'. Even small ones can do damage and the impact of anything larger could be terminal:

'When a meteor hits this planet two things will survive: cockroaches and sitcom . . . ' (*quoted in the* Daily Telegraph)

(The term *meteor* can also apply to 'anything or anybody whose progress is bright but brief'. More usual is the adjective *meteoric* to describe such a progress, often coupled with 'rise', as in 'her meteoric rise to the top of her profession'. Meteors do the reverse of going up, of course, although a belief stretching back as far as the ancient Greeks held that comets and other such objects actually emanated from the earth.)

A *meteorite* is what the *meteor* becomes when it has hit the earth: a 'lump of stone or metal':

A meteorite from the Red Planet had been located in Antarctica, and analysis had revealed the existence of tiny bug-like objects on its surface. (Daily Telegraph)

Embarrassment rating: ○○○, unless you are talking to a scientist. Or unless you are a scientist.

How to avoid: A *meteor* is a kind of shooting sta*r*; a *meteorite* is cold ston*e*. (Note the word endings.)

METER *or* METRE

Both words are to do with measurement, and the slight difference in their endings is a recipe for confusion. In addition, the fact that US usage has only one form for both words (*meter*) makes things more tricky for those Brits who are influenced by American spelling.

A *meter* is a 'measuring instrument': parking *meter*; *thermometer*; *milometer*. A *metre* is the 'basic unit of length in the metric system' (three *metres* in length, a *kilometre* further on). This is the spelling that is also used to describe poetic 'rhythm', the contrasting sounds between long and short or stressed and unstressed syllables in verse.

Embarrassment rating: ●○○ Even careful spellers are likely to be caught out sometimes by this one, and the overall meaning of what you are saying isn't likely to be affected.

How to avoid: A *meter* is a measurer of something. By contrast a *metre* is a unit of distance (note the endings of these words).

METHOD *or* METHODOLOGY

The longer, more impressive-sounding word is sometimes preferred to the shorter, more familiar one – but is it always necessary?

A *method* is a 'procedure' and a *methodology* is a 'system of procedures'. *Methodology* is a popular word in certain writing, usually of a rather bunged-up kind. Its use is legitimate when the writer really means a system of methods, rather than a random collection of them. But much of the time the straightforward *method* is preferable, as it would have been in the example below:

> ☒ *Isolating one issue only and examining the way the press reports on it may be the best methodology* [why not *method*?]. (Guardian)

Embarrassment rating: ◑○○, unfortunately. The user of *methodology*, whether it's needed or not, will probably impress his/her readers or listeners.

How to avoid: Be sparing with *methodology*.

MILITATE *or* MITIGATE

These two verbs are often confused because of their similar look and sound but they have nothing in common.

To *militate*, generally followed by 'against', is to 'have weight', to 'operate':

> *The open range of parts he has taken has also militated against the illusion that we, the public, know him.* (The Times)

Mitigate has something of an opposite meaning – it is to 'lighten', to 'make less harsh' (*mitigating* circumstances in a court of law will reduce the sentence which the defendant would otherwise receive):

The best available instrument for mitigating poverty, Wilson decided, was central government. (Independent on Sunday)

Embarrassment rating: ●●○ These words are slightly outside everyday vocabulary, and anybody using them should be aware of the distinction.

How to avoid: *Militate* is usually followed by 'against' or sometimes 'in favour of', but *mitigate* takes a direct object, as in the example above. You cannot talk about 'mitigating against' something . . .

MISANTHROPIST *or* MISOGYNIST

Both of these terms are to do with dislike and hatred but one has a restricted sexual sense.

Misanthropy is a 'generalised distrust or hatred of everybody', men, women and children:

. . . *in [the film] Max, Noah Taylor's Hitler is a curmudgeon choking with bitterness and letting up on misanthropy only when he's talking about cruelty to birds.* (Daily Telegraph)

Misogyny is specifically 'hatred of women':

And if punk rock was shocking in its day, it had nothing on the misogyny and violence of the gangsta rap that today's teenagers favour.
(Daily Telegraph)

These terms are often applied to attitudes displayed in film, music, etc. but they can be used about people in real life. Those who display such attitudes are the *misanthropist* (or *misanthrope*) and the *misogynist*.

Embarrassment rating: ●●◑ *Misanthropy* is a kind of equal-opportunity position. Most people probably wouldn't like to be accused of it but at least there's a consistency involved. On the other hand, the accusation of *misogyny* carries quite a charge . . .

How to avoid: Be careful about using either term, though it should be said that *misanthropy* has a slightly old-fashioned ring to it (images of Scrooge spring to mind). *Misogyny* contains the Greek root gyne- meaning *woman* that's also found in 'gynaecology'.

MOMENTARY or MOMENTOUS

Both words derive from different senses of the same word, *moment*, but they can convey almost opposite meanings.

Anything which is *momentary* (pronounced with the stress on the first syllable) is very 'short-lived':

> . . . *there was momentary silence among the throng of 40,000, and then they burst into appreciative applause.* (Daily Telegraph)

Momentous (pronounced with the stress on the second syllable) means 'highly significant':

> *Buying a car used to be such a momentous occasion [in India] that it would be whisked straight from the showroom to the temple to be garlanded and blessed.* (The Times)

Embarrassment rating: ●●◐ A genuine confusion arises if an event is referred to as *momentary* when *momentous* is meant, or vice versa.

How to avoid: The sound of the words gives a hint as to their meaning, with the last three syllables of *momentary* (often reduced to *moment'ry*) light and unstressed, while *momentous* moves with an more even plod through its three parts. Anything *momentous* is also significant or serious.

MORAL or MORALE

These similar-looking words are sometimes confused – perhaps because of some subconscious association between behaving well (being *moral*) and feeling good (having high *morale*).

Moral as an adjective means 'connected to questions of right and wrong':

> *'We are not going to be moral guardians and stand in judgement.'* (*quoted in the* Sun)

As a noun, *moral* is used in the singular only in the sense of 'lesson' (the *moral* of a story). In the plural, *morals* describes the 'principles or guiding beliefs' of a person or group, although it tends to have a sexual application only.

Morale characterises the 'spirit of an organised group' such as a body of soldiers or a football team:

> *Their morale was sapped when shells began raining down on them and even the lighter shells pierced the ship's armour.* (Daily Mirror)

Embarrassment rating: ●●◐ An erroneous reference to the low 'moral' of a team could look like a comment on their standards of behaviour.

How to avoid: The pronunciation of each word is a guide to the correct spelling. *Moral* has the stress on the first syllable (to rhyme with 'quarrel') while *morale* is stressed on the second syllable (to rhyme with 'pal').

MUCOUS *or* MUCUS

One of these words is a noun while the other is the adjective derived from it, and it is easy to confuse the two spellings.

Mucus is the noun, describing the fluid secreted by a bodily membrane (e.g. the nose) in humans or animals:

Peter Paul Rubens leaves you with colours clinging, like snail mucus, to the tracks of your mind. (Guardian)

Mucous is the adjective meaning 'mucus-like or slimy':

. . . sulphuric acid is as dangerous as it sounds. Direct contact will burn the skin and play havoc with mucous membranes. (Guardian)

Embarrassment rating: ●○○ Even if the mistake is spotted, it does not obscure the sense.

How to avoid: The '-ous' ending of *mucous* suggests that the word is probably an adjective (compare 'famous', 'notorious', and especially 'viscous', another adjective meaning sticky or slimy); it must be used to qualify a noun, usually 'membranes'. By contrast the '-us' ending for *mucus* is more usually associated with nouns ('callus', 'radius', 'terminus').

MUNDANE *or* WORLDLY

These two words are an interesting example of the way in which synonyms in English can, on the surface, share the same meaning while possessing different underlying senses.

Both terms mean 'of this world', but *mundane* carries the sense of 'everyday' (to the point of being boring):

Most societies at most times have been happy enough to bind together the idea of prayer with the most mundane, business-like realities of life. (Daily Telegraph)

Worldly is often used as part of compound words ('worldly-wise', 'other-worldly') but it also has a meaning of 'experienced in the ways of the world', 'sophisticated':

> *Newspaper foreign editors used to know that the person who understood best the heart of an overseas beat was a foreign correspondent's wife; a good one would be worldly in public affairs . . .* (Guardian)

Embarrassment rating: ●●◐ Many people would take *worldly* as a compliment but would not like to have their lives described as *mundane*.

How to avoid: *Worldly* should be restricted to individuals or material things ('worldly goods', 'worldly possessions') while *mundane* tends to be used about circumstances, events, etc.

NAKED *or* NUDE

This is quite a difficult distinction – and naturally an interesting one.

Naked is the more versatile word with its senses of 'without assistance' or 'lacking ornament' (*naked* effort, *naked* truth) as well as the basic meanings of 'bare', 'uncovered'. *Naked* is generally a less loaded or emotive word than *nude*, which is probably why it was used in the following story about a child:

> *Police were called to a fashionable art gallery last night when concerns were raised over an exhibition featuring photos of an artist's naked daughter.* (Guardian)

Nude has associations with painting, photography and porn, and to that extent it could be equated with being 'intentionally naked' – often for artistic or sexual purposes. Nudism naturally implies a conscious decision to be naked:

> *Japan has a long history of nude public bathing and has only favoured segregated bathing since the end of the Second World War.* (Guardian)

The words aren't quite interchangeable. If you switch round the adjectives in the next example you also alter the balance of the sentence:

> *'I even studied for my own law exams nude to keep the stress down, though unfortunately I wasn't allowed to sit them naked.'* (quoted in The Times)

Embarrassment rating: ●○○, since there is a degree of embarrassment already built into each word!

How to avoid: Were Adam and Eve *naked* before the Fall, but *nude* after it? More than most differences, this one really is in the eye of the beholder.

NAVAL *or* NAVEL

Similar spelling and identical pronunciation sometimes produce a comic confusion over these two.

The adjective *naval* means 'relating to the navy'. The noun *navel* is defined by one dictionary as the 'depression in the centre of the abdomen' but is known to the rest of humanity as the 'belly/tummy-button'. 'Navel-gazing' is self-absorption, fussing too much about your own situation. Be careful over the spelling of this one – either the writer below got the wrong kind of *navel* or southern Californians are very fond of ships and sailors:

> ❌❌ *In a town as full of precious naval-gazing* [should be *navel-gazing*] *types as Los Angeles . . .* (Guardian)

Embarrassment rating: ●●◐ Another red-face error.

How to avoid: The *navel* is in the be*lly*.

NEGLECTFUL, NEGLIGENT *or* NEGLIGIBLE

These words derive from *neglect/negligence* but have moved off in different directions.

Neglectful means 'inattentive', with the implication of failing to care for something or somebody:

> *His busy life at work made him a rather neglectful father.*

Negligent means 'careless', particularly in relation to matters which are your responsibility and for which you may be held accountable. This is a stronger term than *neglectful*:

> *I grew up in a world without panic buttons; now an organisation that fails to provide them for its staff is negligent.* (Daily Telegraph)

Negligible means 'very slight or unimportant' (and therefore able to be neglected):

> *Despite all that fuss, the Oscars had a negligible effect on the American box office.* (The Times)

Embarrassment rating: ●●◐, particularly over the second and third terms. There is a genuine confusion of meaning if, say, an oversight is described as being *negligent* rather than *negligible*, since the implications of the words are almost opposite.

How to avoid: *Neglectful* and *negligent* tend to be used of individuals or groups, while *negligible* applies to events, effects and so on.

NICENESS *or* NICETY

Nice is a very old word with quite a range of meanings. Two of its spinoffs are *niceness* and *nicety*, but in terms of their meaning they are very distant cousins.

Niceness means the 'quality of being nice', 'agreeableness'. There's a blandness to the word or to what it describes, and it's often used with just a touch of criticism:

> *Being Canadian, the authors have a certain orthodoxy of mind that comes from having lived in a country famed for its niceness.* (Daily Telegraph)

Nicety means 'precision' (as when something is judged to a *nicety*) or 'refinement' when it is usually found in the plural form, *niceties*:

> *[He] concludes that [President] Reagan's crude anti-communism was ultimately much more effective than the diplomatic niceties of more sophisticated politicians.* (Daily Telegraph)

Embarrassment rating: ●●○ Swapping the words around in the examples above would produce very different meanings. A person who can display *niceness* in a situation may be totally unaware of the *niceties* of it.

How to avoid: Some manuals on English style suggest avoiding *nice* altogether because it's such a bland all-purpose term, and that might extend to avoiding *niceness* as well. I've always thought that *nice* and *niceness* have had a rather bad press. They remain useful words, carefully used. The same goes for *nicety*. Just remember that this second word has nothing to do with being pleasant . . .

O O O **O** O O

OBJECTIVE *or* SUBJECTIVE

Both adjectives are to do with point of view. The difference between them is probably plain but for the record . . .

An *objective* approach is one which is 'unaffected by personal feelings', 'detached':

From an objective angle she could see that the new bypass being built near her house would benefit the whole town.

Subjective means 'personal', 'taking one's feelings into account':

But from a subjective viewpoint she resented the noise and pollution which the nearby road would cause.

Subjective is occasionally used in a critical way, as in 'You're taking a subjective point of view', with the unstated implication that only the speaker is being *objective* and giving an unbiased account.

Embarrassment rating: ●●○, since the words are opposites.

How to avoid: To be *objective* is to look at matters in an impersonal way (looking at everything, including oneself, from the outside) while to be *subjective* is to regard them from the subject's angle.

OBSOLESCENT *or* OBSOLETE

These words, applied to equipment or machinery and sometimes to organisations, are stages in the same process and there is sometimes confusion over which comes 'first'.

Obsolescent means 'going out of date' (but still usable):

. . . he very soon demonstrated that his skills and airmanship could to some extent compensate for the obsolescent biplane's performance.
(Daily Telegraph)

Something which is *obsolete* is 'old', 'out of date' (and so useless):

Computer-generated effects [in films] may have rendered steel and latex creations obsolete . . . (Independent)

Embarrassment rating: ●●○ As the definitions show, both words have a slightly critical edge but the precise user will want to differentiate between the two states.

How to avoid: Like a number of other '-ent' words – 'emergent', 'nascent', 'adolescent' – *obsolescent* describes something which is in process (in this case, going out of date). The shorter word *obsolete* applies to those things which are already past it.

OFFICIAL *or* OFFICIOUS

Both of these terms originally derive from the same Latin source but they have very different meanings. The second is sometimes used by mistake for the first, perhaps because people occasionally find that *officials* can also be *officious*.

As an adjective *official* describes a 'person or process that is properly authorised':

> . . . *the Elysee Palace in Paris, President Jacque Chirac's official residence* (Guardian)

The noun *official* is used of someone employed by a government department, as 'senior Pentagon officials'.

The adjective *officious*, by contrast, means 'interfering', with an overtone of fussiness:

> *'What are you two talking about?' he asked in his usual officious manner.*

Embarrassment rating: ●●●, if you describe a person as *officious* when you really mean *official*.

How to avoid: Only use *officious* if you intend to criticise or insult.

ORDINANCE *or* ORDNANCE

The one-letter difference between these two words, and the fact that pronunciation hardly distinguishes between them, can cause problems.

Ordinance – more common in the US than the UK – has the sense of a 'ruling' or 'decree' (especially in a local context):

> *In the United States of America there are so-called weed ordinances banning lawns over a certain height.* (Daily Telegraph)

Ordnance has the general sense of 'military equipment' but is almost always restricted in its application to 'artillery and ammunition':

> . . . *the MoD paid out £4.5 million to . . . tribesmen who claimed to have been maimed or bereaved by live ordnance left over from training exercises in northern Kenya.* (Daily Telegraph)

(Ordnance Survey maps are so called because until the end of the 19th century they were commissioned by the Government and produced by its Ordnance Department.)

Embarrassment rating: ●●○ Although *ordnance* grew out of *ordinance*, the two words have moved apart and the mistaken use of one for the other will not convey the writer's meaning.

How to avoid: As indicated above, *ordnance* is probably the more frequent term in the UK – if only because of its everyday appearance on maps of Britain. The connection between an *ordinance* and a ruling might be recalled by the 'i' in the middle of each word.

OUTSIDE *or* OUTSIDE OF

This is a stylistic distinction, with many people preferring to say or write *outside of* even though it's usually unnecessary.

There's not much justification for writing *outside of* when a simple *outside* would do. This is especially the case when *outside* refers to a place:

> *They used to meet outside the building.* (not ***outside of***)

When referring to time, *outside of* is quite often used:

> *They used to meet outside of office hours.* (but *outside* would do just as well)

But when 'apart from' is meant, *outside of* is more acceptable:

> *He had few interests outside of his work.*

There's a faintly American tinge to the expression, which is probably why some people prefer it.

Embarrassment rating: ◕○○ Though *outside of* jars on some.

How to avoid: On the principle that you should use fewer words rather than more, the plain *outside* is usually preferable.

P P P **P** P P P

PANDA *or* PANDER

One of these words is a cuddly-looking animal, the other is a pimp. Take care over spelling.

The *panda* is the 'bear-like animal' from China (as well as a rather less well-known raccoon-like Himalayan creature). It's not to be confused with a *pander* (sometimes spelled *pandar*) who is a 'pimp' or 'go-between' – the word has a slightly literary flavour but is always derogatory. As a verb, to *pander* is to 'gratify', to 'cater to the (low) taste of others':

Maybe when they started price-cutting they felt they had to pander to their lower-brow recruits. (Observer)

Embarrassment rating: ●○○ The bear or the pimp may not object to being misspelled, but the mistake will look comic to those who know the difference.

How to avoid: *Pander* is most often found as a verb and its spelling may be remembered from the sense of 'cater to'. The *panda* is from China!

PEDAL *or* PEDDLE

Identical pronunciation – and perhaps some association between constant movement and door-to-door selling? – cause confusion with these two.

Pedal as a noun describes a 'lever worked by the foot'; as a verb it is to 'operate such a lever':

I pedalled fast to keep the other bikes in sight.

Pedaller is the associated noun (not very often seen).

Peddle, a verb, is to 'sell small items'. When applied to any other kind of trade there is the suggestion of sleaziness or illegality: *peddling* lies, *peddling* drugs. Even when it's used in ordinary contexts it tends to disparage what is being 'sold':

> *Why don't we stick to the line, peddled by literal-minded idiots, that 'all wine smells of grapes'?* (Observer)

(A *pedlar* went from door to door selling goods; the practice may go on but the word has almost disappeared in favour of 'doorstep salesman', etc. The drug pusher or the supplier of doubtful information is a *peddler*.)

Embarrassment rating: ●○○ Your meaning will almost always be clear even if the wrong spelling is used, except perhaps in a statement like 'I pedalled/peddled my cheap bike' – but the same ambiguity would apply if the words were spoken.

How to avoid: In practice, mistakes are likely to arise over when to use 'pedalled' as opposed to 'peddled', and over the spelling of 'peddler'. Try to remember that *peddle/peddler* always sound pejorative, and rarely if ever apply to the wholesome world of cycling. Otherwise this is one to memorise or, if necessary, to look up before writing down.

PEOPLE, PEOPLES *or* PERSONS

What's the difference between *people* and *peoples* – they both apply to large numbers, don't they? And when should one refer to *persons*?

People means either an '(unspecified) number of individuals' or a 'whole national/ racial/ethnic group' (the German *people*, the Maori *people* of New Zealand). The plural *peoples* is restricted to this second sense and applies to the 'nations/racial groups of the world' – it's a slightly formal expression. The plural *persons* is formal and bureaucratic, and the only appropriate place for it is on notices ('This bus seats 54 persons').

Embarrassment rating: ◐○○ But note that *peoples* can only be applied globally.

How to avoid: *People* is – or are – usually good enough. There's a rather stuffy sound to the other two words.

PERPETRATE *or* PERPETUATE

These quite similar-sounding words both contain the idea of 'carrying on/out'.

To *perpetrate* is to 'carry out', to 'commit'. The noun that accompanies the verb is often 'crime' or 'outrage' (just as a *perpetrator* is frequently an 'offender', especially in the US where it may be shortened to the slang *perp*). But the context is not always so serious:

> . . . *the Academy has honoured some truly unspeakable scenery-chewing performances in the Joan Crawford tradition, mostly perpetrated these days by Mr Geoffrey Rush.* (Spectator)

To *perpetuate* is to 'sustain', to 'make last':

> *She avoids the moral high ground too, and never perpetuates the traditional literary myths of romantic love and happy endings.* (The Times)

Embarrassment rating: ●◑○○ There is a very slight overlap of sense between the two words but a more significant distinction of meaning. To *perpetrate* a mistake is to do it once, to *perpetuate* a mistake is to do it repeatedly.

How to avoid: The link between *perpetuate* and *perpetual* suggests the long-term associations of the first word. Similarly, the connection between *perpetrate* and *perpetra*tor helps to clarify the meaning of that verb.

PERQUISITE *or* PREREQUISITE

The similar beginnings and identical endings of these two words may occasionally cause confusion. In addition, both terms describe something which is conditional or dependent.

A *perquisite* is a 'benefit arising from employment'. The word is usually shortened to *perk* – as in 'perks of the job' – and would only be spelled out in full in fairly formal contexts:

> *Among the perquisites of this position are frequent foreign travel and a generous entertainment allowance.*

A *prerequisite* is a 'condition that must be met beforehand':

> . . . *cost-effective production and a strong balance sheet are merely the prerequisites for survival.* (The Times)

Embarrassment rating: ●◑○○ There would be a genuine ambiguity of meaning if the 'prerequisites of a job' were confused with the 'perquisites of a job', but, where the second word is not colloquially shortened to *perks*, it tends to be substituted now with a more accessible equivalent like 'benefits'.

How to avoid: A *prerequisite* is a condition, qualification, etc. which is *requi*red.

PERSECUTE *or* PROSECUTE

The two verbs are sometimes confused, perhaps because they look similar and convey ideas of hostile action, but they have in fact nothing in common.

To *persecute* is to 'maintain a campaign of harassment' (particularly for political or religious reasons):

In Soviet Russia dissidents were persecuted and frequently imprisoned.

To *prosecute* is to 'bring before a court of law':

First-time offenders may be warned by the police rather than prosecuted.

(*Prosecute* has the less familiar meaning of to 'pursue in order to accomplish'; in this sense a war or a political campaign can be *prosecuted*.)

Embarrassment rating: ●●○ In a police state, it would be possible to be both *persecuted* and *prosecuted* (for some imagined offence). But otherwise, *persecution* – at least when it results in explicit harassment – is outside the law, if not actually against it.

How to avoid: The legal associations of *prosecute* are suggested by officials such as the prosecutor, prosecuting counsel, etc.

PERSON *or* PERSONA

The Latin word for 'person' is *persona* in expressions such as 'persona non grata'. But in English a person and his/her persona are not at all the same thing. What difference is produced by the addition of an 'a' to one of them?

A *person* is just a person, a 'human being' (and the word often carries a slightly dismissive note). But a *persona* (plural *personae*) is something else – a 'public image', the 'face' assumed when dealing with the outside world' (the term originally comes from the field of psychology but is now widely used in general contexts):

A former chairman of Granada whose businessman-not-arty-farty-type persona had politicians eating out of his hand, Robinson persuaded Gordon Brown to give money to the arts. (Guardian)

Embarrassment rating: ●○○ In practice, I don't think this confusion is likely to occur but it is useful to be clear about the distinct senses of the two words.

How to avoid: Everybody is a *person*; many people have *personas* for public consumption. The 'a' in *persona* and public face help to provide a link.

PERSONAL *or* PERSONNEL

The spellings of these two words are sometimes confused, with the first being used in place of the second.

Personal is an adjective only, meaning 'relating to the individual', although it very often carries the additional meaning of 'private':

He was unwilling to reveal his personal reasons for rejecting the job.

Personnel is a collective noun which describes the 'workforce' in a particular organisation. It's a bureaucratic word – rather impersonal in fact:

The downturn in the economy led to cuts in the factory personnel.

Embarrassment rating: ●●● if *personal* is incorrectly used as a noun describing a workforce, since the error results from straightforward ignorance. There would be ambiguity in confusing a 'personal trainer' (a private fitness instructor) with a 'personnel trainer' (someone employed to train staff members).

How to avoid: The difference in pronunciation, with *personnel* stressed heavily on the last syllable, should be a guide to the sense/spelling here.

PERSPECTIVE, PROSPECTIVE *or* PROSPECTUS

This similar-sounding group contains ideas of views and visions.

A *perspective* is a 'point of view'. It's probably most widely used in the phrase 'put into perspective', which derives from the artistic technique of showing on a two-dimensional surface how objects seem smaller in the distance. So *perspective* becomes a way of assessing the relative importance – or lack of importance – of something, usually a problem:

. . . his recent spell out of the limelight has given Harry time to rethink his priorities, with his family putting bad reviews into perspective. (Daily Mirror)

The adjective *prospective* refers to the future and means 'expected', 'probable':

Slim employees, bar the surgeons, are seen as a demoralising presence for prospective patients. (The Times)

A *prospectus* is the 'outline of some project which will materialise in the future' or it describes the advertising bumf issued by schools, colleges, etc. (To complicate the situation slightly, a *prospect* can also mean a view.)

Embarrassment rating: ●●○, if reference is mistakenly made to, say, a perspective employer. (Strictly speaking, such a phrase would describe a person like an artist, one who used perspective in his/her work.)

How to avoid: The link between *prospective* and *prospects* (of success) or the (gold) *prospector* suggest the forward-looking nature of the words. *Perspective* is not to do with time but with space.

PERVERSE *or* PERVERTED

Although related, these two words have very different applications and should not be confused.

Perverse describes a person or an action that is 'contrary', 'obstinate', something hard to account for rationally. It would be *perverse* to ask directions from someone in the street and then take a different turning to the one you had been told.

The adjective is often used to describe people's attitude to life:

Resenting other people who do too well, too easily, is one of those national characteristics that Russians take a perverse pride in . . . (The Times)

Perverted has a sexual application almost exclusively, and characterises behaviour or attitudes that are 'deviant'. Even in such a notoriously vague area as sexual definition, *perverted* still carries some weight and is generally applied to activities that are not merely off the beaten track but are also offensive. However, what is *perverted* to one man or woman may be another's standard liberated sexual behaviour. It is a staple term in some newspapers:

The perverted couple are proud of their executive client list. (Sun)

The noun form *pervert* (with the stress on the first syllable) should be reserved for deserving cases, as it were, and not applied indiscriminately as a term of abuse.

As a verb *pervert* (stress on second syllable) is most frequently found in a legal context: to *pervert* the course of justice is to 'interfere with the proper process of the law' (by threats, bribes, etc.).

Embarrassment rating: ●●●, since both words carry a negative charge. The first is comparatively innocent while the second is not. Therefore, to term someone *perverted* when only *perverse* is meant could be construed as insulting, possibly worse. I suspect, though, that *perverse* has become tainted by association and that this term would often be taken as more offensive than it really is.

How to avoid: Both expressions need careful handling for the reasons already given. Think before using either and be sure of your audience!

PHENOMENON *or* PHENOMENAL

Both of these words contain a kind of double meaning, and it may not always be clear which is meant.

At its simplest a *phenomenon* is no more than an 'observable event':

. . . *bluffing about books is a universal phenomenon.* (Observer)

although the word easily shades into its associated sense of 'something extraordinary'. The adjective *phenomenal* is almost always used in this sense and signifies anything 'outstanding':

Internet bank Egg told a story of two extremes today after a 'phenomenal' year for its UK business was washed away by heavy losses in France. (Guardian)

Although *phenomenal* is often used casually for emphasis, particularly in its adverbial form – as in 'phenomenally boring' – it is preferable, at least in formal usage, to restrict the word to events which are truly 'remarkable'.

Embarrassment rating: ○○○ There's no real embarrassment here and the context will generally make clear which of the two senses of *phenomenon* is intended. And, of course, an occurrence such as a solar eclipse is a *phenomenon* twice over – an observable event but also a remarkable one.

How to avoid: Not applicable.

PIQUE *or* PIQUANCY

These related terms, both derived from French, characterise emotions or sensations that are linked by the idea of 'sharpness'.

Pique is 'bad feeling', 'wounded pride':

> *In their pique at being excluded, Italy, Spain and Poland have conjured up a fantasy of the Big Three sitting down together in confident intimacy . . .* (The Times)

(*Pique* is also a verb with the same meaning: to 'wound' or 'irritate'.)

Piquancy, a noun meaning 'sharpness', is often used to describe taste, particularly in its adjectival form (a *piquant* sauce), and generally has positive overtones. But the sensation may not always be so pleasant:

> *No doubt the fact that he had himself faced the death penalty gave a special piquancy to his thoughts on the subject.* (Daily Telegraph)

Embarrassment rating: ●◐○ in, say, a mistaken reference to some dish having *pique* rather than *piquancy*. As with other slightly exotic terms, the onus is on the user to get it right – particularly if that person wants to impress with his/her vocabulary.

How to avoid: *Piquant* and *piquancy* are especially linked to taste, even to *fancy* food. *Pique* comes from a French word for 'pike' which indicates its more uncomfortable associations.

PITEOUS, PITIABLE, PITIFUL *or* PATHETIC

Too many closely related words, all connected to the notion of 'pity'. Bear with me, as they say in call centres, while they're sorted out.

The first three adjectives mean 'arousing pity' or 'to be pitied', although with very slight differences in usage. *Piteous* is not applied to individuals as such but to anything that moves us to feel pity:

> *The searchers heard the piteous sounds of the trapped cat.*

Pitiable and *pitiful* can be applied to people and situations. Of the two *pitiful* is perhaps slightly stronger, suggesting someone who arouses pity through some visible means as well as by inner suffering, while *pitiable* is more to do with the latter:

> *There is moving testimony from the civilian survivors and the equally pitiable aircrew.* (The Times)

Both adjectives are also used to indicate mockery (a *pitiful* attempt).

Pathetic has a milder meaning of 'arousing sympathy', but usually carries an overtone, if not of contempt, then of superiority:

> *Watching a once-admired sports person trying to put a brake on the ravages of time is one of the most pathetic sights imaginable.* (Guardian)

The colloquial use of *pathetic* to mean 'useless', or, more casually, as a term passing judgement on an unsatisfactory situation, can sometimes be a source of ambiguity:

> *There are still oddities like the pathetic minority of women MPs . . .* (The Times)

Here the writer isn't commenting on the quality of women MPs but on the unsatisfactory fact that there are so few of them.

Embarrassment rating: ○○○ with the first three since they are pretty well interchangeable, with the qualification that *piteous* tends to be used about sights, situations, etc. rather than directly applying to individuals.

How to avoid: Not much to avoid here although *pathetic* needs to be handled with care, since it can be ambiguous (see above) in a simple phrase like 'a pathetic showing'.

POPULOUS, POPULAR *or* POPULIST

Three words connected to 'the people' and all deriving from the same source but with distinct meanings.

Populous indicates that an area is 'densely populated' (all cities are *populous* by definition), while *popular* means 'in favour', 'liked by many, or involving many people':

> *Yeltstin was a politician hugely experienced and especially gifted in seeking and, until recently, holding popular support . . .* (Guardian)

Populist (noun and adjective) generally occurs in a political context and describes 'somebody who aims to appeal to the majority' (by offering to cut taxes, put more police on the streets, etc.):

> *Mr Blunkett, who usually plays the populist to keep control of the centre ground of public opinion, has been the liberal in this instance.* (Guardian)

Embarrassment rating: ●●○, if the first and second are mixed up, or the second and third. A *populous* place (i.e. a heavily populated one) is not the same as a place which is *popular* (e.g. as a holiday destination) – although, of course, a single spot may be both. Similarly, a *popular* announcement by a politician, if such a thing is possible, would be different from a *populist* one. The first is genuinely welcomed while the second may look like an attempt to curry favour with the public.

How to avoid: Only a place such as a country, state or city can be *populous*, whereas *popular* can apply to people, ideas, musical tastes or decisions. The ending '–ist' often carries a negative taint (as in 'racist', 'sexist'), and *populist* is no exception.

PORE *or* POUR

The two verbs are sometimes confused, partly because they sound identical but also because both are frequently followed by 'over'.

To *pore* is to 'examine carefully':

> *The couple also pored over a copy of the* News *of the World which had been pushed through their letterbox.* (Sun)

To *pour* is to 'make flow':

> *He was a generous host when it came to pouring out the drinks.*

The usual mistake is to use this second word when the first one is meant:

> ☒ ☒ *As late as page 191 Augie is still pouring* [should be *poring*] *over magazines in search of "vocational hints".* (Guardian)

Embarrassment rating: ●●○ This is a mistake which is quite easy to make, usually when *pour* is put instead of the less familiar *pore*. The meaning should not be affected, although some readers of the *Guardian* quote above might have stopped to ask what was being poured.

How to avoid: The less common spelling may be recalled by some association between another type of *pore*, the very small opening, and the kind of close examination which is suggested by *poring* over something. There is also the association between *pouring* and liquids, both of which words share a letter 'u'.

PORT *or* STARBOARD

One of the 'which-way-round-is-it?' differences.

Port is the left-hand side on ships (and on aircraft) while the *starboard* side is to the right, when facing forward.

Embarrassment rating: ●●○ Moderate, perhaps moderate to high depending on whether you're at the controls of a ship or aircraft or simply looking for the cabin seat allocated to you. While some sailing terms like 'leeward' and 'windward' stay safely in the realms of specialist vocab, I think that *port* and *starboard* are fairly mainstream.

How to avoid: For anyone who doesn't already know the difference, the easiest way to remember is that *port* and 'left' have the same number of letters. Also, the port light on a ship or aircraft is red – the colour of port wine.

PORTENTOUS *or* PRETENTIOUS

There's some overlap between these two weighty words but also a distinction.

Portentous comes from *portent* and so means 'ominous' or 'full of significance'. But it usually has the sense of 'self-important' too, and is rarely meant in a complimentary sense:

> *Many movie DVDs now include an often portentous voiceover from the film's director in which he explains his creative impulses when making the movie.* (The Times)

Pretentious also means 'self-important' shading into 'pompous':

> *What was, by all accounts, a powerful bit of theatre was reduced on screen to a pretentious potboiler.* (Observer)

Embarrassment rating: ●○○ But if you want to calibrate your insults finely then you may prefer to term something *portentous* rather than the more direct *pretentious*.

How to avoid: See above.

PRACTICAL *or* PRACTICABLE

Many people are conscious that there's some fine distinction between these two but are unable to pin it down.

A *practical* person or idea is a 'sensible and realistic' one. When applied to a plan, it suggests not only that it can be realised but also that it has merits:

> *Within half an hour she came up with three practical ways of getting round the problem.*

Practical carries the additional senses of 'good at making things' and 'down to earth' or 'actual' (as in *practical* experience as opposed to theoretical knowledge).

Practicable is not used about people, and indicates merely that something 'can be achieved', and not necessarily that it ought to be:

Within the next few decades it is expected that manned flights to Mars will become practicable.

(The adverb *practically* carries the additional sense of 'almost', 'nearly': as in 'practically finished'. There is potential for a small ambiguity in a sentence such as 'the map was practically useless', which could mean either that the map was almost useless, or that it was useless for any practical purpose such as finding one's way – but could, for example, be hung on the wall as decoration.)

Embarrassment rating: ●○○ But there is a difference between describing a plan as *practical* and calling it *practicable*, and the second term is lukewarm compared to the first.

How to avoid: *Practicable* carries the sense of *able* to be put into practice. It cannot be used to describe people.

PRACTICE *or* PRACTISE

This is one of a group of word pairs which change by one letter between noun and verb (see also 'advice/advise', 'licence/license', etc.), and is probably the pair which is most often confused.

The *practice* spelled with a 'c' is the noun:

There are parallels between Indian and British business practices.

while the *practise* with an 's' is the verb:

The band practised for most of the day.

(US usage, very sensibly, is *practice* for both noun and verb.)

Embarrassment rating: ●●○ This is perhaps a more excusable confusion than that between *advice* and *advise*, since the sound does not change according to whether the word is noun or verb.

How to avoid: Go back, as always, to the 'advice/advise' parallel to determine the spelling of *practice/practise*.

PRAY or PREY

These two verbs are sometimes confused, with the first being used in error for the second. It's true that they sound the same but in this case that's not much of an excuse.

To *pray* is to 'beg for' or to 'ask during worship':

Praying for the American government, it turns out, could well be a full-time occupation. (Daily Telegraph)

To *prey* (on) is to 'kill for food' or to 'exploit' (with the suggestion of terrorising):

. . . he was a thief, and one who preyed on the most vulnerable and unsuspecting of victims – the women who trusted him.
(Daily Telegraph)

(The victim is the *prey* while the attacker is the *predator*.)

Don't confuse these two simple verbs or you will end up with a sense you never intended:

⊠ ⊠ *Bug expert Phil de Vries . . . wends his way around the globe, to be prayed* [should be **preyed**] *on by the 'scariest bugs on Earth'.*
(Guardian)

Embarrassment rating: ●●● This is simple ignorance or, more likely, carelessness.

How to avoid: *Pray* goes with *pray*er; *prey* with *pre*dator.

PRECIPITATE or PRECIPITOUS

Two similar words, one to do with speed, the other with steepness. Perhaps it is the effect of what would occur to anyone falling over a cliff which produces the quite frequent confusion!

Precipitate, as an adjective, describes an action that is 'rushed', 'headlong':

. . . in the face of this onslaught the British units were in precipitate retreat . . . (The Times)

As a verb it means to 'produce abruptly':

. . . the idea that psychological stress can precipitate sudden death . . .
(The Times)

Precipitous means 'steep':

The railway cutting was extremely deep, and unusually precipitous.

However, *precipitous* is quite frequently used to describe an action which, in strict correctness, should be called *precipitate*:

☒ . . . *the precipitous* [should be ***precipitate***] *rush by stores to forsake the high street in return for out-of-town sites* . . . (The Times)

Embarrassment rating: ●◑○ Many people will not detect the mistake and will still get the meaning since the context generally makes it clear. However, there is still some life – and value – in the difference between *precipitate* and *precipitous*, and the distinction is worth preserving.

How to avoid: The sound of each word hints at the meaning: in *precipitate*, the syllables are crowded together, all of them short; in *precipitous*, the word seems to tail away, softly falling out of sight . . . Failing that, rocks, slopes, and drops are all *precipitous*, and all share a letter 'o'.

PRESCRIBE *or* PROSCRIBE

A one-letter difference changes one word into its near opposite.

To *prescribe* is to 'direct', to 'lay down as a rule':

The doctor prescribed plenty of rest and exercise.

To *proscribe* is to 'ban': a *proscribed* activity is one that may be banned by law though sometimes the word just carries the sense of 'frowned on':

A serious smoker, she also pays eloquent tribute to the proscribed glamour of nicotine. (Observer)

(The nouns forms are, respectively, *prescription* and *proscription*. This second word is fairly rare.)

Embarrassment rating: ●●○, if one mistakenly refers to the doctor *proscribing* something. In fact, although doctors are in the business of *prescribing*, they cannot *proscribe* but must merely give advice.

How to avoid: *Prescribe* is a much more usual word than *proscribe*, so it is this first sense/spelling which will generally be encountered, and it can be remembered from the associated spelling of *prescription*. *Proscribe* has sinister roots since it derives from the practice in ancient Rome of writing out for public display a list of those who were to be executed or outlawed.

PREVARICATE *or* PROCRASTINATE

These verbs sound alike, but I suspect that the two are occasionally confused because doing one of these slightly shifty things sometimes involves doing the other.

To *prevaricate* is to 'avoid giving a straight answer'. Not as outright as lying, it is still evading the truth:

> *When the four-year-old demanded to know why the baby got to sleep with me in my bed, I whimpered and prevaricated . . .* (Daily Telegraph)

To *procrastinate* is to 'delay', 'put off' (particularly doing something which should be done):

> *[The airline] procrastinated, asked for copies of his tickets, and said it was consulting its office in St Lucia.* (Daily Telegraph)

(The noun forms are *prevarication* and *procrastination*.)

Embarrassment rating: ●◑○ Both terms are critical although, arguably, *prevarication* is worse than *procrastination*. Or should it be the other way round? There's an accusatory ring to both – 'You're prevaricating/procrastinating!' – and the 'offences' somehow sound the worse for being contained within rather long, Latinate words.

How to avoid: *Prevaricate* contains the idea of *vari*ation or not holding steady and so being evasive; it comes from the Latin verb meaning to 'walk in a crooked or knock-kneed fashion'. As for *procrastinate*, that derives from the Latin word 'cras' meaning 'tomorrow'. As with some other aids to memory, the effort of calling this to mind may be greater than simply remembering the two words.

PRINCIPAL *or* PRINCIPLE

The slight difference between the ends of these two words and overlapping definitions to do with guidance/leadership make confusion almost inevitable. Everybody will have mixed up this pair at some point.

Principal is both noun and adjective, and means 'chief', 'most important':

> *The principal things to remember, she was told, were to keep her speech short and relevant.*

The most frequent application of the noun is to describe the 'head of a college or a school' (this is particularly a US usage), or to refer to the 'main actor(s)' in a play or the main singers in a musical production. An additional noun meaning of *principal* is 'money on which interest is paid'.

Principle is a noun only, and means 'basic belief':

There are principles here, they insist, and they should be examined before too much is given away. (Guardian)

The word can also be used in the sense of a 'guiding idea':

Business Class is a new arrival in Russia, although the principle of better treatment for the few is not. (The Times)

Embarrassment rating: ●◐○ Anyone switching the words round on paper is likely to be understood, although there could be an ambiguity in a reference to the principle/principal of a project.

How to avoid: Only *principal* can be used of people. Only *principal* can be stuck in front of a noun (e.g. *principal* objections), and like main, its synonym, it contains an 'a'. But if a term such as rule, truth or law can be substituted in the sentence, then *principle* is likely to be the correct spelling.

PRISE *or* PRIZE

For once this is a trap which is more apparent than real. The identical pronunciation of these two sometimes causes the second spelling to be used in place of the first – and indeed it wouldn't be wrong to do so.

To *prise* is to 'force (open or away from)', using something as a lever – e.g. a crowbar or money:

Norton is on his way to BBC1 as part of a big-money deal that prised him from Channel 4 . . . (Guardian)

Prized could be used in the example above, but *prised* in more usual in British English. (US spelling is *prize* only.)

A *prize* is a 'reward', and the verb means to 'place a high value on':

Perhaps the shared appreciation of the tulip stems from the fact that both countries [Holland and Japan] prize the little land they have. (Guardian)

Embarrassment rating: ○○○ But *prise* is the preferred British form in the sense of 'lever'.

How to avoid: Not really applicable but see above.

PRODIGY *or* PROTÉGÉ

Two terms which are occasionally confused, perhaps through a similarity of sound as well as underlying ideas of youth or immaturity.

A *prodigy* is a 'wonder'. Once used about signs and omens, it is now applied only to people. It's often associated with children who show very great talent in some field (usually chess, maths, music, and sometimes sport):

> *The thirteen-year-old prodigy Magnus Carlsen of Norway caused another sensation on Thursday night when he came close to defeating the world number one Garry Kasparov.* (Daily Telegraph)

Like almost all words which characterise someone or something remarkable, *prodigy* risks being devalued if overused. Football, in particular, seems to be littered with more prodigies than you could kick a ball at. The word should not be confused with *protege* (more correctly spelled *protégé*), which describes a 'person who is under another's patronage or protection':

> *Following Ramsay's success, Marcus Wareing, another celebrity chef and one of Ramsay's proteges, was installed to run the famous Savoy Grill at that hotel.* (Daily Telegraph)

Embarrassment rating: ●◑○ While it is possible for someone to be both a *prodigy* and a *protégé*, the words have distinct definitions so that to confuse one with the other is to obscure meaning.

How to avoid: A *protégé* is a person under another's *protection*. The word doesn't usually stand alone and naturally goes with the identity of the patron or protector – i.e. X is Y's *protégé*. By contrast, a *prodigy* may well be working by him- or herself. The associated adjective 'prodigious' reinforces the meaning.

PROGRAM *or* PROGRAMME

There is a tendency to use the increasingly familiar first spelling for all occasions in British English. A combination of general American influence together with the computer application of the word are probably responsible for this.

In the US, all *programs*, theatre, television, computer, are just that – *programs*. British English has a spelling difference between the *programme* which you buy in the theatre, watch on TV, etc., and the *program* which runs on a computer. Rather as with the US spelling of 'center', occasionally found in the UK, there's a tendency to use the *program* spelling now for any meaning.

Embarrassment rating: ●●◐ for oldies at least. This is probably a generational difference, since younger people – used to computer terminology from day one (as they say) – are likely to be happier with the *program* spelling. Not that this makes it correct.

How to avoid: The British spelling should be preserved. I can't think of a strong reason for this other than that we should, sometimes, hang on to what is our own.

PROPHECY *or* PROPHESY

There's no problem with meaning here but sometimes a confusion over spelling.

Prophecy, meaning 'prediction' and pronounced to rhyme with 'see', is a noun:

The sect's prophecy that the world was about to end was generally ignored.

To *prophesy*, to 'foretell', is a verb (pronounced to rhyme with 'sigh'). The verb doesn't carry quite the religious/messianic overtones of the noun, and can be used in the sense of 'forecast':

The company prophesied continued growth for the rest of the year.

Embarrassment rating: ●◐○ It's common to see the misspelling 'prophesies' (instead of *prophecies*) for the plural noun. And because it's the same form as the present tense of the verb it doesn't look 'wrong'.

How to avoid: This follows the pattern for 'advice/advise' and 'licence/license' – that is, the 'c' spelling is the noun form while the 's' one is the verb. (See 'advice/advise' entry for further discussion.)

PSEUDONYM, PEN NAME *or* NOM DE PLUME

This isn't a very important difference, perhaps, but a few people might wonder whether there's any distinction between these terms . . .

A *pseudonym* is a 'fictitious name', sometimes one assumed by writers but often by other people to ensure anonymity or protection:

One participant agreed to speak to me if we used a pseudonym.
(Guardian)

A *nom de plume* is the same as a *pen name*, specifically a 'writer's assumed name' (as Eric Blair took the name George Orwell at the beginning of his literary career). Oddly, *nom de plume* is not actually used in French – it joins a little list of phrases which you don't find in that country, including 'son et lumière'. French or not, there's something slightly frivolous about the phrase, and Orwell wouldn't have been caught dead using it about himself. It therefore seems appropriate to describe the assumed identity of this web woman (who might be a man) who might be a callgirl (or not):

> . . . *'Belle de Jour', the nom de plume of a working girl whose blog has just landed her a five-figure book deal.* (Independent on Sunday)

Embarrassment rating: ○○○ Although *nom de plume* is a bit twee.

How to avoid: *Pseudonym* is acceptable for everyone – police informers, celebrities in hiding, writers struggling to make a living.

PURPOSELY *or* PURPOSEFULLY

These adverbs both describe a style of doing something. Though related, they're not identical.

Purposely means 'by intention', 'deliberately':

> *He purposely left the door open so that he could listen to them.*

Purposefully describes a purposeful way of doing anything, i.e. 'in a decided fashion', 'with a sense of purpose':

> *Suspecting he was listening, she crossed the room and purposefully closed the door.*

Embarrassment rating: ●○○ There is some overlap between the words but also a gap, as the examples above show.

How to avoid: The form of *purposefully* suggests its meaning, 'full' of purpose. It is a more intense and energetic expression than *purposely*.

Q Q Q **Q** Q Q

QUASH *or* SQUASH

The second word can almost always be used in place of the first, but the first has a more restricted application.

In a legal context, to *quash* is to 'make invalid' (convictions can be quashed or overturned). It has the more general sense of to 'crush out of existence' but not in a literal sense:

The records were put out in an attempt to quash revived controversy over Mr Bush's Vietnam war-era service in the National Guard. (Daily Telegraph)

Apart from noun senses like 'fruit' and 'ball game', *squash* as a verb has the same meaning of to 'crush flat'. There's a more 'physical' quality to *squash*, which can be used both metaphorically and literally (as here):

Apparently, Wilkinson is cursed with a small entrance to the channel that houses the nerve, squashing it. (Daily Telegraph)

Embarrassment rating: ○○○ Nil, if one refers to 'squashing a legal conviction'. But high in a reference to 'quashing a nerve'.

How to avoid: Only abstracts – convictions, controversy, etc. – can be *quashed*.

RRRRRRR

REBOUND *or* REDOUND

These verbs have essentially the same underlying meaning but they are not fully interchangeable.

To *rebound* is to 'spring back'. Even when not used literally, which it generally isn't, the word retains a kind of physical spring:

> *They also had a bitter defeat to rebound from – they played the Soviet team a week before the Olympics in an exhibition and lost 10–3.*
> (The Times)

To *redound* is also to 'rebound' or 'be reflected back', but this rarer word is found in more dignified contexts. Balls don't *redound*, but words and behaviour do – to your or someone else's advantage, disadvantage, etc.:

> *Denis's policy always was to do what redounded to the credit of his wife.*
> (Daily Telegraph)

Embarrassment rating: ●◐○ But one shouldn't use *redound* in many contexts. For example, the word would not be correct in the *Times* quotation above.

How to avoid: *Rebound* is usually the safe choice.

RECOURSE, RESOURCE *or* RESORT

The three words are closely linked, and a dictionary will usually define them in terms of each other. However, there are small differences in their usage even if it's tricky to sort them out.

To have *recourse* to something means to go to it as a 'source of aid':

> *We had recourse to the Russian speaker in our group when we landed at the airport.*

Resort could be used as the verb in the sentence above ('We resorted to . . . '), giving the same meaning. This is more usual than the equivalent noun construction ('We had resort to . . . ').

A *resource* is also a 'source of help', but the word doesn't normally convey the idea of turning to something in an emergency or a difficulty. More often it carries the related sense of a 'means' that one can draw on (a means of financial support, a way of filling one's time, etc.):

Time didn't hang on his hands after retirement: he had plenty of resources.

Resource can also be a verb, usually in participle form: 'a properly resourced library'.

Embarrassment rating: ◑○○, since the words are close, at least in their noun forms – as in 'Bluffing was his chosen recourse/resource/ resort when in trouble'. Note, however, that one can't say 'we had resource to . . . ' but only ' . . . recourse/resort to . . . '

How to avoid: This is a bit of a maze. *Resource* and *resort* are the more usual words, while *recourse* requires more careful handling.

REGARDLESS *or* IRREGARDLESS
One of these words does not exist.

Regardless means 'without regard to', 'without taking into consideration':

The strength of his [Ken Dodd's] stage presence wins you over, regardless of the gags. (Guardian)

Irregardless does not – or at least should not – exist. But people occasionally use it in exactly the same sense as *regardless*. This non-word has probably come about through a confusion with 'irrespective' and/or a desire to create a more emphatic form of *regardless*.

Embarrassment rating: ●●●, since this mistake reflects pure ignorance.

How to avoid: There's nothing to avoid, except a display of the above.

REGRETFUL *or* REGRETTABLE
These two adjectives, with their connections to remorse and sadness, are sometimes confused in their applications.

Regretful relates only to people, and means 'capable of showing' 'regret':

Under cross-examination the defendant claimed to be regretful over what he had done.

Regrettable applies to incidents or situations (but not directly to people) which are 'causing regret':

Then, in a regrettable turn of events, the company decided to close the factory.

The same distinction applies to the adverbs:

Regretfully, she closed the front door for the last time.

Regrettably, credit card debt is also the most widely available . . . (Independent)

Regretful doesn't mean causing regret:

☒ *. . . it's disappointing and regretful [should be **regrettable**] that the Scottish Executive is going to have to charge English students more.* (quoted in the Guardian)

Embarrassment rating: ●●◐, if an individual is described as *regrettable* or an event as *regretful*. This is a fairly elementary mistake of usage.

How to avoid: *Regretful* could be rephrased as 'full of regret' – and this is a state which can only be experienced by humans. *Regrettable*, like 'deplorable', must be restricted to events or situations, or to words and actions; it cannot characterise a person's emotions.

REIGN *or* REIN

Identical pronunciation and a shared sense of 'control' can cause confusion between these two.

To *reign* is to 'rule over':

Acceding to the throne in 1760 at the age of 22, George III reigned for nearly 60 years. (Daily Telegraph)

To *rein* is to 'control with reins' (used of a horse, young child, etc.) but it is most often used figuratively with 'in' to mean 'restrain':

But the Pakistanis have done little so far to rein in the thousands of Taliban operating from Baluchistan. (Daily Telegraph)

This second word and sense are sometimes confused with the first, as here:

☒ ☒ *News that Richard Desmond is out of the running for the* Telegraph *titles suggests that he may be reigning* [should be **reining**] *in his ambitions . . .* (Observer)

Embarrassment rating: ●●◐ These are fairly elementary words, and any mistake tends to conjure up images of monarchs on horseback.

How to avoid: *Rein* is frequently followed by 'in', the last two letters of the word. The link between kings and their *reigns* is reinforced by the fact that both are spelled with a 'g'.

RELIABLE *or* RELIANT

This is one of those 'which-side-of-the-coin-is-it?' differences. Any confusion is probably deepened by the three-wheeler known as the Reliant Robin.

Reliable describes a person or system or object which can be relied on, and carries the sense of 'dependable', 'trustworthy':

> *It's a very reliable car – we haven't had a breakdown in five years.*

Reliant (followed by 'on') applies to the people who do the relying and so means 'dependent':

> *In the period before the war, US journalists were far too reliant on sources sympathetic to the administration.* (Observer)

Embarrassment rating: ●●●, if an individual who considers himself to be *reliable* is erroneously described as *reliant*.

How to avoid: It's the difference between 'dependable' and 'dependent' (but note the '-ant' ending to *reliant*).

RESPECTIVE *or* IRRESPECTIVE

This is not a confusable in the standard sense since problems arise here not so much over the distinction between the two words as over the proper use of *respective* and *respectively*.

Respective means 'with respect to'. *Respective* and its adverbial form *respectively* are generally used when items in two lists are being matched up and indicate that the first item in list a) is paired with the first in list b) and so on:

> The Specialist, *starring Sylvester Stallone and Sharon Stone, as, respectively, an explosives expert and a revenge seeker . . .* (Guardian)

Respectively has a function here as it makes clear which star takes which role. But the word is often used unnecessarily, as it is here:

☒ *. . . a bemused Inzamam-al-Haq and a clearly irritated Rahul Dravid, the respective captains, were forced to deny that they were playing cricket under orders from their governments.* (Daily Telegraph)

(Readers already know this is about India and Pakistan but there's no earlier reference in the sentence to the teams captained by the two cricketers and therefore nothing to connect them to – 'captains' by itself would have done.)

Irrespective means 'without regard to':

Everyone else has to share out anything left over, irrespective of age and closeness to retirement.

Embarrassment rating: ◐○○ when *respective(ly)* is used unnecessarily, as in the *Telegraph* excerpt above. Its presence in the sentence is merely irritating, like a piece of grit.

How to avoid: Before using *respective*, ask whether it has any useful job to do in the sentence.

RESTFUL, RESTIVE *or* RESTLESS

All three adjectives derive from *rest*, and the first and second are sometimes confused even though their meanings are opposed.

Restful means 'soothing', 'tranquil', and is applied, not to people, but to experiences that may have a calming effect, such as listening to a piece of music:

Going on holiday with two young children isn't exactly a restful experience.

Restive describes someone 'twitchy', 'reluctant to be controlled':

The Prime Minister challenged the more restive Tory MPs to accept that Britain had a strategic interest . . . (Independent)

There is more than a shade of difference between the adjectives *restive* and *restless*. This latter word means simply 'unable to stay still'; unlike *restive* it does not imply that anyone is attempting to exercise control:

These days the black rings [under the eyes] are rarely the effect of all-night partying but more from restless nights with a teething baby. (Guardian)

Embarrassment rating: ●●○ These are very familiar words, even if it's tempting to see *restive* as a synonym for *restful*.

How to avoid: *Restive* and *restless* can only be used of people and animals; *restful* of events and experiences.

RING *or* WRING

Both of these words have a variety of meanings but there's one area in which the two come close – the idea of encircling with the hands – and this can lead to mistakes.

To *wring* has several meanings, including to 'twist' (as in, *wring* one's hands) and to 'exact' (*wring* a confession from someone). *Ring*, too, has a range of meanings from 'encircle' to 'call on the telephone'. One can *ring* a bird round the leg as a means of identification. But what the writer of the following meant was *wringing*:

> ❌❌ *Ringing* [should be **wringing**] *a wounded bird's neck is simply ending its agony quickly and humanely.* (Daily Telegraph)

Embarrassment rating: ●●● because the mistake looks careless or just plain ignorant.

How to avoid: As far as I can see, the only bodily bits one can *wring* are the neck and hands. So whenever these two parts come into contact with this word, the writer needs to ensure he/she has the spelling right.

RISKY *or* RISQUÉ

These two words, one English, one French, amount to the same thing. Where and when is the French one used?

Risky means 'dangerous':

> *The heavy snow and icy roads made for a risky drive home.*

Risqué – generally with an acute accent on the 'e' – comes from the French *risquer*, which (surprise, surprise) translates as 'risk'. This word is only used in a sexual context. It describes a joke, picture, etc. which is 'suggestive'. It has a slightly dated hint of ooh-la-la naughtiness about it, which is obviously what English speakers once liked to associate with the French:

> *In a world where lap-dancing bars have become the fashionable form of risqué entertainment for businessmen, there's a danger that the bunny*

girl with her tail and floppy ears will seem tame, if not ridiculous.
(Scotsman)

Embarrassment rating: ●●○, though I'm not sure that these would be inadvertently confused. Anyone using *risqué*, probably with a wink or a leer, is likely to be aware of its sexual overtones.

How to avoid: Not applicable.

S S S S S S S

SANCTION *or* SANCTIONS

This is an oddity, since one sense of *sanction* seems almost to contradict another sense of the word.

As a verb to *sanction* means to 'give permission'. It is a formal word:

The board sanctioned him to open discussions with the rival company.

But *sanction* is so frequently associated with its noun sense of 'penalty' that the more positive associations of the word have more or less been lost to view, and it is not unusual to find a sentence like this:

☒ *The board sanctioned* [should be *reprimanded*] *him for his unofficial approach to the rival company.*

This is an incorrect use of the verb, but the mistake isn't surprising since people assume that *sanctions* mean punishment. Actually, the singular noun *sanction* can mean 'permission' or 'approval' – but, in practice, *sanctions* is almost exclusively used in the plural to describe the 'formal penalties' which follow from some infringement of laws or rules, as in economic sanctions that are being imposed, lifted, eased, etc.:

Three of her opponents now face sanctions for their roles in a 'malicious and frivolous' conspiracy against her. (The Times)

Embarrassment rating: ●○○, because a contradictory tangle of meanings lies round these words. Since *sanction* is so frequently understood in a negative sense, users should be alert to possible ambiguity in statements like 'She was sanctioned for such and such . . . '. This is quite likely to be understood as 'She was penalised for . . . ' rather than the more correct 'She was given permission for . . . '.

How to avoid: As a noun *sanction(s)* will nearly always suggest some kind of penalty, forfeit, fine, etc. As a verb, the word should be used with care.

SHALL *or* WILL

The difference between these two verb forms is generally side-stepped now, either by shortening both words to *'ll* (I'll, she'll), which buries the difference, or simply by using *will* across the board. But there is a difference . . .

. . . which is neatly illustrated by the old story of the two experts on English grammar who drowned. One threw himself into the river intending to commit suicide. To the people standing on the bank, he shouted, 'I will drown and no one shall save me!' The other grammar expert fell in by accident. When he saw that no one was making a move to help him, what he called out was, 'I shall drown and no one will save me!' Yes, I know, this may be a very contrived situation – like a panda walking into a café – but it does hint at the *shall/will* difference.

The distinction between the two is that, when all that is being expressed is simple futurity, *shall* 'should' be used with the first person singular and plural (I/we) and *will* with the second and third persons (you/he/she/they):

I/we shall see you tomorrow.

You/he/she/they will be at the station at 5.30.

The *shall/will* link with particular pronouns is reversed when the sentence contains an element of compulsion or intention or determination: in short, anything that makes it more than a simple statement about the future. In these cases the first person (I/we) takes *will* while the others are followed by *shall*.

'I will do it, and there's no way you can stop me!'

'You shall go to the ball, Cinderella,' said the fairy godmother.

Embarrassment rating: ○○○, for the reasons given above.

How to avoid: In practice these fairly subtle distinctions are no longer observed, although most people would register that, in the 'Cinderella' example above, it is more forceful when the fairy godmother says 'You shall go to the ball . . . ' rather than 'You will go to the ball . . . '.

SHEAR *or* SHEER

Two words which are identically pronounced and whose spelling is easily confused. In addition, for the verb forms, there is a shared idea of movement, perhaps an abrupt one.

To *shear* is to 'clip' (as in sheep-*shearing*) and to 'cut':

The polar bear can shear straight through bone and tissue, thanks to its elongated canines and rough-edged molars. (Daily Telegraph)

The adjective *sheer* means 'downright', 'absolute':

Nowhere in America is there a greater sense of the sheer intoxication of supreme global power than at investment banks such as Goldman Sachs . . . (Daily Telegraph)

As a verb to *sheer* means to 'swerve', 'turn from':

He came prepared for a confrontation but sheered away from one at the last moment.

Embarrassment rating: ●●○ It's a definite error of spelling/sense to refer to a 'shear drop' or to talk of 'sheering sheep', even though your meaning will probably be understood.

How to avoid: *Shears* are what are used for *shearing*. *Sheer* is the only spelling which can be used in an adjectival context – a *sheer* drop – and also the correct one to describe a swerving movement. It may help to remember that s*heer*, like 'steep' and 'veer', has a double 'e'.

SHOO-IN *or* SHOE-IN

There's not much of a trap here perhaps, but there is confusion over which is the correct version of this popular US import.

A *shoo-in* – the term was US slang originally and derives from a rigged horse race – is the 'inevitable winner of a race', a 'sure thing':

Thank goodness the laws out there prevent foreigners from standing for President because King Jaw himself, Arnold Schwarzenegger, would be a shoo-in. (Guardian)

But a different spelling, *shoe-in*, is quite often seen – although, strictly speaking, it is wrong. Interestingly, the mistake, which most likely comes from some association between fitting and shoehorns, may eventually push out the correct version.

❌ *For all that, the incumbent President is no shoe-in.* (Daily Telegraph)

Embarrassment rating: ○○○, since there is apparent disagreement over which is the preferred form of this word.

How to avoid: This is a slightly informal piece of language but increasingly found in written English. The *shoo-in* spelling is still more accurate. Some association between horse races and the 'shooing' sound made to animals indicates the spelling.

SHOULD *or* WOULD

The difference between these two verb forms follows that for 'shall/ will' (see earlier entry). It's a minor point of language but quite an interesting one.

Should can be used for the first person singular or plural:

I/we should like to thank the speaker.

while *would* is appropriate for other pronouns:

You/he/she/they would have arrived by now but for the snow.

The tendency is to use *would* in all cases ('I/we would like to . . . ') and the formulation with *should* now sounds a little formal though it may be appropriate in some contexts.

Should should, of course, be used when the meaning of 'ought to' is intended:

You really should try and see it.

Embarrassment rating: ○○○

How to avoid: *Would* can be used all the time, except where the sense of *ought to* is required.

SIMPLE *or* SIMPLISTIC

A pair of closely related words. There is a temptation to use the second because it 'sounds' better even though the context may not justify it.

Simple has a range of meanings from the positive ('plain', 'unpretentious') to the negative ('gullible', 'silly'). But sometimes *simple* is just too simple to make the right impression, and so we reach for *simplistic*. The two terms are not the same. *Simplistic* means 'naive', 'oversimplified' and is almost always used in a critical sense. A *simple* plan may be a good one precisely because of its simplicity, but a *simplistic* plan can never be good because it fails to take account of the complexities of a situation. Although there's a slightly patronising edge to *simplistic* – since it's applied to other people's ideas and hardly ever to our own – it does carry a meaning which should be kept distinct from the straightforward *simple*:

> *'It's clear from my own work that I believe in a multicultural democracy, but to go from that position to say someone is morally good or bad is either unnecessary or simplistic.' (quoted in the* Guardian)

A lot of people gravitate towards *simplistic* when *simple* would do just as well or even be preferable:

> *And on the most simplistic* [why not **simple**?] *level – the one at which a TV critic necessarily operates – it just didn't compute.* (Observer)

Embarrassment rating: ●○○ People are not likely to pull you up for using *simplistic* – as long as they are not the targets of the word.

How to avoid: If tempted to use *simplistic,* always ask yourself whether it is really justified. It may look good but does it mean anything other than *simple*?

SITTING *or* SAT

Sat **is increasingly used where better English would demand** *sitting*.

This is an irritating mistake for anyone old enough to remember the way things used to be. Once, in a golden age of correctness, people were described as *sitting* round a table while a baby might be *sat* in its high chair. In other words, to be *sat* is to be put in your position (either by being directed to it or by being physically lifted onto a seat). It's true that some forms of dialect English have always used *sat* in place of *sitting,* but now that everyone else has started to do the same the usage is on its way to becoming standard. A pity, as it makes it sound as though we're all kids waiting to be plonked down in our places:

> ☒ *That's a very long time for anyone to be sat* [should be **sitting**] *around at home all day waiting and worrying about an illness.* (BUPA advertisement)

Embarrassment rating: ●◑○○ Some people wince a little when they hear 'He was sat in that chair' rather than 'He was sitting . . . ', but perhaps they – we – are just being oversensitive.

How to avoid: There is a distinction worth observing here, and the careful speaker would want to avoid giving the impression that he/she has been placed in some seat rather than voluntarily choosing to sit there. This 'error' is worse in writing than in speech.

SOMETIME *or* SOME TIME

Pronunciation runs these two together, whatever the sense. On paper this is a fairly subtle distinction, but it is one that careful users of English will want to observe.

The single word *sometime* is an adverb, meaning 'at an unspecified or unknown point in time':

'Come up and see me sometime' was Mae West's catchphrase.

As an adjective *sometime* means 'former':

She was a sometime magistrate and mayor of the town.

Some time (two words, adjective + noun) means 'for a period of time', usually quite a long period:

For some time now we've been thinking of moving house.

(Compare with *We must move house sometime*.)

Embarrassment rating: ●○○ The positioning of *sometime/some time* in the sentence is a pretty good guide to which meaning is intended.

How to avoid: The *some time* version is usually preceded by a preposition such as 'for', 'at', etc.; *sometime* (single word) is often followed by an expression of time such as 'next week', 'soon', 'in August', etc.

STATIONARY *or* STATIONERY

The endings of these words are pronounced the same, and it is easy to put the wrong one. A classic confusable.

Stationary (adjective only) means 'not moving':

The actor then asked the group to move the table with their minds. The table remained stationary, but the actor suggested it was moving. (Daily Telegraph)

Stationery (noun only) defines the paper, pens, etc. used in a workplace.

Embarrassment rating: ●○○, because the error may well go unnoticed and the sense will not be affected.

How to avoid: *Stationery* is what is bought from a station*er's*. I suspect that the term has been at least partly replaced by the all-purpose 'office supplies'. So most appearances of this pair of words are likely to be in the *stationary* sense/spelling.

STAUNCH *or* STANCH

This is an example of a false difference, in that people may believe there is a distinction between these two words when it's really a matter of common usage.

Either spelling can be used when the verb sense of to 'halt the flow of' is required (to *stanch/staunch* the flow of blood), though *staunch* is more usual. For the adjective meaning 'firm', 'reliable' – a *staunch* ally – the second spelling is almost always found in preference to the first.

Embarrassment rating: ○○○, although *staunch* is the preferred form.

How to avoid: *Staunch* is always right.

STIGMA *or* STIGMATA

These words change meaning between the singular and the plural.

A *stigma* is a 'mark of shame or disgrace', although the word is generally used less intensely than that definition suggests:

> *The bus has finally shed the stigma it acquired in the 1980s when Margaret Thatcher remarked that a man over 30 who was still catching the bus was a failure in life.* (The Times)

The plural version of the word, *stigmata*, is only found in a religious context since it refers to 'the five wounds which Christ received on the cross' (from nails and spear). Certain holy people such as St Francis of Assissi are claimed to have developed stigmata-like marks as a reflection of their devout lives.

The verb to *stigmatise* – meaning to 'brand with shame' and so to 'condemn' – is popular in our culture just now. Simultaneously, we're all guilty and we're all victims.

Embarrassment rating: ●●●, if you were to refer to the *stigmata* of being discriminated against.

How to avoid: Anyone aware of the plural form of the word is unlikely to make the mistake of confusing it with the singular. Oddly, *stigma* is such a usual word that an alternative like 'shame' or 'disgrace' is probably more forceful.

STRAIGHT *or* STRAIT

Identical pronunciation and a blurring of meanings between 'narrow' and 'unbending' sometimes cause these two to be confused.

The adjective *straight* means 'direct', 'without a curve' and so by extension, 'honest'. The noun use is mostly found in a racing context and in the singular:

The favourite was ahead all the way down the final straight.

Another principal noun (and adjectival) use is a slang or informal one to mean 'heterosexual'.

Strait is an out-of-date adjective meaning 'narrow', 'confining', and is now used only as part of a couple of longer words, *straitjacket* and *straitlaced*.

As a noun, almost always in the plural, *strait(s)* describes 'a narrow stretch of water between two seas' ('the Straits of Taiwan') or has the sense of 'difficult circumstances', often with 'dire' in front of it:

After the house sale fell through they found themselves in dire financial straits.

Embarrassment rating: ●●◐ The meaning will probably remain clear but there's a red-face element in any mistake: for example, a reference to the Straights of Gibraltar could imply that the writer is picking on the heterosexual population of the Rock.

How to avoid: *Straight* is the standard form/spelling of the singular noun and of the adjective; when the word is found in the plural, *straits* is the much more likely form.

STRATEGY *or* TACTICS

These terms, originally military, refer to planning on a large scale and a small scale. But which is which?

Strategy has long since moved from its origins as a word of war (where it means 'generalship', 'campaign planning') and now encompasses any 'large-scale and long-term planning'. In the 1990s especially it broadened out to become a favourite term in education and the 'soft' sciences, producing expressions such as 'classroom strategies', 'learning strategies', etc.:

It is the responsibility of the coach to adapt his training and selection strategies to best suit the demands on his players. (Daily Telegraph)

Tactics – very often used in the plural – underpin *strategy*, that is, they are the 'means to reach a goal', the detailed manoeuvres that enable a strategic plan to be realised:

Other tactics [to exploit a film] include leafleting campaigns and even the setting up of Christian coffee bars next to cinemas.
(Independent on Sunday)

Embarrassment rating: ●○○, although anyone wanting to play the part of an armchair general or a soccer supremo needs to get the difference straight.

How to avoid: While it's true that *strategy* and *tactics* tend to blur into each other, the first should be reserved for the grand plan and the second for the fine detail.

SUGGESTIBLE *or* SUGGESTIVE

Two terms connected to *suggestion* but with widely different uses. Both are slightly pejorative.

Suggestible means 'open to suggestion' and so 'gullible' or 'easily influenced':

The hypnotist found some suggestible guests for his next performance.

Suggestive can mean simply 'evocative' (without defining exactly what is being evoked); often followed by 'of', it can be a feature of more formal/technical writing:

In 1859, when the Origin of Species *had come out, the evidence from fossils was suggestive but very incomplete.*

But *suggestive* generally defines comments which contain a double meaning or have a sexual undertone:

The writer was a diffident, ceremonious man unlikely to risk suggestive remarks to his upright publisher. (Guardian)

Embarrassment rating: ●●○, since these words convey different notions; and a *suggestive* report could be ambiguous, meaning either *indicative of something*, or just *full of innuendo*.

How to avoid: *Suggestible* (with the same '–ible' ending as 'gullible') is used of people, often in the context of hypnotism. Applied to remarks and evidence *suggestive* could have a neutral meaning but much more frequently characterises risqué comments.

TTTTTTT

TAIL *or* TALE

These two words are easy to confuse. Maybe it's because they sound the same and share three out of four letters. Maybe it's because of the old saying ' . . . and thereby hangs a tale' – meaning that there is a story yet to be told, but somehow conjuring up an image of a donkey or other animal with a *tail*.

A *tail* is the 'posterior extremity of an animal'. It has a slang application to buttocks and/or genitals. And in cricket, *tail* describes the players who are put on to bat at the end.

A *tale* is a 'story', often one which is spoken rather than written down and sometimes with overtones of childhood (as in *The Tale of Peter Rabbit*). It can be true or fictitious or just plain malicious (in the sense of 'telling tales').

Embarrassment rating: ●●○, since these are ordinary words and to put them in the wrong context – e.g. to mistakenly write of 'the storyteller's tail' – conjures up a comic image.

How to avoid: The idea of a *tail* as a kind of 'line' could be reinforced by the similarity of its spelling to tr*ail*. And there is a link between *tal*king and *tales*.

TEMERITY *or* TIMIDITY

Two nouns which are opposites. It is perhaps the false echo of 'timorous' in *temerity* which sometimes encourages misunderstanding of the first.

Temerity means 'daring', with the suggestion of rashness. It is more usually applied to, say, challenges to authority than cases of physical daring:

The defendant had the temerity to question the sanity of the judge in open court.

Timidity points to an opposite attitude: 'lack of nerve', a shyness that makes its possessor unassertive:

Timidity made him reluctant to speak out even when his own interests were being threatened.

Embarrassment rating: ●●○, since any confusion gives completely the opposite aspect to whatever is being described.

How to avoid: The meaning of *timidity* is plain enough, but some association between *temerity* and *temp*er may help to fix the shared idea of hot-headedness.

THAT *or* WHICH

There's a tendency to assume that these two can be used inter-changeably, but this applies only in certain sentence constructions.

That and *which* may be used for each other but only in cases where *which* is not preceded by a comma (i.e. only in defining clauses, not in descriptive ones – see entries for 'which/,which/who/,who' for definition and further discussion). You cannot use *that* in a defining clause. For example, *that* (or *which*) is right in the following sentence:

The city firms that had been invited to tender for the work complained that they had been given too little time.

But it would be wrong if the sentence were rephrased as follows:

☒ ☒ *The city firms, that* [should be **which**] *had been invited to tender for the work, complained that they had been given too little time.*

There are also stylistic reasons for using *that* simply as a variation on *which*. In the following example, a repetition of *which* within the space of six words is avoided by putting *that*:

. . . *the British and French governments, which own the state railways that in turn own Eurostar* . . . (The Times)

Embarrassment rating: ●●○ if *that* is used where it shouldn't be. It may seem pernickety to restrict the use of *that* to defining clauses only . . . but it's simply correct English!

How to avoid: Since *which* will always be 'right', the play-safe advice would be to stick to that word. *That* can be used for variation, however. It cannot be preceded by a comma.

THEIR, THERE *or* THEY'RE

Uncertainty over the spelling of these three words, particularly the first two, is very common.

Their is the possessive form of the pronoun 'they' – indicating something that belongs to 'them':

They wanted the cash to prop up their collapsing empire . . . (Sun)

There is an adverb of place ('over there') or is used to start a sentence or introduce certain verbs (especially 'to be'):

'There were moments when we were in real trouble.' (quoted in the Sun)

They're is the elided or contracted form of *they are*, and should be used only in informal contexts:

'They're sick as parrots over the 10–0 defeat.'

Embarrassment rating: ●●● This is a basic mistake.

How to avoid: *There*, when it contains the idea of place, is the opposite to 'here' – the same letters with an added 't'. *Their* always entails possession, and the last four letters of the word give 'heir', someone who shortly expects to come into possessions. *They're* can only be used in contexts where 'they are' would make sense – so if you are unsure whether this is the appropriate spelling, try using the full-length phrase. If it works, then it may be right to put *they're*, although it should be said that this shortened phrase is not quite as acceptable as similar contractions like 'I've' or 'he's'.

THROES *or* THROWS

The first word mainly occurs in one particular phrase, and its unfamiliar look sometimes causes people to confuse it with the much more usual *throws*. There may also be half-conscious associations between ideas of force and motion.

Throes (always found in the plural and nearly always preceded by 'in the') are 'spasms' or 'pangs of pain' – they were originally birth pangs. The word retains something of this old meaning, since it applies to painful processes which are not yet complete:

Iran is in the throes of a bitter power struggle between reformers and the ruling conservative clergy . . . (The Times)

Throes shouldn't be confused with *throws*, plural of the noun *throw* ('casting', 'act of throwing', 'a loose covering'), as it is here:

☒☒ . . . *she would have seen a city in the throws* [should be *throes*] *of a festival unmatched anywhere in the world.* (Observer)

Embarrassment rating: ●●◖ Although *throes* may be an odd old word, the expression 'in the throes of' has the status of a cliché, so there's not much excuse for getting it wrong.

How to avoid: It may be tricky to avoid but anybody who writes 'in the throws of' is on automatic pilot. If taken literally, the phrase makes no sense. What's being thrown? Where's it going?

TITILLATE *or* TITIVATE

There's a Carry-On-Ken-Dodd quality to both these words and they are rarely found in a serious context. The second word is sometimes mistakenly assumed to have 'naughty' overtones.

To *titillate* is to 'tickle', to 'mildly excite', almost always with a sexual application:

The Windmill had exposed naked female flesh for the previous wartime generation, but the Lord Chamberlain insisted that the Windmill flesh must not quiver or titillate a nanomillimetre. (The Times)

The similarity in sound between *titillate* and *titivate* – or an artificial emphasis on the first syllable of the second word – may suggest a sexual meaning here too, but in fact *titivate* is to 'tidy', to 'make smarter':

I want them to think well of me and the garden. So I have been going round tidying and titivating . . . (Observer)

Embarrassment rating: ●○○, since these words are almost always used tongue-in-cheek and any confusion is likely to add to the humour. That said, it would be odd and misleading to talk about *titillating* one's kitchen.

How to avoid: Tickle and *titillate* both contain 'l's. There is a faint connection between *titivate* and reno*vate*.

TORPID *or* TORRID

Two similar-looking words with meanings that are distinct, almost opposed. I suspect that for most people, the present writer included, their precise meanings remain a little cloudy without the aid of a dictionary.

Torpid means 'sluggish':

The hot weather made the animals torpid.

Torrid means 'scorching', 'parched':

The torrid climate meant we couldn't go out during the day.

(The most usual application of *torrid* is in its associated sense of 'hot with passion', and the word joins the honourable little roll call of terms that signal sexual content in a film, play, etc. Others include 'sensual', 'explicit', 'frank', and the old favourite 'steamy'.)

Embarrassment rating: ●●○, since the words do convey near-opposite meanings (contrast a *torpid* love scene with the *torrid* variety).

How to avoid: *Torrid* rhymes with 'arid', one of its meanings. *Torpid* comes from *torpor*, a state of numbness or lethargy.

TORTUOUS *or* TORTUROUS

Both of these words suggest something unpleasant or worse, and pronunciation sometimes blurs them into one by overlooking the second 'r' in *torturous*.

Tortuous means 'twisting' or 'highly complicated':

We almost got lost on the tortuous mountain path.

Torturous derives from *torture*, and means 'causing severe physical or mental pain':

I spent a torturous hour jammed into the tiny one-man canoe.

Torturous, in theory a much more literary word, tends to get misused for *tortuous* because of the pain inevitably associated with anything lengthy, complex or laborious.

Embarrassment rating: ●○○ Both words could be applied to the same thing. Becoming involved in a legal process, for example, might be both a *tortuous* and a *torturous* experience. (In fact an Internet search reveals that the phrase 'tortuous process' has only slightly more hits than 'torturous process', though *tortuous* is undoubtedly what is intended.) However, they have distinct meanings and should not be confused.

How to avoid: The derivation of *torturous* from *torture* is a key to the spelling of this word.

TRAVELLER *or* TOURIST

Two words which mean almost the same thing but which carry different overtones.

The difference between these two could take a book, or at least a whole chapter, to sort out. A *traveller* (US *traveler*) is 'one who travels' (and the term also has the specialised sense of 'travelling salesman or saleswoman'). There's a sense of purpose to the word, as in 'business traveller', and often of adventure. Bookshops and newspapers have travel, not tourist, sections. A *tourist* is 'one who travels for pleasure', a 'sightseer'. There's sometimes a touch of criticism in the word, particularly in a phrase such as 'health tourist', which implies travelling with the sole purpose of taking advantage of some facility or amenity of a country, e.g. the NHS.

Embarrassment rating: ●◐○○ Most *tourists* would probably like to think of themselves as *travellers*, but many *travellers* – especially the intrepid, go-it-alone variety – would be aggrieved to be called *tourists*.

How to avoid: It is a matter of choice rather than of avoidance here. Maybe it boils down to a question of how we see ourselves: 'I'm a traveller, you're a tourist, but he/she takes package holidays'.

TRIUMPHANT, TRIUMPHAL *or* TRIUMPHALIST

Three words relating to victory, one in a positive sense, one neutral and one critical. Care is required to tell them apart.

Triumphant means 'rejoicing in victory', and generally applies to individuals, teams, etc. and their words and reactions after they've won:

> *The team was triumphant after their fifth victory in a row.*

Triumphal describes rather the process of 'commemorating a victory'. So an arch or a column – or a march – could be *triumphal*.

Widely used now is the adjective *triumphalist*, suggesting 'gloating in victory', and the noun *triumphalism* – these words carry a critical note because they convey a cocky revelling in success:

> . . . *alcohol, spite or triumphalism, three of the key ingredients in the media industry.* (Independent)

Embarrassment rating: ●●○ There is a risk of misunderstanding if the wrong term is used; a *triumphant* occasion could be very different from a *triumphalist* one.

How to avoid: *Triumphant* can be applied to people or occasions, while *triumphal* is used of buildings, objects, etc. *Triumphalist* (with the negative '–ist' ending) tends to describe people's attitudes.

TROOPER *or* TROUPER

Two words which are pronounced identically and which describe 'ordinary' members of large groups. Ideas of service and a sort of workaday resilience cluster round each term.

A *trooper* is a 'private soldier' (and in the US also a state policeman). The soldier's reputation for swearing explains this comment about Tim Henman:

> *Tim Henman has smashed many more rackets and uttered a lot more of the language of troopers in the heat of the battle than people realise.* (Guardian)

A *trouper* is 'someone who plays in a troupe of actors or other performers', usually admired for his/her longevity and resilience:

> *They weren't manufactured and studio-polished to mime on* Top of the Pops; *they link to an older trouper tradition.* (The Times)

There's sometimes a slightly mocking note to the application of *trouper* (warhorse is often what's meant). But this headline about all-round entertainer Des O'Connor, quoted in the *Guardian*, presumably intended to applaud his sticking power rather than his soldiering:

> ☒ *"What a trooper [?should be **trouper**]!" read one O'Connor-related headline this week.*

Embarrassment rating: ●◐○ Although there is potential for ambiguity when the words are spoken aloud – 'He/She is a trouper/trooper' – the context and tone of voice will almost always indicate which is meant. But if the words are mixed up when written, the meaning may be obscured.

How to avoid: The *trooper* spelling can be reinforced by the associated words, 'troop', 'trooping', and compounds such as 'troop carrier'. But any context involving public performances, especially variety ones, is likely to involve the *trouper*.

TRUSTEE *or* TRUSTY

Both of these nouns are related to trust but you would not be thanked for confusing them.

A *trustee* – pronounced to sound the double 'ee' – is a 'person who is entrusted with managing property or an organisation' (often for charitable purposes). A *trusty* is a 'person in jail who has earned special privileges' (usually through good behaviour), although I am told that the word has not been used for many years. As an adjective, *trusty* means 'reliable', although for some reason it's hard to imagine the word being used without a touch of irony. Is it because it evokes old Technicolor epics where valiant knights called out for their 'trusty steeds'? Or because a disgraced ex-Cabinet Minister talked of defending himself with the 'trusty shield of traditional British fair play' shortly before being jailed for perjury?

Embarrassment rating: ●●● if you happen to refer to someone high up in a charitable organisation as a *trusty*.

How to avoid: Care should be taken over the spelling and pronunciation of *trustee* – the double 'e' ending indicates that he/she is the recipient of trust (compare addressee, legatee, etc.). As indicated above, *trusty* is not much used now, at least in a serious sense. A more acceptable adjective is 'trustworthy'.

U u U U u U u U

UNDERLIE *or* UNDERLAY

The 'lie/lay' distinction is a recipe for disaster (see relevant entry for an attempt at explanation), and this related pair is no exception.

To *underlie* is to 'lie beneath'. The present participle/adjectival form is *underlying* and the past tense form is *underlay*; the word is normally applied to abstracts such as ideas and principles:

But September 11 shattered the assumptions that underlay Bill Clinton's world view. (Daily Telegraph)

To *underlay* is to 'lay under' – i.e. to 'place something underneath something else'. The past tense form is *underlaid*. This verb is rarely found, and *underlay* is more often used in its noun sense to describe the 'felt, rubber, etc. placed beneath a carpet'.

Care needs to be taken over the right past tense form of these verbs. 'Underlied' doesn't exist – what the writer of the following meant was probably either *underlined* or some garbled idea of *underlying*:

⊠ ⊠ *For centuries, clergy have from their pulpits been preaching messages that underlied [?should be **underlined**] anti-Semitic sentiment in societies worldwide . . .* (The Times)

Embarrassment rating: ●●○ It's easy to make a mess of this, but the error still stands out even if most readers won't be able to pinpoint exactly what's wrong.

How to avoid: *Underlying* is quite straightforward but the other forms of the word (*underlie/underlay*) are trickier, as are *underlay/underlaid*. Better to avoid this lot altogether unless you're sure of what you are doing.

USE *or* UTILISE

This is a bit like the 'begin/commence' distinction, with people choosing the longer word because it looks more impressive.

Utilise suggests an active putting to use of whatever one can find:

Robinson Crusoe utilised the resources of his desert island.

Use is a plainer term:

She used her knowledge of languages to get by.

Utilise is often used because *use* doesn't sound sufficiently weighty. But the shorter word is normally good enough.

Embarrassment rating: ●○○, although there are occasions where *utilise* would be just silly ('Did you utilise the car today, dear?').

How to avoid: Use *use*.

V

VALUABLE *or* INVALUABLE

The 'in-' prefix to *invaluable* sometimes causes people to assume it is the negative form of *valuable* (probably by analogy with 'incorrect', 'indecisive', etc.).

The opposite of *valuable* ('having worth') is 'valueless' or 'worthless'. People may occasionally use *invaluable* in this second sense, but its correct meaning is 'not capable of being valued' or 'beyond price' – and therefore very valuable indeed. It tends not to be applied to objects – if the *Mona Lisa* was ever stolen (again) it would be described as priceless, not *invaluable* – and the word is normally coupled with abstract words like 'experience' or 'information':

He may be 30, but the Welshman's importance to United is still every bit as invaluable as at any time during his wonderful career. (Daily Telegraph)

Embarrassment rating: ●●◐, because to erroneously describe something as *invaluable* when you really mean to say that it is worthless is, in effect, to say the opposite of what you intend.

How to avoid: Remember that 'in-' intensifies *valuable* so that whatever is so described becomes more important than ever.

VENAL, VENIAL *or* VERNAL

The first two words are quite similar in sound and both have overtones of wrongdoing.

Venal means 'open to being bribed' and so 'corrupt':

Perhaps the most venal example of anonymous quotes occurred in the false story . . . which alleged that the Democratic presidential contender, Senator John Kerry, had had an affair with a journalist. (Guardian)

Venial, usually used with 'sin' or 'offence', means 'forgivable'. (In Catholic theology it is contrasted with a 'mortal sin' which deprives the offender of spiritual grace.) When used in an everyday context it tends to suggest nothing more than a minor infringement:

Don't your dieting friends have a slight air of religious fervour? We've fashioned a world of venial sins where the only commandment is Thou Shalt Not . . . (Guardian)

Neither word should be confused with *vernal*, meaning 'connected to spring'. Once a poetic term, this word is perhaps not much used now except in 'vernal equinox', the date in late March when the night and day are of equal length.

Embarrassment rating: ●●○, since a *venal* offence is by definition worse than a *venial* one and putting these words the wrong way round may mislead.

How to avoid: *Venial* is frequently associated with sin (both words contain an 'i') and tends to occur in a religious context. *Venal* derives originally from a Latin word *venum* meaning 'goods for sale', which is how it comes to be associated with corruption.

W W W **W** W W

WAIVE, WAVE, WAVER or WAIVER

A group of words which look alike and are quite often confused. The
gesture of *waving* possibly links up to the underlying idea behind
waive and *waiver*.

To *waive* is to 'forgo', to 'hold back from claiming an entitlement':

> . . . *the satellite trucks and radio reporters who have come to see his fortress
> of parking . . . to have him graciously waive the £1.20 charge for the first
> hour.* (Guardian)

A *waiver* (noun only) is the 'act of waiving' or, more usually, a
'document which shows this', that is, it indicates that the possessor is
exempt from some fee or charge.

Wave has a variety of meanings including to 'signal' and to 'move in
an undulating way' and cannot be used in the sense of *waive*. To *waver*
means to 'grow unsteady', to 'falter':

> *I was going to need some help – someone to kick my weak-willed, unethical
> butt whenever I wavered and started to show signs of giving up.*
> (Guardian)

The two senses and spellings, *waver* and *waiver*, can be confused:

> ❌ ❌ . . . *Defence Secretary, Donald Rumsfeld, who last week insisted
> America 'must not waiver [should be **waver**]' in regard to Iraq.*
> (Independent)

Embarrassment rating: ●●◐ if the mistake appears as it does in the
Independent quote above because *waver*, in the sense of to 'falter', is a
familiar word. Also found is the misspelling *waver* instead of *waiver*,
and I imagine this error comes from some idea of 'waving through' –
that is, permitting someone to go through uncharged.

How to avoid: *Wave* and *waver* are associated through ideas of motion
and instability. To *waive* or to provide with a *waiver* is to give a permit
(note the 'i's in each word).

WASTE *or* WASTAGE

These two words relate to something unused or unneeded but there is a wide difference between them.

As a noun or verb *waste* characterises activities which are extravagant or useless (a *waste* of money, to *waste* time) while the adjective *waste* describes anything which is 'unused' or 'rejected' (*waste* ground, *waste* paper). *Wastage* refers to 'inevitable loss through use or decay'. So there will always be a *wastage* of water from a reservoir through evaporation, however much care is taken not to *waste* any. Some genius came up with the expression 'natural wastage' to describe the process whereby companies can reduce their workforce through retirement, death on the job, etc. rather than through compulsory redundancy. It's a wonderfully sterile phrase.

Embarrassment rating: ●●○ To confuse the two may produce a genuine ambiguity of meaning. For example, there is a real distinction of meaning between 'natural waste' (the contents of a sewage farm) and 'natural wastage' (the phasing out of unneeded workers).

How to avoid: The idea of a slow and natural loss, contained within *wastage*, may be reinforced by 'leakage'.

WEATHER, WHETHER *or* WETHER

These three words, two of them part of basic vocabulary, are quite often mixed up, with confusion over when or whether to include two 'h's.

Weather is 'atmosphere', sun, rain, etc. *Whether* is a conjunction introducing the first of one or more alternatives (*whether* . . . or). And a *wether* is a 'castrated ram'.

A *bell-wether* – which can be male or female – is the leading sheep in a flock, followed by the others because it has a bell hung round its neck. The word therefore means a 'leader' or 'trend-setting item'. Bell-wethers are oddly popular at the moment, although it's not always clear what point is being made by this rustic image:

On the Aylesbury estate, the bell-wether of Blair's conscience, things are not
that bad . . . (Guardian)

('Bell-weather' is wrong, though used sometimes perhaps because of some association with wind chimes.)

Embarrassment rating: ●●◐, if only because the first two words are such standard English. The least-used of the three, *wether*, is the only one to be spelled exactly as it sounds.

How to avoid: There is no simple way of remembering these. *Weather* has the 'a' of *a*ir or *a*tmosphere – and its middle letters when rearranged spell 'heat' – but this may be a case where it's more trouble to memorise the memory aids than the words themselves.

WHICH *or* . . ., WHICH; WHO *or* . . ., WHO

This isn't a conventional confusion in the terms of this book. There is, however, a significant difference in application between the *which* which stands by itself and the *which* which is preceded by a comma. The same goes for *who* and , *who*.

Essentially, the difference is that between a defining (*which*) clause and a descriptive (, *which*) clause. If this isn't clear – and it probably isn't – then consider the following examples. Defining clause first:

The painting which was in the attic was valued at £5,000.

(This was the attic painting: the place where it was found defines it. The implication of the sentence is that there were other paintings elsewhere which were more – or less – valuable. So the next sentence might go: 'But the painting in the cellar fetched £10,000'.)

When commas are put in, the meaning of the sentence changes and a descriptive clause is produced:

The painting, which was in the attic, was valued at £5,000.

(Here the clause introduced by *which* is simply descriptive. The painting happened to be in the attic rather than somewhere else.)

The same distinction applies to *who* when it stands alone and , *who* preceded by a comma. As an example, take these two sentences:

The men who were in their 20s were ordered to report for duty the following day.

(Only those in their 20s were required, not those who were 30, 40, etc.)

The men, who were in their 20s, were ordered to report for duty the following day.

(The men happened to be in their 20s. The sentence doesn't imply that age was necessarily a factor but merely reports on it as an incidental detail.)

Embarrassment rating: ●○○ We're breathing fairly rarefied air here. Nevertheless, there is a distinction in meaning between the *which* or the *who* with a comma and the ones without, and the careful user will want to observe it to avoid ambiguity.

How to avoid: This is one that takes a bit of skill to tell apart. But if you can drop the clause beginning with *which* or *who* then a comma is needed.

WHISKY *or* WHISKEY

Two drinks with a certain amount in common, and a one-letter difference.

The standard English spelling of *whisky* (i.e. the stuff distilled in Scotland) doesn't have an 'e':

It all explained why whisky is so important to Scotland: it's nature's great anaesthetic. (Independent)

But the *whiskey* which is produced in Ireland or America takes the 'e' (and this is the standard US spelling):

After the first bottle of Paddy Whiskey was drunk he opened up to us. (Observer)

Embarrassment rating: ●●○ There are three or four constituencies in play here: the Scots, the Irish, the Americans, to say nothing of the serious *whisky* (or *whiskey*) drinkers. Using the wrong spelling with any one of them might have consequences . . .

How to avoid: The version from Ireland or America is the one spelled with an 'e': *whiskey*.

WHO *or* WHICH

When to use *which* as opposed to *who*?

Who is used for individuals:

The man who broke the bank at Monte Carlo . . .

while *which* tends to be for events, objects, etc.:

There was a historic battle which took place on this spot.

Countries and human groups sometimes take *who*, and there is an indeterminate area where either *who* or *which* can be used:

Our products are inspired by other cultures who have used plants safely and effectively for centuries. (Body Shop advertisement)

Similarly with animals: reference to an individual animal (particularly a pet) will probably be followed by *who*, but a collective noun (flock, herd) will take *which*.

Embarrassment rating: ●○○ Most people instinctively pick the 'right' word and the wrong choice – e.g. 'a person which . . . ' – just sounds wrong.

How to avoid: Play it by ear. Sometimes using 'that' can get you out of a tight spot, for example when you have a phrase like 'a company or individual which . . . ' (or 'who'?).

WHO *or* WHOM

Enter the *who/whom* debate and you enter a little minefield of anxiety, at least for those who are concerned with accuracy. So, when should one use *whom* and – just as important – when should one avoid using it?

Absolutely correct English requires the consistent use of *who* as the subject of a verb, while *whom* is found as the object of a verb or following a preposition:

> *. . . it is Gayle King, her best friend, to whom she once gave a million dollars for a Christmas present, who stands in as her sister.* (The Times)

(*whom* is the object of 'gave' while *who* is the subject of 'stands')

But it is much more normal to find *who* in speech rather than the technically correct *whom*:

> *'I'm becoming – definitely have become – as interested in who I work with as what I work on.'* (*quoted in the* Independent on Sunday)

Indeed, being 'right' in speech can sound a bit stilted and unnatural:

> *'Whom are you going to allow to finance it?'* (*quoted in the* Independent on Sunday)

The general use of *who*, when *whom* would be grammatically correct, is increasingly common in writing:

> *When our partners, who* [should be **whom**] *we've sworn never to leave . . .* (The Times)

> *. . . a respected House historian who* [should be **whom**] *Mr Gingrich had summarily dismissed after 12 years' service . . .* (The Times)

And a large *Guardian* headline (over an article on factory farming) – 'Who's killing who?' – almost certainly opted for the 'wrong' form of the word to avoid the slight fussiness that can sometimes be suggested by *whom*.

Using *who* when it is the direct object of a verb (as in the last three examples) is more acceptable than using it after a preposition. Here convention definitely favours the switch to *whom*:

> . . . *he started with no preconceptions about Mountbatten, about whom he knew little . . .* (The Times)

although it is not hard to find cases that don't follow convention, particularly where the writer is aiming at a conversational tone by putting the preposition after the verb:

> . . . *since she minds enough about who you sleep with to want it to be her, exclusively, and for good . . .* (GQ)

If this was the end of the story – with *who* being all right in most circumstances, and *whom* being the preferred form after a preposition such as 'to' or 'about' – then life would be simple. But unfortunately the *who/whom* uncertainty often produces a situation where the attempt to write correct English actually leads to more mistakes. It is quite easy to put *whom* because the construction of the sentence makes it look as though the object form of the word is correct. This tends to occur after verbs like 'think' or 'believe', as in the following examples:

> ☒☒ *The other's from unmarried friends from way back, whom* [should be *who*] *we thought were like us (happily unmarried, but bound by a clutch of deliberate offspring) . . .* (Independent)

> ☒☒ *Meanwhile GPs, whom* [should be *who*] *the Government assumed were eager to take on hospital work such as small operations, are giving warnings . . .* (Independent on Sunday)

In each case *whom* is the subject of a verb, and not the object of one, and so *who* should be used:

> . . . *unmarried friends . . . who . . . were like us . . .* (subject of 'were')
> . . . *GPs, who . . . were eager . . .* (subject of 'were')

The simplest way to establish which form is correct is to recast the subordinate clause as a separate sentence – e.g. 'The Government assumed that they . . .'. Using 'they' (rather than 'them') indicates that 'who' is right.

The following examples show how it should be done:

Kathy Mitchell . . . the one who brush salesmen always hope will open the door . . . (Guardian)

. . . Czech model Adriana Sklemarikova, who pals said he was set to wed. (Sun)

Embarrassment rating: ●◐○ because the gap between correct usage and what generally happens is wide. But if you put in a piece of formal prose 'This is a person about who . . . ', you are showing either that you don't know the right usage or that you don't care. And there are still people who do know and do care, and they may be the ones reading your words. The reverse error – putting *whom* where *who* is right – is less obvious, but still something to avoid.

How to avoid: Read the advice and guidance given above!

WHO'S *or* WHOSE

Two 'grammar' words, *who's* and *whose*, with identical pronunciation and very similar spelling.

Who's is the contracted form of *who is*. *Whose* is the possessive form of *who*. Although the words sound the same they have completely different functions, neatly illustrated by this line from a play:

"Who's this old relic, whose side is he on?" (*quoted in* The Times)

The usual mistake is to put the contracted form, *who's*, in the place of the possessive, *whose*, as in these examples:

☒☒ *The Icelandic pop pixie [Bjork], who's [should be **whose**] new single, Army Of Me, soared into the Top Ten last week . . .* (Daily Star)

☒☒ *. . . they too demand to know on who's [should be **whose**] side he will be fighting.* (The Times)

Embarrassment rating: ●●● Although this is a mistake we can all make in haste it's still considered by most people to be a major grammatical howler, on a par with confusing *it's* and *its*.

How to avoid: This one is quite hard to forgive as it's so easy to check: just replace *whose* or *who's* by the full-length version, i.e. 'who is'. If this makes sense in the context, then you can use *who's* if you wish. If it doesn't make sense, then the right spelling is *whose*.

WILE, WHILE *or* WHILST

There are two different problems here. One is to do with confusion over *wile* and *while*, the other is to do with the choice between *while* and *whilst*.

As a noun *wile* describes a 'trick', but there's often something pleasant or seductive about it:

> Here he [the author Michael Faber] has got down and dirty with Victorian England, creating a heroine who, like Becky Sharp, lives on her wits, using her feminine wiles to secure social advancement. (Daily Telegraph)

To *wile*, a rare verb, also means to 'trick' or 'beguile'.

Wile has nothing to do with *while* – or *whilst*. As conjunctions these two words mean exactly the same thing ('during'), but *whilst* has a slightly fussy, pursed-lips quality to it.

Embarrassment rating: ●●○ 'Wiling away the time' was a legitimate spelling in the 18th century, though it will be corrected nowadays. A more serious error would be to refer to a person's 'whiles'.

How to avoid: The adjective *wily* gives an indication of the correct spelling of *wile*. And when it comes to *while* and *whilst*, why not save yourself the extra letter by choosing the first version?

WINNING *or* WINSOME

Two words that both sound positive, even synonymous: unfortunately one can be loaded, even critical.

Winning, apart from its sense of victorious (the *winning* team), can mean 'engaging' or 'persuasive': a *winning* smile, a *winning* speech. *Winsome* has absolutely nothing to do with 'win'. Although it can carry the sense of 'attractive', it is almost always used in contexts which suggest something rather 'cute and calculated':

> . . . wearing a lot of pink, or anything with a frill can come across as affectedly winsome, a bit like twirling your hair or giggling too much.

(Guardian)

Embarrassment rating: ●○○ *Winsome* will always carry an implied criticism but dictionaries give very little warning about this.

How to avoid: If in doubt stick to *winning*.

WREAK, WRECK *or* REEK

Wreak and *wreck* have very similar spellings and meanings, *wreak* and *reek* are pronounced the same: all three have strongly negative meanings. A recipe for glorious confusion.

Wreak and *wreck* are often mixed up because their meanings are close, although they are pronounced differently (*wreak* with a long 'ea' sound, as in 'week'). To *wreak* is to 'bring about harm', to 'inflict vengeance':

Wherever the storm went, it wreaked a trail of havoc.

To *wreck*, on the other hand, is to 'destroy', or to 'spoil something so completely as to put it out of action':

'I lasted exactly seven minutes in 1995 before I wrecked my shoulder against Japan . . . ' (*rugby player Keith Wood, quoted in the* Daily Telegraph)

To *reek* is to 'give off smoke or fumes' and generally applies to unpleasant smells or, metaphorically, to anything unattractive or corrupt. This term is also confused with *wreak* despite having a quite different meaning because the two words are pronounced the same. The right use is:

After all, no one will want to buy into a brand that reeks of doom and closure. (Guardian)

The wrong use is:

❌❌ *The new album still wreaks* [should be *reeks*] *of post-9/11 terrors. Rhymes has found solace in Jamaican agriculture.* (Guardian)

Embarrassment rating: ●●○ Despite the difference in meaning, these can be hard to untangle. It's easy to mispronounce *wreak* as *wreck*, by analogy with words like 'threat' or 'tread'.

How to avoid: Stick to the phrase 'wreak havoc' and leave more ambitious variations strictly alone (avoid particularly plunging into the murky waters of the past tense, which is *wreaked*, not *wrought*). Another rule of thumb: if you can follow your verb by 'of' then you must be dealing with *reek*, not *wreak*.

YIN or YANG

Yin and *yang* are Chinese terms describing the complementary (but opposed) principles which underlie religion, medicine and so on. The two go together like a horse and carriage – but which is which?

Yang is the 'active male principle', light and warm, while *yin* is the colder and more passive 'feminine principle', each necessary to the other, held in a state of balance and tension, etc. As with various imports from Chinese culture, such as *feng shui*, originally serious ideas have been largely reduced to advertising props or lifestyle adornments for the west:

> How clever of [hotel] owner Anouska Hempel to reflect 'the bi-polarity
> of the world between yin and yang, black and white, hot and cold . . . '
> (Daily Telegraph)

Embarrassment rating: ●○○ If you can't sort out your *yins* from your *yangs*, don't worry – unless you are in seriously New Agey circles. A little face might be saved by ensuring you pronounce *feng shui* correctly (say 'fung shway').

How to avoid: *Yin* contains -i-, as does fem*i*nine: *yang* contains -a-, as does m*a*sculine.

YOKE or YOLK

These two words sound the same, and share three out of their four letters. Moreover, *yoke* is not a word that we come across very often in these days of industrial farming, so the likelihood of getting it confused with the contents of the breakfast egg is high.

The noun *yoke* is 'anything that joins items/people/animals together', with a verb meaning of 'link'. In a concrete sense the *yoke* is a 'frame that fits round the neck' (of oxen, for example) and, metaphorically, it can also stand as a 'symbol of oppression or slavery':

. . . neither was there any sign of the joyous self-expression of a people jubilant at the overthrow of the colonial yoke. (Daily Telegraph)

Yolk is the 'yellow part of an egg'. The first word is occasionally used where the second is meant, as here:

☒☒ *I hit one egg so hard that it dented the yoke* [should be *yolk*]. (Daily Telegraph)

Embarrassment rating: ●●○ – *yolk* in particular can look very comical in the wrong context since *yoke*, in its figurative sense, is often used to give a sonorous literary ring to a sentence.

How to avoid: The *yolk* of an egg is yellow – and like 'yellow' it contains the letter 'l'.

YOUNG *or* YOUTHFUL

Both words mean roughly the same, but using *youthful*, despite its being a positive term, could cause mild offence in the wrong context.

Young tends to be neutrally descriptive but *youthful* carries overtones of 'fresh and vigorous'. It's quite often used not about the young (who are naturally youthful) but about older people who've retained – or clung onto – the habits, attitudes, etc. of earlier days. If you describe someone as having a *youthful* appearance the implication is that they look younger than they are, often surprisingly so. But in other contexts the word may not always be complimentary.

Embarrassment rating: ●●○ Anything to do with age is a potential minefield.

How to avoid: Never use *youthful* of anyone over 30.

YOUR *or* YOU'RE

Two extremely common words that sound the same and have very similar spelling.

Your is the possessive form of the pronoun 'you':

Don't forget your toothbrush.

You're is the shortened form of 'you are':

You're not going to believe this!

Reversing these (*you're* toothbrush/*your* not going to) is a bad mistake.

As with the confusions over 'its/it's' and 'whose/who's', the way to check which one is correct is to experiment with the full-length version, in this case 'you are'. If it makes sense then *you're* is correct, if you want to abbreviate the expression. If it does not make sense, then the word you intended to write is *your*.

Embarrassment rating: ●●● A mortifyingly basic grammatical mistake, though one most of us are likely to have committed when writing in haste.

How to avoid: It takes only a second to substitute the full version 'you are' and see how appropriate it sounds. Another test (for the grammatically inclined) is that *your* is always followed by a noun of some description, or an adjective plus noun (*your* address, *your* lucky day), whereas *you're* will be followed by an adjective (*you're* late), 'a/an' or 'the' (*you're* a fool, *you're* the winner), a preposition (*you're* in trouble, *you're* on air), an adverb (*you're* easily the best) or a verb (*you're* shivering, *you're* not listening).

ZZZZZZZ

ZENITH *or* NADIR

This is a which-way-round-is-it? difference which, I must confess, is included here partly for the satisfaction of having an entry under 'z'.

The *zenith* is the 'position in the sky directly over the observer's head', and so comes to mean 'high point', 'most flourishing period':

> *Evans grew up at the zenith of the Welsh coal industry, when one in four men worked in mining.* (Guardian)

The *nadir* is the 'direct opposite of the zenith', and if taken literally would apply to the position under the observer's feet, but it is rarely used in this celestial or astronomical sense and means rather the 'lowest point', the 'worst period':

> *The 2002 A-level marking scandal was the nadir, a shambles of control-freakery, pseudo-privatisation and muddle.* (The Times)

Embarrassment rating: ●●◐, since the words convey precisely opposite meanings.

How to avoid: The *zenith* is the hig*h* position overhead, the *nadir* is the point under the observer.

INDEX OF ENTRIES